Tears of Longing

Harvard East Asian Monographs, 206

Tears of Longing

Nostalgia and the Nation in Japanese Popular Song

Christine R. Yano

Published by the Harvard University Asia Center
and distributed by Harvard University Press
Cambridge (Massachusetts) and London, 2002

© 2002 by the President and Fellows of Harvard College

Printed in the United States of America

The Harvard University Asia Center publishes a monograph series and, in coordination with the Fairbank Center for East Asian Research, the Korea Institute, the Reischauer Institute of Japanese Studies, and other faculties and institutes, administers research projects designed to further scholarly understanding of China, Japan, Vietnam, Korea, and other Asian countries. The Center also sponsors projects addressing multidisciplinary and regional issues in Asia.

Library of Congress Cataloging-in-Publication Data

Yano, Christine Reiko
    Tears of longing : nostalgia and the nation in Japanese popular song / Christine R. Yano.
      p. cm. – (Harvard East Asian monographs ; 206)
    Includes bibliographical references (p.) and index.
    ISBN 0-674-00845-6 (cloth : alk. paper)
    ISBN 0-674-01276-3 (paperback)
    1. Enka—History and criticism. 2. Popular music—Japan—History and criticism.
I. Title. II. Series.

ML3501.Y3 2002
782.42164'0952—dc21

2001039594

First paperback edition 2003

Index by the Jaida n'ha Sandra

∞ Printed on acid-free paper

Last figure below indicates year of this printing
  12 11 10 09 08 07 06 05 04 03

Acknowledgments

No one writes a book without incurring large debts, and this book is no exception. First, I thank those funding agencies and institutions that supported my fieldwork and writing: the Crown Prince Akihito Scholarship (especially Mr. Ralph Honda, for his wit and encouragement), the Japan Foundation Dissertation Fellowship, the Center for Japanese Studies at the University of Hawai'i, the William P. Lebra Scholarship, the Foreign Language and Area Studies Fellowship Fund, the Inter-University Center for Japanese Language Studies Fellowship Fund, the Northeast Asia Council of Association for Asian Studies, and the Edwin O. Reischauer Institute of Japanese Studies at Harvard University.

My heartfelt thanks go to my teachers: Takie Lebra, who suggested this topic and subsequently helped to shape it with incisive critique and infectious enthusiasm; Sharon Minichiello, for her continuing, multifaceted support; Alice Dewey, who read this work as both a dissertation and a book manuscript. Corky White stands alone as a friend and bon vivant, whose generous spirit and intellectual energy have taught me much.

I extend special thanks to my enka teachers: in Honolulu, Mr. Harry Urata, for his long-standing friendship, humor, and spirit; and in Tokyo, Mr. Hisashi Noda (and his wife), for his welcoming kindness, eagerness, and intensity. Both have invested much of their lives in enka, and I hope this book does justice to the time they relinquished for me.

During my fieldwork, my life was enriched by friendships with Sachiko Frauenknecht and Reiko Mori. My sincere appreciation also goes out to those in the enka world who went beyond politeness to help me: Mr. Sakurai Takeshi of NHK, Jiromaru-san of the Mori Shin'ichi Kōenkai, Kimata-san of the Yashiro Aki Fan Club, Ishikawa-san of Kitajima Jimusho, and members of Noda sensei's karaoke circle.

I also extend special thanks to those at the Reischauer Institute and Harvard University for making my year there so special and productive: Helen Hardacre, Galen Amstuth, Ruiko Connor, Tim George, Aviad Raz, Kyu-Hyun Kim, and Adam Kern. Thank you also to the anonymous reviewers of the Asia Center Publications office at Harvard University and to John Ziemer and Linda Howe, whose editing advice has made this a better book.

I am grateful to students at the University of Hawai'i who have listened to parts of this book and given me feedback: Jeffrey Maret, Matthew Carlsen, and Gaku Kinoshita. Thanks go as well to those who have helped in various ways in preparing this work: Yoko Kurokawa, Yumiko Tateyama, Takaki-sensei, Kitsutani-sensei, Marlene Patton, Brandon Ledward, Jaida n'ha Sandra, and Paul Li.

I have presented portions of this work to colleagues at the following institutions and organizations, whose stimulating input has left its mark: Harvard University, Columbia University, Stanford University, Yale University, Bowdoin College, the University of Washington, Haverford College, the University of Hawai'i, the East-West Center, the Japan Society (New York), the Japan-America Society (Honolulu), and the International House of Japan.

Other friends and colleagues have also left their imprint, both directly and indirectly: Nancy Cooper, James Roberson, Nobue Suzuki, Laura Miller, Carolyn Stevens, Joe Tobin, John Zuern, Mike Hayes, Jane Moulin, Karen Jolly, Kōichi Iwabuchi, Shūhei Hosokawa, Aaron Fox, Nina Etkin, Miriam Stark, and Joanne Izbicki.

Last, but in no way least, I thank my family for their support and forbearance: my grandparents, now gone, who never had to talk of heart because they lived it daily, and my parents, whose humor, encouragement, and constancy have been invaluable. My biggest thanks go to Scott, who has seen this through from start to finish with patience and grace, sometimes at the sacrifice of his own work, and to Eli and Marika, now both miraculously taller than I, whose laughter and tears have provided necessary distraction. These last three have been my mainstay.

Contents

List of Tables		ix
List of Figures		ix
List of Music Examples		x
Prologue		1
Chapter 1	The Cultural Logic of Enka's Imaginary	13
	Collective Remembering, Collective Forgetting	14
	Localizing the National, Nationalizing the Local	17
	Patterning Forms Through Kata	24
Chapter 2	Inventing Enka: Definitions, Genres, Pasts	28
	Defining "Enka"	29
	Meiji Era (1868–1912)	31
	Taishō Era (1912–1926)	33
	Shōwa Era (1926–1989)	35
	Heisei Era (1989–present)	42
Chapter 3	Producing Enka: Lessons in Perseverance	45
	The Enka Industry: Metaphors for the Nation	46
	The Making of a Singer: Imaging the Imaginary	54
	The Making of a Hit Song	73
Chapter 4	Enka on Stage: Patterning the Practices of Intimacy	77
	Live Performances: Creating a Display of Patterned Intimacy	78
	Mediated Performances: Broadcasting Intimacy	82

Chapter 5	Clichés of Excess: Words, Music, Bodies, and Beyond	90
	Textual Kata: A Modern Musical Recasting of *Waka*	92
	Musical Kata: Aural Processes of the Past	103
	Bodily Kata: Gendered Display	114
	Beyond Kata: Cliché and Its Limits	122
Chapter 6	Consuming Enka's Imaginary: Listening, Singing, Doing	124
	Enka's Appeal	125
	Kōenkai and Fan Clubs	127
	Karaoke	141
Chapter 7	Enka as Engendered Longing: Romance, Furusato, "Japan"	148
	Romancing the Nation	149
	Longing for Furusato	168
	"Japan"	178
Epilogue		181
Appendix A:	Major Record Companies That Produce and Market Enka	187
Appendix B:	Regular Mass Media Enka Programs in the Tokyo Area, 1992	191
Appendix C:	Listing of Songs in the Corpus	193
Notes		205
References		227
Index		247

List of Tables

3.1	Recording Sales by Genre and Format, 1992	47
3.2	Japanese Popular Music: Solo Singers, 1991	55
3.3	Japanese Popular Music: Solo *Shinjin*, 1991	56
5.1	Word Frequency in Song Texts	94
5.2	Compositional Kata (CK)	106
5.3	Performative Kata (PK)	110
5.4	Male and Female Poses	115
5.5	Female Enka Singer's Patterned Body Movements	119

List of Figures

1.	Fans Waiting for Doors to Open at Shinjuku Koma Gekijō	xiv
2.	Nippon Columbia Auditions, 1992	60
3.	Singer at Her Debut Party	72
4.	"Mori Shin'ichi in Asakusa," a Publicity Event	131
5.	Mori Shin'ichi Greeting His Fans	137
6.	Poster of Mori Shin'ichi Outside Shinjuku Koma Gekijō	140
7.	*Taishū Engeki* Performer Walking Near Congratulatory Displays	160

List of Music Examples

1. Rhythmic Chordal Accompaniment: Sone Yoshiaki — 104
2. Rhythmic Chordal Accompaniment: Kawai Personal Keyboard — 104
3. Accented Repeated Notes: Excerpt from "Kokoro-zake" (Sake of the Heart) — 107
4. Accented Repeated Notes: Excerpt from "Settchūka" (Flowers in the Snow) — 107
5. Sung Repeated Notes: Excerpt from "Funa-uta" (Sailor's Song) — 108
6. Melodic Ornamentation Preceding End of Phrase: Excerpt from "Hi no Kuni no Onna" (A Woman of Volcanic Land) — 108
7. Musical-Emotional Leaps: Excerpt from "Kita no Yado kara" (From an Inn in the North Country) — 109
8. Musical-Emotional Leaps: Excerpt from "Tsugaru Kaikyō Fuyu-geshiki" (Winterscape of the Tsugaru Straits) — 109

Tears of Longing

Fans Waiting for Doors to Open at Shinjuku Koma Gekijō

Prologue

Wednesday, June 16, 1993, 12:45 P.M. Exiting the east gate of the massive Shinjuku train station, one of the hubs of the Tokyo megalopolis, I dodge umbrellas held high to ward off the dripping rain of tsuyu (the early summer rainy season). Talk of Japan's economic bubble bursting fills the newspapers, but there is little evidence of it yet on the streets of Tokyo. As I cross Shinjuku Dōri, I glance down toward Kinokuniya Bookstore, but I have no time to browse today. Instead, I head toward Kabuki-chō, described by one tourist guide book as "one of the raunchiest, wildest, and most fascinating nightlife districts in all of Japan" (Reiber 1990: 157) and by another as Tokyo's "sleaze center" (Conner and Yoshida 1984: 180). It is comparatively tame by day, yet hucksters await potential customers outside their strip joints, peep shows, and massage parlors. I bypass karaoke bars, conveyor-belt sushi restaurants, and shops displaying over thirty varieties of doughnuts. My destination in this polyglot mix is at once a location, an institution, and an event. I am heading to the Shinjuku Koma Gekijō theater to catch a matinee performance of fifty-seven-year-old Kitajima Saburō, a veteran male singer, during his month-long run.[1]

Outside the theater, long lines of fans, who have, in effect, been waiting since Kitajima's last appearance at this same theater a year ago, wind around the corner and down the street. Many have traveled for hours by tour bus or train and paid from ¥2000 ($18) to ¥9500 ($86) for a ticket to today's performance.[2] I stand out not for my face, since I could be anyone's daughter or neighbor, but for my relative youth, height, and brightly colored clothes. Most of the fans, women and men in their fifties and sixties, are well under my five-feet, six-inches and are attired in somber dresses or dark, slightly worn suits. Judging by the signs on the tour buses I see idling at a distance, I conclude that many are from less urban areas—Nagano, Niigata, Shizuoka. They wait, their hands, far more used to working than lying idle, at their sides. At 1:30 P.M., there is a flurry of excitement as the doors open and the crowd rushes in. The orderly lines give way to brief mayhem, and I feel shoulders against my back and insistent shuffling at my sides. As people take their seats, the snacking begins—sushi, rice crackers, dried cuttlefish, deep-fried potato croquettes, fish cakes, pickled vegetables. The rustling of plastic bags and containers mingles with the general din of half-conversations, grunted replies, and appreciative lip-smacking. Fifteen minutes before the show is scheduled to begin, the house is nearly full.

I glance at the program, which announces the usual format: period drama, intermission, song show. By the time the lights dim and the curtains part, at 2:05 P.M., most of the food and drink have been consumed. Hands and mouths free, the crowd murmurs, some even shouting in delight and waving enthusiastically as their star appears on stage. They do not applaud him so much as greet him as if he were a friend, a brother, an uncle, or a father. He looks like them, although his clothes are those of their grandfathers or great-grandfathers. Gleaming skyscrapers are less than a kilometer away, but we are being transported to eighteenth-century Edo (premodern Tokyo). Kitajima plays the sword-fighting wanderer who fends off twenty assailants in the name of justice and then picks up his belongings and goes on his way. By the end of the hour-long period drama, which is only the first half of the show, the audience has laughed and cried with "Sabu-chan" (their affectionate nickname for Kitajima), the tough guy with the heart of gold. His tears—for his hometown, for the mother has not seen for seventeen years, for the lover from whom he has had to part—are theirs. In sharing his tears, the audience becomes his.

During the half-hour intermission, I browse through the array of kyarakutā gudzu (character goods) displaying Kitajima's picture and signature, which members of his fan club are selling at a booth in the lobby: sweatshirts (¥10,000/$91), decorative wall panels (¥50,000/$455), handkerchiefs (¥1000/$9), telephone cards (¥1000/$9), folding fans (¥2000/$18). Adjacent to this booth is a stand sponsored by Crown Records, the company for which Kitajima records, selling cassettes, compact discs, and videotapes. Business is brisk, despite the threat of economic recession. I buy a prepaid telephone card, one of the least expensive articles, which, I rationalize, would at least prove useful in an emergency.

When the lights go down again, the crowd eagerly anticipates the spectacle of the "hit parade," the song portion of the program. Kitajima does not disappoint. His songs express many of the same themes as the earlier historical drama: hometowns, mothers, lovers. In their pathos and sentimentality, they remind me of American country and western songs, although the music sounds completely different. He sings stoically of the ties that bind men to men, of the "path of a man" and what it means to be a man. Kitajima's costumes range from a white sequined tuxedo to the hakama (traditional Japanese male formal wear). The stage effects, too, are stunning—laser-emblazoned images, flashing strobe lights, fireworks, and as a finale, a twenty-foot-high rolling festival mikoshi (palanquin), on top of which Kitajima stands, singing. None of this goes unappreciated by the audience, who come to see the spectacle almost as much as to hear the singer. The music Kitajima sings, the songs audience members relish, the cassettes Crown Records sells, are enka, the focus of this book and the point where music, emotion, gender, and, as I argue, one version of nationhood converge in contemporary Japan.

Enka, a popular Japanese ballad genre that originated in the early twentieth century, combines Western instruments with Japanese scales, rhythms, vocal techniques, and poetic conventions in melodramatic songs of love, loss, and yearning. To the Japanese public, enka sounds timelessly old, although it is still actively created and consumed. The erasure of passing time is in fact part of its attraction. A 1993 hit is deliberately contrived to be easily mistaken for a 1953 one, and for the duration of the song, the forty-year gap is neatly erased. What helps to achieve this timelessness are not only the sounds and the images of enka but also—and most important—its sentiment. Here are hometowns left long ago but not forgotten, lovers parted, mothers remembered for their sacrifices. Amid the tumult and complexity of today's Japan, which faces challenging questions of political leadership, economic recession, and globalization, these affairs of the heart, dredged up from a reconstructed past, seem wonderfully simple, direct, and untarnished. What ties listeners to these songs is not so much a particular turn of melody or twist of phrase but an engagement in what, throughout this book, I call an "imaginary," which holds up to public view a communally broken heart.

Let me say at the outset that I do not approach enka as a fan of the music. Indeed, my own distance from it makes it all the more suitable as the focus of a study of what George Lewis (1987; cf. Bourdieu 1984) calls "taste cultures," especially as they intersect with concepts of emotion, gender, history, identity, and here, nationhood. My purpose in studying enka is twofold. First, I am interested in the emotions and their construction in particular cultures (Lutz 1988). In enka, among all the popular music genres in Japan, emotion runs particularly high. Enka is known as a form of *naki-bushi* (crying song), songs whose merit is measured by their ability to elicit tears. One composer calls enka "songs that make many tears flow [*namida o takusan nagasaseru uta*]." In this book I analyze those tears—their commercial production and promotion, and their individual and collective consumption.

This is not to say that enka's tears are wholly different from those of earlier Japanese narrative forms or those of other cultures, since they share much in common. What I wish to explore here, however, are the ways in which these tears are culturally constructed to suggest a boundary of difference through which Japanese define themselves to themselves and signify who they are. As one enka lyricist puts it, "The Japanese are a people who like to cry [*Nihonjin wa nakitai minzoku*]." I take his statement, and others like it, as invocations of an identity that is based in emotion. Enka's tears become collective tears that define a racial, a cultural, and even a national community.

This brings me to my second, related interest in studying enka, which is its reputation as *"nihon no uta"* (song of Japan), an expression of *"nihonjin no kokoro"* (the heart/soul of Japanese), and even *"dentō no oto"* (the sound of Japanese tradition) (see, e.g., Anonymous 1987: 14; IASPM-Japan 1991: 12). Amid the nationalistic cultural fervor of the 1970s, the record industry promoted enka as one emblem of national culture. Amid this larger project of collectively imagining what it means to be Japanese, the labels "nihon no uta" and "nihonjin no kokoro" thrust enka and its talk of emotions into the spotlight of this public construction of Japaneseness (Anderson 1983).

Enka is one dimension of Japan's national self-image, and like all such images, it glosses over, even masks, certain parts of that national self in order to shape a homogeneous whole. On stage, within clouds of synthetic fog and swirling lights, these songs provide a seductive spectacle of a past, superimposed on the present, that evokes nostalgia for a world in which cultural nationalism is unnecessary. In its representation of the collective imagination, enka offers up highly charged individual pasts bundled together and recast as the nation's own. This book examines this enka version of "Japan" as a reified past that is consumed in the present.

Enka and its consumption pique our interest as social practices of active, personal choice. One may "do" enka as an individual, as a spectator in an audience, as a member of a fan club, and as a student in a classroom of amateur singers. That "doing" takes many forms and requires varying levels of personal investment: buying tapes, requesting songs, tuning in to television and radio programs, listening to and watching performances, joining fan clubs, singing at karaoke bars. By "doing," one participates in a form of commercially produced national culture. This is not to say that all who "do" enka necessarily give the same meaning either to their actions or to the genre itself. For some, enka is merely an excuse to perform on a karaoke stage. For others, however, it may be a way to recover the intimate memory of an engaged heart, even if that intimacy brought heartbreak. For still others, it calls forth a sense of Japan's past and their own entitlement to that past.

The Japan of which enka sings builds upon, and is itself built by, a nostalgically framed collective memory. The aim of this book is to analyze this nostalgia, this deeply embedded relationship between a nation and its past(s). The sentimental music of enka evokes issues of class, power, and history and ties them together through the intimacy of emotion. What this book asks, then, is this: If enka provides one version of an imagined Japan, who is doing the imagining and to what purpose? In other words, whose "Japan" is this?

Some consideration must be given to those who control the production and marketing of enka. The power behind the industry is overwhelmingly male: Men compose, manage, and create enka throughout the entire production and distribution process. Although female singers outnumber male singers by almost two to one, the words, the music, and the singers' images are under the control of men. Thus, I argue, the voices of enka become a chorus of male expression. Through record-company-led fan clubs, whose membership is primarily female, men also control the organized consumption of enka (see Chapter 6). The axes of subjugation and manipulation fall along predictable lines: male over female, producer over consumer, manager over singer. And yet there is also power in the choices consumers make and in the meanings and uses they give these songs—what Michel de Certeau and Henry Jenkins have dubbed "textual poaching" (de Certeau 1984; Jenkins 1992), that is, fans' appropriation of media texts for their own uses. Rather than take a strictly ideological approach, I look for what William Kelly has called the "multiple zones" of interaction that surround any cultural product (quoted in Treat 1996a: 6).

Enka becomes one of a bundle of characteristics that identify, through their consumption, a particular life-stage in Japan. Sales of enka lagged far behind the levels of other genres in the 1990s—4 percent of all recording sales in 1992, shrinking to just over 1 percent by the end of the decade (Oricon 1993, 1998)—but according to fans and industry sources, its place within national culture is confirmed by AM radio, karaoke, and cable broadcasting. One particular supporter of enka is the state institution NHK (Nippon Hōsō Kyōkai; Japan Public Broadcasting), which schedules regular radio and television broadcasts and concerts.[3] These sites of consumption focus on attracting middle-aged and older adults, the primary fans of enka. In contrast, an activity like gateball is considered exclusively and appropriately of interest to the elderly (Traphagan 2000: 126).

Although some fans have listened to enka since early adulthood (and even longer), many others claim to have turned to it only as middle-aged and older adults. For them, listening to enka becomes part of a general turning toward "things Japanese," what Lise Skov and Brian Moeran call the "consumption of tradition" characteristic of the "'old-age end' of the media market" in Japan (1995: 8). Fans characterize their interest in enka as a stage in the process of moving from youthful consumption of Euro-American-influenced music and goods to more nativistic "Japanese sensibilities" in later adulthood. What is striking is the inevitability with which enka and "Japan" are paired. Fans explain their turning to enka in terms of a musical taste that lay dormant, waiting only for their life experiences and, for some, a sense of their own innate Japaneseness, to catch up to its lyrics and music. They are prodigal sons and daughters who return to "Japan" (and thereby to enka) during this later stage of their lives. One enka lyricist in his late fifties recalls his eventual shift to enka in these terms: "When we were young, our idols were first Elvis Presley, then the Beatles. We all did this, listening to [Western pop] music, and enjoying it. But when we hit our forties, somehow the pop music from abroad didn't appeal anymore, and we naturally [*shizen ni*] began searching for something else. It was enka." This book attempts to understand the process and the meaning of this shift to enka by older consumers.

When I asked an enka composer in his sixties whether or not non-Japanese could appreciate enka, he said that they might understand the words (at a dictionary level) and even like the music, but that a true appreciation of the genre was something only Japanese come by "naturally." According to him, this appreciation rises out of the very soil into their souls. The same arguments have been heard delimiting the ability of non-Japanese to speak Japanese, to fully understand Japanese aesthetics, or to muster the *hinkaku* (dignity) befitting the top rank of a *yokozuna* (grand master of sumō wrestling), and they do not bow in the face of foreigners' fluency in speaking Japanese, foreign achievements in the Japanese arts, or the victories of non-Japanese sumō wrestlers.[4] Language, art, sport/ritual, food, music, and emotion, as sites of racial exclusivity, become critical tropes of identity, which surface in talk of *kokoro* (heart/soul) as Japan's intangible, essential spirit.

Although enka's main audience is primarily an older one, enka forms a ubiquitous layer in the national soundscape. Promoted as the center of national culture through state-run media networks such as NHK in a geographically compact country with a high population density and relatively limited media options, enka becomes at the very least what I call "music overheard": one may not be a fan of enka but one cannot help having some general exposure to it or knowledge of it. In Japan I am constantly surprised by nonfans' familiarity with enka songs and singers; with enka's reputation as an expression of *"nihonjin no kokoro"* (heart/soul of Japanese); with the titles and tunes of some of its greatest past and present hits; and with the names, faces, and gossip surrounding its stars. Certain media mechanisms, such as NHK's annual New Year's broadcast of the Kōhaku Uta Gassen (Red and White Song Contest; see Chapter 4), ensure such "overhearing." Other ways enka may be "overheard" include daily morning television *"waido"* ("wide"; celebrity gossip) shows; "sports" newspapers and magazines that print the latest entertainment news and scandals; cable broadcasting into bars, sushi restaurants, and other nighttime entertainment businesses; and karaoke. "Music overheard" is not uniformly multidirectional but points instead to several loci of control, all of which define a society's mainstream. Enka's ubiquity is thus the result of a highly manipulable, power-laden distribution of cultural resources.

Enka's fans are said to constitute not only a life-stage group but also a class and regional group. According to its reputation, enka is most popular in rural areas and among blue-collar workers, but this claim overlooks the many white-collar urban office workers who sing enka nightly in karaoke bars and karaoke *bokkusu* ("boxes"; private rental booths). Blue-collar workers and rural areas thus become the loci of "otherness"—a "vanishing periphery" (Ivy 1995)—that coexists with the white-collar urban world of Japan's international achievements. To enka's fans, this "other" Japan and its music represent a "truer" and more fundamental indigenous Japanese culture.

In fact, many in Japan, particularly young people and intellectuals, actively contest enka's claim to national status, arguing that enka, an older, reputedly blue-collar, rural genre, retains outdated values and concepts. Japan, they say, has moved well beyond this feudalistic world to gain a foothold in the international economic and political arena. They dismiss enka as an anachronism whose place within present-day Japanese society is peripheral, not central. They prefer to project an image of a Japan that looks forward rather than backward. One of the ironies of enka as national culture is the degree to which the genre and its fans may be criticized, even mocked, not simply as old but as *furu-kusai* (literally, "smelling of old"; outdated). These opposing viewpoints, structured in part along generational lines, form the very core of the competing and highly polarized internal debates about modernity, internationalization (*kokusaika*), and "Japan" itself that are characteristic of contemporary Japan.

The debate goes on behind closed doors. Japan does not include enka among the examples of "official national culture" it offers either internationally or domestically. Instead, its cultural ambassadors include kabuki, *koto* (zither), the tea ceremony, flower arranging, even sumō wrestling, all of which perform "Japan" to an international (primarily European and American) audience. This Japan presents itself with colorful dramaturgy, refined aestheticism, spirituality, and exoticism on a grand scale in performances that also play to a domestic audience, marking class, history, prestige, and the official national culture. Japanese popular culture industries, meanwhile, export another, unofficial image of Japan in youth-oriented *manga* (comics), *anime* (cartoons), and "cute" products such as Pokémon and Hello Kitty, as well as cars, sushi, karaoke, and electronic appliances. Alongside these official and unofficial presentations of a national self are other images of Japan and Japanese. Among its Asian neighbors, for example, bitter memories of Japanese colonial rule and wartime atrocities linger. For other international eyes, the image of Japan is one of mixed accomplishment: the Japanese are technological wizards but robotic workhorses, and sometimes, xenophobic global citizens.

Enka buys into none of these images. These songs are small performances of the heart meant to play primarily, although not exclusively, to a home audience. Through a wash of tears, enka contradicts official international cultural images: not Japan as number one, but Japan as vulnerable to the subtlest affront; not Japan as cute or smiling, but Japan in tears and by its own definition (nihonjin no kokoro, "heart/soul of Japanese") at its most Japanese. This construction may be interpreted as a kind of "self-orientalism": Japan exoticized for its own consumption, synopticized in its own stereotype.

Other factors further complicate enka's status as the site of national culture. Whether direct from Japan or in the form of stylistically similar melodramatic ballads in other indigenous Asian languages, enka or enka-like music can be heard on juke boxes, in karaoke, and over the broadcast airwaves in Taiwan, Korea, Hong Kong, and parts of Southeast Asia (Ching 1996). What is curious—and significant—is that, within these Asian locales, people claim enka or its counterpart as their own music sung for generations, a legacy of the colonial period. Teresa Ten, a female enka singer born in Taiwan in 1953, has been quoted as saying, "I grew up in Taiwan listening to Japanese songs, so I cannot think of Japanese songs as being foreign music. Japan's music is Asia's music" (Anonymous 1995: 13). More accurately, perhaps, what Ten expresses is the degree to which Japan's popular culture has become part of the popular culture of its former colonial subjects.

The performance of enka as an expression of national culture is made all the more ironic by the appearance of non-Japanese singers on the enka stage, including both "hidden" Koreans long resident in Japan and passing as Japanese, and overtly Korean and Taiwanese singers from Asia. Just as the Japanese music industry has been exporting enka to other Asian countries, it has since the 1980s also been importing new singers from these countries, especially Korea and Taiwan. Teresa Ten was one of them,[5] and others include the Korean male singer Chō Yonpiru (debuted 1982) and the Korean female singers Kye Unsook (debuted 1985) and Kim Yonja (debuted 1988). In view of its various links throughout Asia, one might ask whether enka should more appropriately be called "the heart/soul of Asia." The answer depends on how and when the Japanese music industry, which jumps from "Japan" in one instance to "pan-Asia" in the next, decides to address the issues of boundaries and difference.

Critical issues, such as waning domestic popularity, dependence on state support, internal divisions, and pan-Asian markets and singers, are among the contingencies within which enka must be situated. In this book, Chapter 1 lays the groundwork for what I call the "cultural logic of enka's imaginary" by introducing the basic argument linking popular song, emotion, patterned form, and the nation. Chapter 2 examines the invention, definition, and place of enka in the history of modern popular music in Japan. Chapter 3 looks at ways in which the commercial production of enka contributes to its reputation as a nostalgic version of national culture grounded in emotion. Chapters 4 and 5 analyze the characteristic patterning of the genre and the ways in which these patterns render emotion both formulaic and real. Chapter 6 examines two modes of consumption, fan clubs and karaoke, both important ways in which individuals personally involve themselves in the enka world. Finally, Chapter 7 presents the imaginary of enka as it links emotion and the nation through nostalgia and romance. The book ends where it began, at Kitajima Saburō's concert at the Shinjuku Koma Gekijō theater in Tokyo, but, as I hope, having reached a larger destination.

The fieldwork on which this book is based took place primarily in the Tokyo-Yokohama area of Japan from August 1991 through July 1993, with later research sojourns in Honolulu, Hawai'i, and parts of Japan through June 2000. Although I have updated certain aspects of the work since its first writing in 1995, I have kept the body of the research intact, in part to serve as a historical record of this aspect of Japan in the early 1990s and in part because of my conviction that many of the processes I observed, recorded, and analyzed remain fundamentally unchanged today.

Geinō-kai (the entertainment world) is a closed-door world in Japan, and the segment of it that produces enka is notorious for being even more tightly closed than most. My study is by necessity broad, as is its design, since no business establishments would allow me sustained access to their operations when they could foresee little economic profit for themselves. I therefore cast a wide net in carrying out a multi-sited ethnography anchored in sounds rather than places, institutions, or people. In my fieldwork I have been an enka fan club member, a karaoke student, an observer of the training and recording process, a live concert and studio audience member, a media viewer, an amateur performer, an interviewer, and an interviewee.[6]

My net spreads ever wider. As I meet Japanese overseas, many of them now listening to enka with increased interest, I see ways in which this music continues to be reconfigured outside its homeland. As I go to karaoke bars and to singing lessons in Hawai'i and listen to older Japanese-Americans sing enka—not as their parents did but as they have chosen to do, often taking lessons from a local expert in what might be characterized as a new kind of interaction with leisure, performance, and "Japan"[7]—I see enka forging new identities and connections. These Japanese-Americans of my parents' generation ask me, who never sang or listened to this music as a child, "What is enka? What does it mean?" I find this reversal of positions unexpected and even poignant. The ties of enka stretch and bind, sometimes ironically so. My purpose here is to question those ties but at the same time to embrace them in an effort to understand the processes and the conditions through which they work.

CHAPTER ONE

The Cultural Logic of Enka's Imaginary

Japan has long been fascinated with itself, but no more so than during the late nineteenth and twentieth centuries, when national introspection has been framed within issues of modernity.[1] Whether modernity is approached as a matter of technological achievement, global capitalism, or mass-mediated public culture, its competing definitions have thrown into high relief the subject, and the subjectivities, of Japan as a construct that is embedded within these definitions. Periodic reiterations of national-cultural definitions have resulted in slogans and categories contrasting Japan with "the West." Whole fields of cultural production—from clothes to food to toilets—have become dichotomized as Japanese (*wa-*) or Western (*yō-*), defining difference while also shaping national-cultural boundaries (Tobin 1992: 24–25).[2] These dichotomies coexist as competing choices in a menu of shifting identities and affiliations.

The question of identity is further complicated by Japan's ambivalent attitude toward "the West," which has been characterized variously as one of admiration and disdain, envy and contempt, infatuation and fear, a reverential view of the foreign that Yoshino Kōsaku calls "exocentrism" (quoted in Hosokawa 1999: 520) and ethnocentrism. The musicologist Hosokawa Shūhei argues that these opposing attitudes are "constitutive of and complicit in Japanese modernity" (ibid.). The primary point is that however Japan defines *wa-* and *yō-* and wherever it places them within cultural hierarchies, the two are kept marked and separate as if by a tacit agreement to continue to differ. In many (although not all) spheres of consumption, "Japanese" and

"Western" elements coexist as fundamental oil-and-water differences, unresolved and unresolvable. As a consumer, for example, one chooses to lodge in a Japanese inn or a Western hotel, to squat above a Japanese toilet at a train station or sit on a Western one, to eat rice or bread for breakfast. These choices are not neutral: these actions of the body are strategic assertions and practices of identity.[3] It is not that sitting on a Western toilet makes one more "Western" but that repeatedly choosing to do so when a Japanese version is also available serves as a small bodily signifier of one's choices, both to oneself and to others. Nor does it matter that what some might consider Japanese, for example, tempura, has European/Portuguese roots, or that what others might consider Western, for example, spaghetti, has Asian connections. What matters are the meanings and categories already in place, the continuing concern with markers of distinctiveness.[4] The presence of these choices suggests multilinear paths to coexisting, often competing, modernities. Each choice involves interlocking fields (e.g., Western clothing/steak/toilets with seats) that extend to the smallest details (e.g., nail polish color or perfume fragrance). One steps into the prefabricated scene much like an actor speaking lines in a play or a carnival-goer placing his or her face in the cutout of a cardboard frame.

Enka feeds into this dichotomization as part of the "introspection boom" of the late 1960s and 1970s, which repeatedly asked one question: "Who are we Japanese?" But what is the logic behind this introspection, this practice of identity-making? What lies behind the Japanese construction of "Japaneseness"? What is at work when Japan becomes "Japan"? And, as I asked earlier, whose "Japan" is this? These are the questions that shape my approach to enka.

Collective Remembering, Collective Forgetting

The cultural logic of "Japaneseness" builds upon processes of nostalgically framed expression and desire.[5] Kathleen Stewart identifies nostalgia as a cultural practice that increases in importance as social life becomes diffuse, ambiguous, and fragmented (1992: 252). But the nature of this cultural practice varies according to where one situates oneself in the cultural landscape: nostalgia could be "schizophrenic exhilaration" in response to the multiplicity of images, or it could be "pained, watchful desire" framed by loss (ibid.: 253). Enka lives between these two extremes. Rather than evoking "memory with the pain removed" (Lowenthal 1985: 8), enka invokes the memory of pain prolonged into a state of aestheticized desire, the experience of life lived on emotional edge.

Fred Davis's (1979) proposal for a "sociology of nostalgia" is crucial in analyzing the sources, expressions, and meanings of nostalgia within group life, although Davis does not address different conceptualizations of nostalgia itself or how it is perceived by different members of the same group. Enka, for example, is not simulated nostalgia for a fictive past, as John Treat's (1996b) analysis of the Japanese writer Banana Yoshimoto suggests. Yoshimoto may write longingly of stereotypical happy families, but these families exist—as dreams, images, and memories—only in her stories. Here, nostalgia has no referent.

The enticement of enka is that it suggests a forum for collective nostalgia, which actively appropriates and shapes the past, thereby binding the group together. Enka encodes within nostalgia a historical moment of self-reflexivity, establishing a particular relationship with the temporal past that distances it from, while also placing it firmly in, the present. It is not the nostalgia described by Christopher Lasch, which "is all too eager to pronounce the past dead and gone and shed a sentimental tear in its memory" (1984: 69–70). Rather, it is nostalgia compartmentalized, assigned a place, just as "things Japanese" are kept categorically separate from "things Western."

What is past and distant becomes a kind of "internal exotic," a resource at once removed from people's lives yet central to their version of national-cultural identity (cf. Ivy 1995).[6] Borrowing the concept of "frontier," which, as Tessa Morris-Suzuki (1998) shows, was important in creating a sense of the Japanese nation in the nineteenth and twentieth centuries, one can posit enka as a kind of ironic frontier: it pulls the margins in to serve as a version of the center. Enka's internal exoticism, its domestic "frontierness," works on several levels. Setting songs in past times and remote areas of Japan establishes a sense of temporal and spatial otherness. Moreover, the characters that inhabit the enka world—bar hostesses, gangsters (*yakuza*), sailors—are today marginalized. Their actions, concerns, and emotions—the conflict between *giri* (duty, obligation) and *ninjō* (human feelings), a theme found in numerous kabuki plays and other narratives associated with Japanese tradition—become links with the past. These internal features may be considered exotic to mainstream Japanese life in the present. As Marilyn Ivy (1995) points out, "Discover Japan," the tourism campaign launched by Japan National Railways in the 1970s to encourage domestic travel to the more remote areas of the country, follows this same cultural logic.[7]

Nostalgia's function within this framework is to preserve distance—but to preserve as well a yearning to transcend it. In fact, distance itself, a "desire for desire," as Susan Stewart puts it (1993: 23), becomes nostalgia's sustaining mechanism. The erasure of distance threatens the very need for desire. Enka is thus not so much a "custodian of the past," as Carol Gluck (1993: 65) suggests, as an active exoticizer of many pasts.

This concept, the "internal exotic," finds parallels in Stewart's theory of the souvenir, the "portable" exotic, a piece of the faraway one can bring home, which simultaneously maintains distance and collapses it (1993: xii). The souvenir asserts its exoticism even when thrust into new settings. Thus, enka becomes the souvenir that brings the margins closer together in order to define the personal, or the subjective, and the national. Maintaining enka's "otherness" is a deliberate production and marketing tool.

Manipulating the past is not unique to Japan, as the extensive literature on the invention of tradition shows (Hobsbawm and Ranger 1983). But according to Robert Smith, Japanese "are unusually adept at it" (1983: 9), by which he does not mean to imply duplicity but to suggest a thoroughgoing rigor in shaping not simply the past but also the present and the future. What I call *tsukutta mono* (things made), a concept I borrow from an interview with a record producer, is helpful here in understanding the general Japanese attitude toward manipulation. Tsukutta mono suggests that 1) the human world functions most smoothly when one controls one's surroundings, including people, objects, and ideas; 2) the natural world is best appreciated when the human hand has shaped it to suit its own tastes (Kalland 1995); 3) human effort is the fundamental unit of value (cf. Singleton 1995); and 4) acceptance of these "truths" is part of being a mature human being (cf. Plath 1980). Manipulation becomes a way to valorize, aestheticize, and harmonize with one's physical and social surroundings. Obviously, this kind of cultural explanation masks various sociopolitical processes, especially hegemonic ones; at the same time, however, one must not overlook the concept of tsukutta mono in analyzing both the processes of manipulation and attitudes toward it. In the context of this study, tsukutta mono is a frank expression of the goal of the music industry, which regards its products—songs, singers, and images alike—as objects of "making" and manipulation (see Chapter 3).

Among "things made" and manipulated are collective memories. I take Marita Sturken's notion of "cultural memory"—memory that is shared outside the avenues of formal historical discourse yet is entangled with cultural products and imbued with cultural meaning" (1997: 3)—as critical to an understanding of enka's place in the lives of its listeners. Cultural memory accrues through public gatherings and utterances, memorials and anthems, televised concerts and ballads—and through the sometimes heated contestation that surrounds them. Popular song, particularly a nostalgically informed genre of popular song such as enka, becomes a "technology of memory," an active shaper of memory rather than merely its vessel (ibid.: 9). Each song creates a snapshot of individual experience that is publicly displayed and collectively recalled. Moreover, this technology of memory is also a commercial commodity, bought and sold in a marketplace of competing memories. Thus, popular song and the memories it shapes must be considered not only within the social framework of national, cultural, and personal concerns, but also within an economic framework of business decisions and profit-making.

Constructing the past is as much a matter of collective forgetting as of collective remembering (Sturken 1997: 7). The amnesiac quality of nostalgia continually surprises. It selects which details to obscure in order to naturalize memory, history, and identity and then build its own phantasmic utopia. Memory itself suggests the ongoing interaction of what Jonathan Boyarin calls the "creative collaboration between present consciousness and the implicit shaping of consciousness, its selection of the contours that experience or have expression of the past" (1994: 22). The politics of memory lies in accommodating its purposes. The conundrum here is that memory is neither entirely individual nor wholly collective; it is an embodied social practice that constantly creates and tests identities (ibid.: 26). Memory becomes the substance of identity as well as its legitimation. The processes of remembering, forgetting, and, in effect, inventing, are central to enka and to its role in the larger project of creating a national culture (cf. Fujitani 1993). Enka, a genre that looks old and sounds old, thus assumes dual roles: it is a technology for creating national and cultural memory and it is an archive of the nation's collective past.

Localizing the National, Nationalizing the Local

In enka, the focal point of nostalgia and memory is *furusato* (hometown), literally, "old village," but generalized since the 1970s and 1980s to refer to the idea of originary, emotive space: homeland (Reader 1987; Robertson 1991: 5, 14).[8] Jennifer Robertson's (1991) excellent work on furusato as a trope of Japanese nostalgia in the 1980s analyzes the politics of place-, history-, and tradition-making during that period. Although the "furusato boom" of the 1980s has ended, in cities as well as rural areas enka continues to convey the sound of furusato—over the radio, on television and in cable broadcasting, and in karaoke.

Furusato is conveyed through other sounds as well, in particular *min'yō* (folk song), which occupies a privileged status in Japan as a preindustrial rural "folk" art.[9] Celebrated in concerts, competitions, and preservation societies, min'yō is part of national culture, but its status is higher than that of enka and its place more esoteric. Enka is commercial music, professionally produced and distributed from urban centers. Although many of its singers are said to come from the countryside, its relationship to regional Japan is based in the sentimentality and nostalgia of distance. Min'yō, on the other hand, might be recorded professionally, but it retains its link to "the folk" through its rootedness in amateurism (sometimes semiprofessionalism) and regionalism.

"Homelands," a concept borrowed from cultural geography, is useful in discussing the furusato element in enka. Richard Nostrand and Lawrence Estaville, Jr., citing interlinking factors of place, power, and history, define homelands as "places that people identify with and have strong feelings about" (1993: 2–3). Both furusato and homelands share the sense of an ascribed rootedness, of belonging not by choice but by way of "natural" bonds of blood, birth, and soil. In the case of Japan, however, homeland has retained both the specific meaning of one's family's rootedness to a particular place and the more generalized sense of "national family" rootedness in a mythic Furusato Japan (Robertson 1991: 32–37; cf. Ivy 1995). Conceiving of the nation as homeland lends it an affective immediacy and intimacy often lacking in the larger political sphere.

In Furusato Japan, place is given meaning through discursive practices that include song. As Henri Lefebvre emphasizes, place is not mere land area, it is "a projection onto a (spatial) field of all aspects, elements and moments of social practice" (1991: 8; Keith and Pile 1993). I would argue that in contemporary Japan, the meanings given to place through the concept of furusato have transformed the local into the national. Regional spaces, once individuated through sometimes minute differences, have been incorporated into the national project of homogeneity and majority making (cf. Gladney 1998; Weiner 1997). In defining the meaning of these spaces, provincial regions such as northern Honshū, with its harsh winters and strong folk traditions, have been generalized as center(s) of a "true" national identity and particularized as the idiosyncratic periphery of the nation-culture. These spaces are at once core and periphery, internal and exotic, whole and part. One of the most effective conduits of these spatial/national meanings and identities is enka.

NHK, Japan's national public broadcasting system, is here considered part of "the apparatus of discourses, technologies, and institutions (print capitalism, education, mass media, and so forth) that *produces* what is generally recognized as 'the national culture'" (Donald 1993: 167). Enka is not, of course, the only, or even the most prestigious, component of national culture. Prestige, as I have noted, can be found in Japan's "cultural ambassadors": kabuki, koto (zither), flower arranging, the tea ceremony, and sumō wrestling. Enka stands apart, less refined perhaps, but hardly less confined and self-conscious before an audience of insiders. As James Donald suggests, the nation, by which he means a "sense of" the nation, is an effect of these cultural technologies, not their origin (ibid.: 167). The process of nation-making that concerns us here is not one of sheer invention or fiction (cf. Gellner 1983). As Benedict Anderson's by now well-known argument puts it, "Communities are to be distinguished, not by their falsity/genuineness, but by the style in which they are imagined" (1983: 6). Enka is a factor in Japan's "styling," the process of imaging and imagining that is fundamental to the symbolic production of the "nation as community."

The cultural logic of "enka as national culture" arises from its discursive production of "values, dispositions, and differences" reified as "Japan" (Donald 1993: 167). Through its analysis of the twinned concepts of romance and furusato-homeland (see Chapter 7), this book examines how these values, dispositions, and differences link enka to the nation. Enka, this "homeland in song," fuses the local to the national, thereby giving the imaginary a sense of place.

One of the most effective ways in which regional localities have been nationalized is through a process of incorporation: various urban-rural divides become less relevant than a single center-periphery divide. The symbolic split in twentieth-century Japan is therefore not so much city vs. country (although this is still a relevant dichotomy) as it is Tokyo vs. not-Tokyo,[10] labeled variously *chihō* (provinces), *inaka* (rustic countryside), and *kokyō/furusato* (hometown), each of which gives different nuances to the sense of place. *Chihō*, which defines lands that are outside Tokyo, is most neutral; *inaka* imparts a sense of cultural backwater as well as physical distance; *furusato* is the most emotionally binding. Areas labeled with these "not-Tokyo" terms include cities such as Sapporo, Hiroshima, and Fukuoka, whose populations total well over one million (Ueda 1992: 36). With the incorporation of rural areas into what has been constructed as a Tokyo-centric national urban culture, the urban-rural split carries less and less meaning (Ivy 1993; Kelly 1993).

At the same time, the concept of rusticity otherwise associated with an urban-rural split becomes reconfigured here as a Tokyo-provinces divide, and, within Tokyo, as a *yamanote-shitamachi* (uptown/foothills-downtown) axis of difference. Therefore, although urban centers such as Osaka, Nagoya, Kobe, and Hiroshima may not be rural, they are "rustic"—that is, not-Tokyo—in Japanese terms. Outside the boundaries of Tokyo there is also a sharp drop-off: even cities such as Yokohama and Kawasaki, less than an hour away on Tokyo rail lines and visually contiguous with its urban landscape, are considered "rustic." What is important to consider, then, is a concept of "rusticity" that is based not on population density, strict geographic location, or even economic base, but on cultural distance from a single national center, Tokyo. On this cultural map there is no real in-between, no real suburban.

Dorinne Kondo's astute analysis of difference as an idea constructed around the yamanote-shitamachi axis clarifies some of the issues surrounding enka (1990; also Bestor 1989; Dore 1958; Seidensticker 1983). Shitamachi connotes far more than geographic areas within Tokyo; it becomes a significant characterization of the class, lifestyle, ethos, and aesthetics of these areas: working-class, artisanal, preindustrial, informal, straightforward, cooperative, intimate, warm, emotional, Edo-period *chōnin* (townspeople) panache (Kondo 1990: 57–68). For the purposes of this study, however, what is most significant about shitamachi is that, while it is supposed to be the locus of the "truly Japanese," as Kondo is careful to point out, this characterization involves some ambivalence: as much as non-shitamachi may look fondly upon shitamachi and its people, they would never want to become shitamachi dwellers (ibid.: 68). Like enka, shitamachi is a nostalgic "reminder of who they [white-collar middle-class] are—the repositories of what is 'traditionally' or 'truly' Japanese—and of what they have lost" (ibid.: 72). Rusticity (and enka, the music linked with it), which brings different kinds of cultural capital together in an uneasy tension, is both reviled as a cultural backwater and celebrated as a cultural repository.[11]

Regional differences, often built upon the smallest details but zealously upheld, are also a factor in the construction of furusato in song and in other forms of public discourse, and become part of its general texture. Various regions of Japan are characterized not only by language, food, folklore, music, and scenery, but also by the look and character of the people who live there. But more than texture is at work here. Through their regional and subregional differences, residents become bound to local spatial identities; but when these differences come together under the umbrella of furusato, then being a "local" means being a national citizen. Difference becomes the basic thread—separate, distinct, and representative—of the national fabric. As Ivy points out, "Representative value becomes a mobile sign, detachable from locale but dependent on perpetually evoking it" (1995: 13). These interrelationships between sign and signified, part and whole, are the crux of the matter here. Yet separate does not mean equal; the distribution of power and control over national culture is not shared evenly by center and periphery, by urban and rural, or even by various regions within peripheries.

As a result of this uneven balance of power and control, rural communities need to negotiate their own identities within the competing ideologies emanating from urban centers. Kelly (1986) documents a rural community in northern Honshū whose inhabitants respond to pressure to adopt *gōrika* (rationalization) in their agricultural techniques while continuing to value nostalgic evocations of themselves (and other rural communities) as repositories of Japan's past. Even when communities are not strictly rural, they constantly invoke furusato as the model of authenticity, which links them not only to pastness and tradition but also to sociality and morality. Therefore, as Robertson (1991; also Moon 1989) argues, *furusato-zukuri* (furusato-making), a government policy of the mid-1980s that aimed to produce a sense of the past in these communities, became a deliberate production of "tradition," emotion, and virtue. Enka, reinvented as a genre of Japanese "tradition," has played a role in this process. In fact, "traditionalism," defined by Theodore Bestor as "the interpretation, creation, or manipulation of contemporary ideas about the past to bestow an aura of venerability on contemporary social relations" (1989: 4), informs communities, songs, and ideas that seek to legitimate themselves.

The notion of homeland is related to another concept frequently invoked in Japan, that of *shimaguni* (island country). Enka also supports what Dru Gladney (1998) calls "majoritarian discourse"—Japan's continuing self-definition as shimaguni, isolated, unique, and homogeneous, a land and culture unto itself. Moreover, Japanese are said to have the mentality of island people, looking inward rather than outward. These constructions shape a culturalism that ignores Japan's present internationally embedded condition as well as its past experiences of permeable boundaries. Japan may indeed be an island surrounded by water, but water is not an unbridgeable barrier. Yet the persistent myth of shimaguni transforms Japan into a homeland with nowhere else to go.

The homeland presented in enka builds the nation from its individual blocks. As the local narrows down to the specificities of individual mothers, distinctive hometowns, and regional food, language (or dialect), and song, locale becomes a critical link to the larger constructs of racial blood, "virtual" furusato, and national culture. Underlying much of the ideology expressed in enka is a firm belief in a collective sense of the Japanese people, an "us-ness" frequently invoked in daily conversation as *"wareware Nihonjin"* (we Japanese people). This "us-ness" forms a canon of belief known collectively as *nihonjinron* (treatises on being Japanese). Flourishing in the late 1960s and 1970s, a time when Japan could be said to have emerged from its postwar dependence on the United States, nihonjinron was (and remains) a powerful ethnocentric ideological tool. At its center is a strong belief in the homogeneity and uniqueness of the Japanese people, the Japanese language, and Japanese culture. Harumi Befu delineates six main features of the nihonjinron canon: 1) ecology (geographic determinism; Japan as a resource-poor island subject to frequent natural disasters); 2) subsistence economy (wet rice cultivation that necessitates cooperative social organization); 3) social structure (group orientation organized in hierarchical structure); 4) psychology, in particular, *amae* (dependency); 5) language; and 6) ethos, in particular, an emphasis on the spiritual side of the Japanese character (1993: 109–13).[12] In its own explicit reification of "Japan," enka encompasses many of these same assumptions.

But enka encompasses much more, including emotion, which influences and shapes the cultural logic of its imaginary. In the analysis that follows I examine enka in terms of "emotional style," defined by Dwight Middleton as "the normative organization of emotions, their indigenous classification, form of communication, intensities of expression, contexts of expression and patterns of linkage with each other and with other domains of culture" (1989: 188). The concept of "emotional style" embeds emotion firmly within a particular society at a particular time. My aim is not to characterize "the Japanese" as a composite of timeless patterns—shame culture, social embeddedness, dependency (Benedict 1946; DeVos 1973; Doi 1971; Lebra 1976)—but to deal with song as one of many forms of "emotion talk" in Japan, and with enka as emotion talk that is linked to identity-production. Moreover, I consider the emotional style presented in enka within its broader sociopolitical framework, what Raymond Williams has called "structures of feeling" (1965). These structures situate emotion within ideological, political, and economic forces. Enka may be held up as one way in which emotion becomes implicated in the highly ideological act of producing "the nation."

This form of cultural nationalism contrasts sharply with the overt nationalism that prevailed before World War II. As Darrell Davis (1996) shows in his analysis of Japanese art films, the aggressive nationalism of the 1930s may be seen in the monumental film style built around "a certain Japanese aura," which infused the country's feudal heritage with spiritual, even sacred, attributes. Enka's nationalism, however, concerns not the public Japaneseness of the 1930s but a kind of private, painful longing, which its proponents would say is more characteristic of Japan in general. What links both of these versions of national-cultural identity together is their emphasis on spirituality. One version of spirituality is the warrior,[13] the other, the lover. As Davis puts it, "in the end, it [Japan's spiritual self-image] is an appeal to the holiness of Japan, over against the secular blandishments of Western materialistic corruption" (1996: 10).

In the face of Japan's assertions that it is a classless (or, at least, a middle-class) society, enka provides stubborn testimony of the covert structures that continue to support stratification. Enka is often presented as a "taste culture" (Gans 1974) associated with the blue-collar working classes, or *taishū bunka* (laboring classes culture), and class does in fact become part of its rhetoric of emotion, past, and place. The process of designating one class/taste culture as the national culture is critical here, but even more interesting is the process of deciding which one. According to Pierre Bourdieu's (1984) theory that class is structured around consumer distinctions, one would expect a national culture to be drawn from the tastes and lifestyles of the dominant class. Indeed, Gerald Creed and Barbara Ching (1997) speak of the domination of the urban gaze and its devaluation of the rustic as a source of national-cultural identity. In Japan, however, through an internal exoticization, taishū bunka has become a version of national culture that keeps enka simultaneously at the margins and in the center of national-cultural identity.

Through a series of transformations, the folk/rural/working class is defined as the "real" nation (cf. Sorensen 1997: 41). The ideology at work here suggests a deliberate heterogenizing of social strata that is akin to Stewart's sense of nostalgia as "desire for desire." Blue-collar distinctions keep enka separate and "exotic," and this same separateness characterizes the construction of Japaneseness. The story the Japanese tell themselves about themselves becomes one private face of the nation. It is not a face with which all Japanese would agree or even one all would accept, but it persists as "music overheard," as ambient public culture.

The relationship between "international Japan" and "domestic Japan" may be contextualized by the very performativity of Japanese social life and the identities expressed through the contrasts between *tatemae* (public face) and *honne* (private feelings); *omote* (surface, front side) and *ura* (underside, back side); *soto* (outside) and *uchi* (inside) (cf. Bachnik and Quinn 1994; Doi 1986; Goodman and Refsing 1992).[14] The "domestic Japan" that enka helps to define draws on "*honne* culture" constructed as Other: working-class, feudal past, distant rural homeland. When Other is reconfigured as Self, enka expresses the ambivalent contradictions of these different "Japans" (cf. Ohnuki-Tierney 1990).

Patterning Forms Through Kata

Emotional expression in enka takes the form of stylized formulas I call *kata* (patterning; patterned form).[15] The concept, from the traditional arts of flower arranging and the tea ceremony, the martial arts, and kabuki, is here extended to include patterning in Japanese culture in general.

Theodor Adorno's (1990) well-known critique of Western popular music analyzes formulaic structures as the product of capitalist industrial production, which seeks to standardize its commodities. His criticism is based on a Marxist economic determinism and the "duping of the masses" as well as on a eurocentricism that devalues repetition in favor of originality. While it is true that standardization and patterning lend themselves to more efficient production of commercial music, how people in various cultures regard that patterning may differ. According to Simon Frith, the fixedness of popular music is intrinsic to recording technology, which effectively captures and replicates one particular performance in time (1987: 61). What I am seeking, however, are ways to understand not only Adorno's standardization and Frith's replication, both certainly very much a part of the genre, but also people's attitudes toward these processes and their precedents in traditional arts. Analyzing these patternings as kata, rather than simply reducing them to aspects of capitalist production or technological replication, shows how they give form to and aestheticize the emotions they express.

My emphasis on kata may understandably result in a structuralist approach, but I would justify that approach as one that is already deeply embedded within this cultural form. In enka, kata exist on several levels at various stages of production, performance, and consumption. They display varying degrees of "patternedness" that can include the smallest nuance of breathiness, the lifting of a heel, and the streaming of tears, as well as the sounds, sights, and situations that evoke those tears.

There are good reasons for choosing kata over the English words "pattern," "style," or "formula." First, kata emphasizes an embeddedness in daily life. Linguistically, there is both a character for formal kata and a verbal suffix, -kata (written in syllabary), that denotes a patterned way of doing things. Second, kata emphasizes surface form and beauty: the viewer's attention is drawn to the surface of the staged event and to the effects produced by the performers. This emphasis on form and effects gives a highly theatrical sense to performance and a performative sense to daily life. Third, kata emphasizes detail, which makes of a knowledgeable audience a highly refined one, acutely aware of the finest differences and their aesthetic effects. Fourth, as a system of theatrical display, kata places emphasis on technique, on the process of doing: a performance becomes a presentation of presentation. The audience enjoys the product and the process of transformation. Fifth, kata separates the whole into discrete, patterned units, which create a recognizable code of the performance action, a code whose goal is beauty. Through patterns, beauty and emotion are created, perceived, and evaluated.

Sixth, kata is important as a way for art forms to be taught and handed down from one generation to the next. Kata, and the related concept *katachi* (form), becomes a means by which one may "enter" (*katachi de hairu*) an art form: it is a manner of doing, a way of being (Kondo 1990: 106), which creates its own historical links. As Thomas Kasulis explains, "By absolutely standardizing the practice, the student sees the master perform the movement in exactly the same way each time" (1993: 317). Kata becomes not merely a distillation of one individual way of doing things but a historic panoply of teachers past and present, embedding the doer and the doing in a thick diachronic context. Kata at once establishes, constructs, and verifies a relationship with the past.

At the same time that it formalizes, aestheticizes, and historicizes, kata also spiritualizes, and this seventh characteristic may be the most crucial one of all. Working on the external through kata transforms and defines the internal. The two are interrelated parts of the same whole. For this study, what is important is that, unlike much Western thought that gives primacy to what is below the surface and behind the mask as somehow truer and more significant, a theory of kata gives the surface its due. Jacob Raz's explanation of yakuza behavior fits well with this theory of kata: self-presentations "are not merely outward expressions of some inner substance of identity, but a constant process of *creating* that identity, while simultaneously signifying and demonstrating it" (1992: 213). The Western hierarchized dichotomy of form (the false) vs. content (the true) becomes reconfigured as continuous and interpenetrating parts. Here, cultural elements such as tsukutta mono and tatemae/honne can be brought together. Kata is at the same time superficial and profound; it is content attendant upon form (Kondo 1990: 106).

These aspects of kata—surface aesthetic, attention to detail, performativity, codification, historical significance, and transcendence—contradict the approach to emotions, expression, and temporality assumed by many Western scholars. Emotions as kata are at once raw and cultivated, and their very cultivation through time provokes moral and aesthetic admiration. The notion of kata, however, also includes its negation. In the aesthetic realm, the master perfects kata to the point where it vanishes. The creative goal of kata-training is to fuse the individual to the form so that the individual becomes the form and the form becomes the individual.

In spite of what might seem a highly formulaic system of popular "hit-making" in a conservative genre, not all enka songs are hits, nor do all well-trained singers become stars. Herein lie the limits of kata. Teachers of enka teach pattern, while singers of enka speak of *kosei* (individuality, originality), which they consider necessary for success in the enka world. One needs to balance doing things as they have been done before using a standard formula and trying something a little new to gain notice. One must recognize the value of both.

The cultural logic of enka's imaginary uses kata to add new dimensions to what might, on the surface, be interpreted as mere nostalgia. Enka is not a museum that seeks to preserve the past. A genre called *natsu-mero* (from *natsukashii*/nostalgic, *merodii*/melody), which consists strictly of rereleased old songs, serves that purpose. Enka, on the contrary, is always newly created. The music industry is constantly busy: new songs are composed every year, and new singers groomed for their debut. Amid this constant busyness, however, enka denies that the past is past and provides a space within the present where the values, interactions, and emotions associated with the past can continue to exist. It does so in part through furusato, which becomes a spatialized metonym for temporality, but even more important, it does so through kata. By taking the past as patterning, enka is able to evoke the patterning of the past even as it pushes patterns to new limits. This cultural logic situates enka firmly in the present and gives force to its particular version of nationhood.

CHAPTER TWO

Inventing Enka

Definitions, Genres, Pasts

"There is no definition of enka [Enka no teigi wa nani mo nai n desu]."
—Producer/manager of a top enka star

"Before the war, all you heard was ryūkōka [umbrella term for Japanese popular song]. Then some time after the war, everyone said 'Enka, enka!' So, tell me, what is enka?"
—Seventy-year-old Japanese-American amateur singer

"Enka is any kind of [Japanese] popular music which, when you hear it, you know it's Japanese."
—Elderly Japanese-American proprietor of Japanese music store, Honolulu

Although enka is an indigenous popular song genre whose roots stretch back well before 1868,[1] this historical account begins in the Meiji era (1868–1912). During that time, Japan introduced and promoted Western music and instruments in a deliberate, self-conscious attempt to modernize itself in the image of the West. Inasmuch as modernity is shifting and relational, enka is "modern" music that brings Western instruments together with Japanese scales, vocal techniques, and textual themes. Since the 1970s, enka has also come to be regarded as "traditional" music that reaches back to the roots of Japaneseness.

My purpose here is not to situate enka as either "modern" or "traditional" but to examine it as an invention. In using the word "invention," I am aware that, as is true of most inventions, enka is not wholly new; it draws on a name ("enka") and a group of musics with roots in the past. What is new, however, at least since the 1970s, is the combination of the name and the music under the self-validating mantle "heart/soul of Japanese" (nihonjin no kokoro). Enka's credibility as a traditional genre rests on historicizing and naturalizing its progressive evolution. Yet its evolution is not linear but one that has been reconstructed to invoke "tradition." In commenting on the invented traditions of modern Japan, Stephen Vlastos points out, "Traditions of any duration are diastrophic rather than flat and unified; hence they function as multivalent and somewhat unstable cultural signifiers" (1998: 6). This chapter focuses on the instability of enka—as music, as named genre, and as cultural signifier.

Defining Enka

The *Oricon Yearbook*, the standard publication of the Japanese music industry (akin to America's *Billboard*), divides popular music into five broad categories (listed by percentage of sales in 1993): 1) *fōku* ("folk"; urban folk-music inspired music) and *rokku* ("rock"), 77.0 percent; 2) *poppusu* ("pops"; Euro-American derived middle-of-the-road pop music), 10.3 percent; 3) *yōgaku* (popular music imported from Euro-America), 8.1 percent; 4) enka, 4.2 percent; and 5) other, 0.5 percent (Oricon 1993: 3).

As the comments quoted at the beginning of the chapter suggest, defining enka is difficult not only in Japan but wherever the music is heard and sung. One Japanese musicologist defines enka as "popular songs of the *kayōkyoku* [broadly, twentieth-century mainstream Japanese popular music] genre that are said to have Japanese musical and spiritual characteristics" (Gondō 1988: 4). That enka "sounds Japanese" may be the result of certain traits of musical style or poetic conventions (see Chapter 5). Moreover, the listener's sense of what is and is not Japanese shifts over time: conventions change, as do even those boundaries between genres established by the music industry. For example, "Kayōkyoku Chōsa" (Popular Music Survey), a 1968 survey on popular music conducted among Tokyo urbanites, attributed different genres to their favorite singers. Although enka was included as a category, some singers of what is today considered enka were at that time labeled "*mūdo kayō kashu*" ("mood song" singers) (Komota et al. 1980: 64–65).[2]

Defining enka is difficult not only because the genre is slippery but because the word itself has been used to mean different things over time and been written with different ideographs.[3] The two most common meanings of enka, based on different spellings, are "performed song/speech song," its earliest usage during the Meiji period, and "love song," a later usage with strong sexual, even erotic, connotations. The composer Hoshino Tetsurō (n.d.), who distinguishes six different ways of writing the word, has compiled and categorized 105 of his own songs according to these groupings. Altogether I have come across ten different ideographic spellings and definitions of *enka*.

The music industry defines enka by singer, not by music or text (Fujie 1989: 199). The songs sung by "enka singer X" are considered enka by the very fact that they *are* sung by singer X.[4] Of course, not all singers are happy with this situation. As the manager of M.H., a female star, puts it, "The biggest problem is that of placing a singer's entire output into a single genre. This practice is particularly strong in the field of enka. Therefore, an enka singer like M.H. gets into a lot of trouble. For her, it's really an inhibiting thing [*totemo ikigurushii koto na n desu yo*]." The genre restricts a singer's repertoire and likewise becomes defined by what a singer sings. Theoretically, when and if a singer broadens his or her scope, the genre might possibly expand. M.H.'s manager gives an example: "So it may be that the songs that M.H. sings are classified as enka. However, you know her famous 'song X'? That was 1975. At the time it came out, people were criticizing her, saying, 'Why is M.H. singing folk songs?' However, now 'song X' has become a representative enka song. Strange, isn't it?" In this case, a song once considered (and criticized) as being outside the genre has subsequently become central to the genre. More often, the genre becomes a kind of self-censoring, delimiting factor in a singer's repertoire. The conservatism of singers (or, more accurately, of those in charge of producing enka) and audiences tends to cap any expansion of the genre into other modes of expression. That this is "old-sounding" music, then, is no accident (see Chapter 3).

Whether or not enka is defined according to style ("all popular songs that sound Japanese") or performer ("all songs that enka singers sing"), the Japanese public and the popular media continue to use the term as an important catch-all for popular music considered to be of indigenous origin. Thus, in Japan the question of enka's possible Korean roots remains a controversial one. Those who make this claim point to the similarities in musical form and content between enka and many Korean popular songs, the "affinity" of many singers of Korean ethnicity for enka, and the historical link between Koga Masao (1904–1978), the man who created the prototype of enka style, and Korea, his home during part of his early life. Others, who claim that enka has indigenous roots, acknowledge possible Korean borrowings but point to enka's origins in Japanese popular music forms such as *naniwa-bushi* (Osaka song), also known as *rōkyoku* (narrative song). My aim here is neither to verify nor to dispute enka's indigeneity but to recognize enka as a native category that has emerged out of specific historical circumstances.[5]

Meiji Era (1868–1912)

The word *enka*[6] is an abbreviated form of *"enzetsu no uta"* (oratorical song). It originated in the 1880s to describe the antigovernment protest songs sung in the streets in support of the *jiyū minken undō* ("freedom and people's rights movement") of 1874–90, which sought to establish a democratic constitution and a nationally elected assembly. Japanese intellectuals, who had read the works of Western philosophers in translation and embraced their ideals of popular representation, began to call for representative government. In an attempt to suppress the movement, the Meiji government imposed restrictions on public expression. The movement's intellectual leaders, meanwhile, hoping to gain popular support but hindered by the low level of literacy among the general population, sought some form of oral communication that would promote the movement's ideas and ideals. Using a kind of speech-song and taking it directly to the streets would not only avoid government restrictions on published materials and avert police interference at large gatherings, it would also make these ideas more accessible to the public. Enka ("speech-song") was born.

In its attempt to appeal to the general public, the movement also broadened its initial interests to include the problems of farmers and land tax reform. In its original form, enka was half-sung and half-spoken by an *enkashi* (enka singer/caller; otherwise known as *sōshi*, singer/caller) unaccompanied by a musical instrument. In its rhythmic exaggeration of certain syllables, it was musically similar to the cries of street vendors, but its goal was political: to deliver a message in an entertaining way and gain support for a political agenda.

The enkashi, described in these early days as "singing street guerrillas," printed and sold enka lyrics, but did so "hastily in the streets, with one eye always out for the police" (Nakamura 1991: 270). Gradually, however, their role shifted from that of political guerrilla to that of entertainer, and they began to organize into groups such as the Seinen Kurabu (Youth Club), formed in 1890, to write songs and print and distribute lyrics.

An important aspect of enka during this early period was the *kae-uta* (substitution song) tradition of setting different lyrics to the same melody.

Given their lack of musical background, the relative importance of their political message, and the absence of copyright laws, the enkashi used kaeuta as a wide-ranging tool. The resulting enka were collections of verses written by different people but set to one musical form.

With the establishment of the Diet in 1890 and Japan's victory in the Sino-Japanese War of 1894–95, the impetus for protest songs diminished, and enka went into decline. By 1901, the Seinen Kurabu had disbanded. But the onset of the Russo-Japanese War of 1904–5 reinvigorated nationalistic fervor, and the immense popularity of Soeda Azembō's (1872–1944) enka song "Rappa Bushi" (Bugle Call Song) launched a revival. During this resurgence in popularity, enka began to focus less on politics and more on entertainment. Soeda, who had been a member of the Seinen Kurabu since 1892, became the most famous enka composer and performer of the Meiji era.

The earlier, more political enka was closer to stylized speech than to song. But that changed during the Meiji era, when the schools, the military, and other institutions of public life began to adopt Western music in the larger project of creating a "modern" Japanese nation.[7] Through the continuing influence of two particular types of Western-based songs—*shōka* (school songs composed to introduce Japanese children to Western music) and *gunka* (military songs)—enka became more "musical" in the Western sense, emphasizing melody over speech. Soeda Azembō's enka, characteristically describing historical or current events in a personal and emotional manner, drew on these school and military songs to reshape what had begun as a stylized speech performance into a new, more tuneful genre.

In 1907, the violin, a prestigious—and portable—Western instrument, was introduced in enka performance, heralding the age of what was known as *baiorin enka* (violin enka). According to Sakurai Toshio (b. 1910), whom I interviewed in 1993 as the last enkashi still living and performing, the idea of using the violin to accompany the singing came not from the enkashi themselves but from the more intellectual strata ("*erai hito*"),[8] who felt that the instrument would give the genre greater prestige, attract more attention—and sell sheet music. The enka performed during this period consisted of news of contemporary events set to preexisting melodies.

The stylistic forerunners of what is today considered enka include various kinds of *min'yō* (folk song), *naniwa-bushi/rōkyoku* (narrative song), and *kouta* (a ballad form), all of which were accompanied by the *shamisen* (lute). Like baiorin enka, naniwa-bushi flourished among street performers before the advent of electronic media (but has continued into the electronic era through recordings issued by major record companies). Naniwa-bushi recounted familiar stories of the past as well as newsworthy stories of the present, often on a moralistic theme such as *giri-ninjō* (duty vs. human feelings). Its heroes included valiant samurai, chivalrous thieves, charismatic outlaws, dutiful sons, and devoted wives. Although naniwa-bushi was popular in the streets, intellectuals regarded it as an expression of "cheap taste and feudalistic morals" (Koizumi 1980: 551), some of the same criticism leveled at modern enka. The heritage of naniwa-bushi vocal production, singing technique, and ornamentation, along with the subject matter of its texts, has carried over into contemporary enka.

Taishō Era (1912–1926)

Although Japanese *ryūkōka* (popular music) originated during the Meiji, many Japanese scholars consider the Taishō era to be its true founding period, since at that time these songs were well known throughout the country and sung by a broad spectrum of the population (Minami 1987: 469). The ryūkōka of the Taishō era is the musical form most closely linked with today's enka. Contemporary Japan nostalgically reconstructs the Taishō as the period during which modern urban Japanese culture, with its mix of prewar innocence and appetite for the latest fads, began. The Taishō era witnessed a major social upheaval as rural people migrated en masse to the cities in search of work, spawning a new but increasingly common social phenomenon, the lonely urbanite. Ryūkōka, the music of these urban migrants, spoke directly to the personal experience of lost love, separation, and loneliness. Mita Munesuke cites "Sasurai no Uta" (Song of Wandering), written by Kitahara Hakushū in 1917, as the first modern popular song to deal with loneliness, in particular, the loneliness of leaving home (1992: 96).

The Taishō era gave birth to many forms of popular culture, including a new musical genre, *shin-min'yō* (new folk song). Although in various ways this new urban song form mimicked traditional regional folk songs, it was composed by professional urban songwriters and recorded in urban studios for nationwide sale. One of the favorite themes of these new folk songs was that of furusato, glorified as utopian rural hometowns. By the early 1930s, however, shin-min'yō had begun to diminish in popularity as enka, another genre about furusato, emerged. Whereas shin-min'yō referred to specific regions and often mentioned actual place names, enka songs expressed a generalized furusato (Mita 1992) more meaningful to displaced urban dwellers from a variety of regions. From about the middle of the Taishō era, enkashi, who by now were professional singers, were able to make a living in bars singing customer requests.[9]

The growth of radio broadcasting and the record industry in Japan in the 1920s and 1930s popularized ryūkōka and its use of Western instruments, such as the violin, the harmonica, the guitar, the mandolin, and the xylophone, to accompany popular songs. Syncretized pentatonic scales derived in part from Japanese traditional scales provided melodic material. Some texts departed from the traditional 7-5 meter in accord with more Western-influenced musical phrase lengths.[10] And, according to Mita, only since the Taishō era have romantic love songs played such a major role in Japanese popular song (1992: 52). The *"en-"* (speech; performed) of earlier Meiji enka thus became the *"en-"* (romance, eroticism) of Taishō enka.

"Sendō Kouta" (Boatman's Song), with words by Noguchi Ujō (1882–1945) and music by Nakayama Shimpei (1887–1952), is considered the oldest example of popular, commercial, urban Taishō enka (IASPM-Japan 1991: 12). A dark and gloomy song first popularized in 1921 by enkashi, who sold the sheet music, it was recorded and released by several record companies in 1922 and 1923, with great success. Nakayama, among the first generation of composers to be educated in the Meiji school system, was very familiar with Western-based music (Mita 1992: 55). In its use of the syncretic Japanese *yonanuki onkai* (pentatonic scale) in its minor mode, "Sendō Kouta" was the first popular hit influenced by the lessons of Western-based school music.

During this period, a song gained popular momentum as it moved from sheet music to recording to film, each medium building on the previous one. In 1923, a low-budget film based on "Sendō Kouta" capitalized on its popularity (Nakamura 1991: 266). Other songs followed a similar pattern: Tottori Shun'yō's "Kago no Tori" (A Bird in a Cage) of 1924, for example, also achieved nationwide popularity, moving from medium to medium. Performed by enkashi standing near the screen, these songs flourished as background music for silent films in the 1920s (IASPM-Japan 1991: 19–20).

Although what we today call enka emerged in the 1920s, it was included under the broad category ryūkōka, which encompassed nearly all domestically produced popular music. Here were the musical beginnings of urban-based mass culture, which also included newspapers, magazines, advertising, comics, radio, movies, and department stores. This emergent national consumer culture brought industrial capitalism into the homes of ordinary citizens. Popular songs recalling lost loves and distant hometowns became one of its most widely consumed products.

Shōwa Era (1926–1989)

The long, cataclysmic Shōwa era, during which Japan developed its industries and technology, fought and lost a war, and rebuilt itself to international economic prominence, marks the maturing of enka and its "birth" as national music.

Prewar (1920s–1930s)

The introduction and spread of electronic media such as the radio and the phonograph led to a major change in the evolution of enka. In 1925, radio stations in Tokyo, Nagoya, and Osaka—the first in Asia—began broadcasting. The Japanese government immediately recognized the ideological power of these media and placed them under tight control (Kasza 1988: 72), forming the Nippon Hōsō Kyōkai (NHK), which monopolized broadcasting in Japan from 1926 until 1951. Japan's nationalist goals of the 1930s and 1940s included the creation of an electronically unified country. In the early days of broadcasting, however, radios remained a luxury item even among urban dwellers: in 1932, just over 25 percent of urban households and less than 5 percent of rural households owned a radio (NHK *Nihon Hōsō-shi* [History of Japanese Broadcasting], vol. 1, "Rajio no Nendo Betsu Toshi Gunbu Fukyūritsu" [Yearly Urban-Rural Rate of Diffusion of Radios], quoted in Kasza 1988: 88). During the 1930s, the national government decided to distribute radios to rural villages as a means of broadcasting its own messages throughout the country. But the dawn of a national mass media society spelled the gradual demise of street arts and artists such as enkashi.

During this period, as recording technology improved, phonograph records became more affordable for a wider segment of the population. In 1927, foreign investment helped establish all three major recording companies in Japan: Nippon Columbia (American Columbia and British Columbia), Nippon Victor (American Victor), and Nippon Polydor (Deutsche Polydor). Fortuitously, these new companies were able to take advantage of the latest innovations in recording when setting up their own facilities.

Until this time, songs generally originated outside record companies and were recorded and released only if they were already popular. For example,

"Kachūsha no Uta" (Kachusha's Song), with words by Shimamura Hōgetsu (1871–1918) and Sōma Gyofū (1883–1950) and music by Nakayama Shimpei (1887–1952), was recorded by Orient Records after gaining great popularity in Shimamura's 1914 *shingeki* (new theater) dramatization of Tolstoy's novel *Resurrection*.[11] "Habu no Minato" (Harbor of Habu), written by Noguchi Ujō and Nakayama Shimpei, was recorded in 1928 by Victor Records at the suggestion of a women's magazine editor. Benjamin Gardener, the president of Nippon Victor, suggested that his company follow the lead of its American parent company and others in the United States and generate hits of its own. The first such hit was "Kimi Koishi" (You, Sweetheart), produced and recorded in 1928 by Nippon Victor with words by Shigure Otowa (1899–1980) and music by Sasa Kōka (1886–1961). As the movie industry also grew, record companies and movie companies cooperated to release records and movies simultaneously, ensuring maximum public exposure throughout the country.

In the 1930s, popular songs were performed by geisha as well as by enkashi and other professional singers. Although typically trained in "traditional" song and dance, geisha sang ryūkōka to remain competitive with café waitresses and bar hostesses, their more Westernized counterparts,[12] infusing these songs with components of traditional Japanese music from kouta ballads, the genre with which they are most often linked (Dalby 1983: 80; Fujie 1989: 204). Many popular songs of the time also borrowed scales, vocal techniques, and other elements from regional folk song genres. During this decade, naniwa-bushi/rōkyoku also flourished. Because its feudalistic themes lent themselves to a nationalistic ideology, the government encouraged and supported naniwa-bushi throughout the World War II years, and its influence on enka, especially the more conservative subgenre called *do-enka* ("real enka" enka) remains strong.

At the same time, American popular music also influenced ryūkōka. In 1937, the hit "Wakare no Burūsu" (Parting Blues), composed by Hattori Ryūichi and sung by Awaya Noriko, prompted a flurry of "blues" hits. The Japanese version of the blues, however, generally ignored the standard sixteen-measure chord progression and "blue-notes" characteristic of American blues, latching on instead to its melancholy mood, which helped lay the foundation for the enka of the postwar period. Japanese *burūsu* (blues) was characterized by its slow tempo, *yonanuki* minor scale, 4/4 rhythmic structure, and general atmosphere of sadness, all combined with a vague "Western" feel.

The "father of modern enka" is the composer Koga Masao, whose major influence on the genre is reflected in the codified style known as *"Koga merodii"*

(Koga melody). This term refers to songs based on Koga's style, which features dark, introspective lyrics, a slow tempo, guitar or mandolin accompaniment with idiomatic melodic patterns, the yonanuki minor scale, and solo voice.[13] Koga's membership in a mandolin club during his university years influenced his compositional style, as did the years he spent in Korea. The hits "Sake wa Namida ka Tameiki ka" (Is Sake a Teardrop or a Sigh?) of 1931 and "Kage o Shitaite" (Following after Your Image), which illustrate the elements of his style, feature the musical and textual patternings—the kata—of today's enka.

One of the popular song themes of the time was that of "wandering or rootlessness," the antithesis of furusato, hometown, and family. Songs such as "Akagi no Komori-uta" (Lullaby of Akagi) (lyrics by Satō Sōnosuke, music by Takeoka Nobuyuki, sung by Shōji Tarō) and "Nozaki Kouta" (Nozaki Short Song) (lyrics by Imanaka Sakkei, music by Omura Nōshō, sung by Shoji Tarō) accompanied movies and plays based on popular novels about wanderers. In postwar enka, wandering or rootlessness remained an important theme (IASPM-Japan 1991: 10).

During the mid to late 1930s, increasingly volatile political conditions began to affect music and other expressions of popular culture in Japan. Whereas the Japanese public embraced American culture and music in the 1920s and early 1930s, once Japan had embarked on the road to the 1937 war with China, the government attempted to eliminate certain elements that were considered too American. Baseball was purged of American words and newly created Japanese terms were adopted.[14] The government closed the popular dance halls where one could see and be seen listening and dancing to American music. It also shut down foreign-owned record companies and exerted strong control over the remaining Japanese-owned companies, such as King and Teichiku Records. Some Japanese popular singers turned from more overtly American music, such as jazz, to enka.[15] Popular culture echoed the political imperatives of nationalistic militarism.

World War II (1940s)

During World War II,[16] Japan's efforts were increasingly concentrated on achieving victory. Under the National Mobilization Law of 1938, the government took a two-pronged approach to popular music: suppress unwanted elements and promote elements useful to the war effort. In January 1942, immediately following the dramatic entry of the United States into the war, the Information Bureau banned all "enemy [i.e., American] music," such as jazz,[17] as well as Japanese popular songs with sentimental or romantic themes (Shillony 1981: 144). The government also banned all overt expressions of sadness, such as the word *namida* (tears), in lyrics (Mita 1992: 7, 35). It took additional measures to prohibit music it perceived to be heavily influenced by the decadent popular music of the West, banning electric guitars, banjos, and ukuleles, for example, in 1944 (Iritani 1991: 174; Shillony 1981: 144). Yet banned songs, including parodies of official music and romantic ballads, continued to capture the hearts of the citizenry, albeit in private.

Under government directives, popular music turned increasingly to *gunkoku kayō* ("military country" popular songs), including *gunka* (marchlike military songs), which promoted nationalistic, imperialistic ideals. Iritani Toshio explains that daily broadcasts of gunkoku kayō and the national anthem were intended to instill group consciousness in the Japanese nation and foster a fighting spirit (1991: 167). Along with films, jingoistic phrases, and propagandistic posters, popular music became one of the military government's ways of spiritually mobilizing the citizenry for the tremendous sacrifices that would be required during what has been called Japan's "valley of darkness" (Havens 1978: 13; Davis 1996). These songs tended to focus less on the enemy and more on the spiritual strength of the Japanese people themselves (Dower 1993: 40). The government also produced songs promoting more direct war messages, which were then released by commercial record companies. Often, however, these propagandistic songs, dictated from above, never gained true popularity; people tended not to sing them and not to buy recordings (Komota et al. 1981: 127). Even the musicians who performed them turned to jazz and other banned music during their off-hours and found other ways to skirt military rules (Atkins 1998: 367).

On the other hand, some government-sanctioned songs did become popular and are still sung today. These songs tend to dwell on themes such as the family, and especially mother, that, when taken together, form a kind of sentimental education. One example, "Kudan no Haha" (Mother of Kudan [area of Tokyo around Yasukuni shrine, where Japan's war dead are memorialized]) (1939), tells the poignant story of an elderly mother who travels from the countryside to the Yasukuni Shrine, where her son has been enshrined as a war hero.[18]

Songwriters and musicians, along with other entertainers and artists, joined in the patriotic mood. In 1943, both the Japan Patriotic Arts Association and the Roving Musical Patriotic Volunteer Corps were established.

People in the arts helped propagate and glorify the country's wartime goals. As Ben-Ami Shillony remarks, "the patriotic mood generated by an all-out war, on top of the repressive measures of the government, created a remarkable consensus in the fields of thought, literature, and the arts" (1981: 119).

Postwar (1950s–1960s)

The miracle of Japan's postwar recovery is nowhere more dramatically demonstrated than in the contrast between conditions immediately after the war and those in the late 1960s. Popular music likewise exhibited striking changes. The nationalistic musical expression of the prewar period, such as naniwa-bushi, faded quickly as American popular music swept the country amid the overriding presence of the American Occupation forces. "Big Band" jazz was performed live in cities and on military bases, and could be heard throughout the country over the airwaves of the Far Eastern Network (FEN), the American armed forces network. Moreover, Japanese historical accounts credit this bright and lively Western-inspired but Japanese-produced music with spurring the nation forward. One of the first hit songs was "Ringo no Uta" (Apple Song), sung and recorded by Namiki Michiko in 1945. The musical elements of this and other songs of the period—avoiding yonanuki scales and Japanese vocal ornamentation such as *yuri* (a vibratolike "swinging" of the voice to alter pitch)—were heavily influenced by American popular music.

A central figure in boosting public morale was the immensely popular Misora Hibari (1937–1989), who debuted in 1949, at the age of twelve. A child star in the movies, she sang and danced, performing a variety of popular songs. Her portrayal of a streetwise orphan, forever captured on film in *Tokyo Kiddo* (1950), made her emblematic of Japan's postwar period, and her energetic brightness amid hardship became a source of national optimism. It is her association with enka, however, for which she is primarily remembered. Dubbed the "queen of enka," she embodied emotion and pain, remaining the people's singer even as she rose above them (Tansman 1996: 121). Attesting to her enduring popularity is the elaborate Misora Hibari memorial museum built outside Kyoto after her death,[19] as well as the continuing activities of her nationwide fan club.

Although the government suppressed "gloomy songs" immediately after the war, by the late 1940s and 1950s this kind of song had resurfaced. One example, from 1948, is Koga Masao's "Yu no Machi Erejii" (Bath Town

Elegy). This song, which features the yonanuki scale and Koga's characteristic plaintive guitar accompaniment, is said to have begun a postwar performance trend (Fujie 1989: 205). The theme of loneliness also resurfaced in popular song but with an important difference: it "began to change from the loneliness of separation from the hometown, to the even deeper loneliness of people without a hometown, [the loneliness] of living truly alone" (Mita 1992: 104). Whereas songs of loneliness in the 1920s and 1930s expressed the plight of the urban migrant yearning for a rural hometown, in the late 1950s such songs might also express the plight of the rural dweller left behind. During the phenomenal growth of the postwar period, Japan developed a modern transportation infrastructure of highways and high-speed trains, which effectively diminished the distance between urban and rural areas, even as popular songs retained the symbolic city-country separation. Increasing job opportunities in cities brought urban growth and rising material affluence. Before World War II the rural population stood at about 60 percent of the total; by 1961 it had decreased to 45 percent (Bennett 1967: 418–19). For the first time in Japan's history, over half the population lived in cities.

The Broadcasting Law of 1950 established the NHK as a special public corporation intended to serve the needs of various segments of the population[20] and mandated the establishment of private commercial broadcast stations. The opening of commercial radio stations in 1951, and of commercial television stations in 1953, was one of the most significant developments affecting popular music in Japan.[21] Neutralizing the monopoly, although not necessarily the dominance, of NHK, these companies brought new voices to the media airwaves.

In another development of the late 1950s, separate production companies gradually began to take control of record production from record companies (Kawabata 1991: 333). Under this system, production companies managed singers and coordinated lyricists, songwriters, and all other aspects of producing a record. As they grew in size and power, some even took over the copyright of the songs they recorded. As a result, particular songs became linked with particular singers (Fujie 1989: 206). Songs and singers could now be marketed to record companies as a package and their involvement limited to promoting and selling.

In 1966, for the first time, sales of *hō-ban* (Japanese-originated recordings) exceeded those of *yō-ban* (foreign-originated recordings), a trend that continues (Kawabata 1991: 336).[22] This turning of the tide of popularity toward domestic recordings and Japanese-originated music suggests a retreat from the wholesale embrace of American popular music and a retrenchment of domestic styles and genres. In a practical sense, however, this shift also meant that record companies now began to adopt the same kinds of budgets and promotional tactics for hō-ban they had previously used for yō-ban (ibid.: 338).

Japanese "blues" of the 1930s experienced a revival in the 1960s, when singers such as Mori Shin'ichi (see Chapter 6) released a series of "blues" hits. These "blues" hits, as well as the popular songs known as *mūdo-kayō* (mood songs), were slow-to-medium tempo ballads about failed romance that featured Western instruments such as the saxophone and steel guitar. They too have beeen incorporated into today's enka.

Post-postwar (1970s–1980s)

The word *enka* reemerged in the late 1960s and 1970s, during the waning days of the enkashi, when it was used by media and record companies to differentiate between the more indigenous forms of Japanese popular music and other, Western-influenced forms.[23] According to Nagata Gyōji, a popular music critic, after World War II the flood of American popular music into Japan seemed to affect just about all forms of popular music (reference to Nagata in Anonymous 1987: 14). To differentiate more clearly between this American-influenced music and the songs it considered more characteristically Japanese, the record industry chose the word *enka*. In one spelling of *enka*, the *en-* ideograph denotes erotic sexual liaisons, which fit the songs more closely (i.e., Taishō enka), but the industry censored that ideograph and adopted a more neutral one meaning "to present or perform" (ibid.). In this sanitized form, enka became especially widespread as a result of Nippon Victor's advertising campaign for the singer Fuji Keiko, who debuted in 1969 (IASPM-Japan 1991: 12). The music critic Nakamura Tōyō claims that the word *enka* denotes the "most conservative strain in popular music" because of earlier enkashi associations with premodern performance styles (1991: 272). Here, then, in an industry-determined cultural product, sound and sentiment coalesce.

This genre-making—or, as I call it, "genre-izing"—hinges on the music and the meanings given to that music as an invented tradition, but it tends to erase the processes of invention. In the case of enka, the music has historical precedents yet was only identified as a separate genre in the postwar period:

the music sounds "old," but the genre itself is young. Stylistically, according to one amateur singer now in his seventies, enka sounds even more "traditional" in its use of vocal ornamentation and inflection than the prewar ryūkōka of which it was a part. This "genre-izing" process coincides with other examples of cultural nationalism in the late 1960s and 1970s, in particular the emergence of "nihonjinron," discussed earlier, and the prominence of a nostalgic version of furusato in representations of Japanese identity (Robertson 1991: 5). During the introspection boom of the period, enka became one more boundary marker of national taste, this time in the field of popular music.

In the 1970s, proliferating youth-oriented popular music genres served as the backdrop for the emergence of enka. These popular genres included a new "folk" movement, influenced by American urban folk singers such as Bob Dylan and Joan Baez, and *gurūpu saunzu* ("group sounds"; pop groups), influenced by groups such as the Beatles. Performers adopted not only the sounds of Euro-American popular music but also, in some cases, its individualistic ideology, writing their own music and opposing dominant, profit-making business practices (Fujie 1989: 208). Few songs appealed to both the young and the old, and the resulting musical generation gap still characterizes Japan's musical scene (IASPM-Japan 1991: 11–12).

The typical instrumental accompaniment to enka songs during this period included the saxophone (tenor, and later, soprano), trumpet, electric guitar, electric bass, piano, and strings. The ponderous sounds of Koga merodii enka gave way in the 1970s and 1980s to lighter, brighter lyrics and music that veered closer to *"nyū myūjikku"* ("new music"), a term newly coined to describe young adult-oriented (as opposed to teen-oriented), Western-influenced popular music. The darker, more melancholy enka never disappeared, however, remaining under the enka umbrella as one of several types.

Heisei Era (1989–Present)

Enka's various reconfigurations are most obvious in its subgenres, although those I encountered most frequently during my fieldwork reveal often arbitrary distinctions. The type of enka considered most "traditional" is called do-enka ("real enka" enka; in Osaka dialect, the prefix *do-* means "real, true, the extreme"). Influenced most strongly by naniwa-bushi, and therefore displaying a pronounced Kansai (Osaka, Kyoto) regional flavor, do-enka songs focus on themes of giri-ninjō (duty vs. human feelings), morality, and hardship. Musically, they follow the yonanuki (Japanese pentatonic) scale and employ a slow-to-medium tempo, often including a dramatic spoken *serifu* (recitative) between verses. The singing technique for these songs relies on narrative inflections and extra-musical vocalizations such as grunts and growls, which reflect the influence of naniwa-bushi. Men's do-enka—songs expressing a male point of view—tend to be more common than women's (although singers of either sex sing these songs). Well-known contemporary do-enka singers include Kitajima Saburō, Toba Ichirō, Miyako Harumi, Nakamura Mitsuko, and Sakamoto Fuyumi.

Another important subgenre of enka, this one influenced by the burūsu (Japanese version of the blues) and similar melancholy genres, is *mūdo enka* ("mood" enka), which is concerned with the heartbreak of romance. Often written in the yonanuki minor scale to express sadness, these songs tend to be slow, pensive ballads. Singers of mūdo enka employ traditional vocal techniques, especially *yuri* and *ko-bushi*, the vibratolike ornamentation that can produce an effect much like stylized crying. Women's "mood" enka are more common than men's (although again, these songs are sung by members of both sexes). Representative mūdo enka singers include Mori Shin'ichi, Itsuki Hiroshi, Yashiro Aki, and Ishikawa Sayuri.

The last major contemporary enka subgenre is *poppusu-kei enka* ("pops"-style enka), which straddles the line between enka and "new music" or even "pops." Its lyrics tend to be about love and heartbreak, but in a lighter vein. The music tends to be lighter as well, often in a major key with slightly faster tempos and less traditional vocal ornamentation. The singers, who tend to be younger (whether in age or merely in image), include Horiuchi Takao and the Korean singer Kye Unsook.

Of these three major subtypes, mūdo enka is the most common, while do-enka, the most "traditional" subtype, is the least common, but relative popularity is often a reflection of regional preferences. My study is based on the Tokyo area (Kantō plain), but I have been told that in the more conservative and "traditional" Osaka (Kansai region), do-enka is more popular. However, given do-enka's connections to naniwa-bushi, which originated in Osaka, it is not surprising that many consider it the embodiment of Kansai culture.

In recent years, enka has remained popular, but it continues to face difficulties. The number of radio and television programs featuring enka has declined since the 1970s, and some critics also claim that the quality of the songs themselves has declined (Arita 1991). As its fans age, whether today's young people will embrace enka when they too reach their forties remains uncertain. Articles in popular journals and industry publications (e.g., Anonymous 1992c) continue to decry enka's decline in popularity since its heyday in the 1960s and 1970s. But even if enka is no longer as popular as it once was, it retains the loyalty of many older Japanese and its hold on certain population groups, such as truck drivers, farmers, fishermen, and yakuza (organized crime figures, gangsters).

I prefer to think of enka not as "in decline" but as one part of a more segmented market, a trend that began in the 1970s and still continues. That segment, however small in number terms, commands an inordinate amount of cultural weight because of its position, however disputed, as an expression of the "heart/soul of Japanese."

Moreover, in spite of dwindling record sales, a wide cross-section of the population retains a general knowledge of enka as what I have called "music overheard" (see Prologue). The same young people who profess an aversion to enka can still name its major stars and hum many of its tunes. They might sometimes sing enka in karaoke in a parodic way but at other times sing it sincerely, as a culturally acceptable if highly codified expression of particular emotions. Similarly, avowed nonfans might "hear" enka without really listening to it and sing it without embracing it.

The process of inventing enka invokes what Bourdieu has called "genesis amnesia": "history turned into nature, i.e., denied as such" in its collective forgetting (1977: 78–79). Forgetting the origins of enka has been made easier because of its links to the past: to the politically activist enkashi turned raconteurs and the enkashi who sang and sold popular songs. Furthermore, songs we would in retrospect call enka have been sung for decades, from "Sendō Kouta" (Boatman's Song) of 1921 to "Sake wa Namida ka Tameiki ka" (Is Sake a Teardrop or a Sigh?) of 1931 to "Namida no Renraku-sen" (Ferryboat of Tears) of 1965. In the late 1960s and 1970s, reinventing enka served to situate national culture within a specifically popular musical frame: it could be sung, listened to, overheard, manipulated, even bought and sold, but it remained deeply felt.

CHAPTER THREE

Producing Enka

Lessons in Perseverance

Tokyo, June 24, 1992, 11:35 P.M., approaching the fourth hour of a recording session that has continued without a break. Koguchi Junko (pseudonym), a sixteen-year-old female singer recording her debut song, is in tears, but these are tears of frustration, not longing or sadness. She can't seem to get a six-note passage right. The composer plays it for her on the piano. She tries to sing it back to him and fails. Her mother talks with Junko earnestly, but to no avail. The producer tries, also without success. Yet instead of letting Junko take a real break, everyone pushes ahead, asking her to sing the passage just one more time. As the session drags on, Junko's mother sends Junko's father out to buy everyone canned coffee. It finally ends an hour later. Although neither producer nor composer is fully satisfied, they will splice together something acceptable. There is no sense of achievement, only resignation.

What makes the behind-the-scenes production of enka significant are the ways in which the particular modes and behaviors associated with it reflect, or are said to reflect, certain themes of "traditional" Japan: perseverance, effort, spirit, repetition, and rank. Enka is singled out as different from the rest, an underdog with low sales, a long-lived genre that does not go in for passing trends, a conservative anachronism that in a high-tech industry still relies on face-to-face interaction. Most significant here is the fact that these characteristics become constructed as ways to link enka with notions of "Japan." Enka not only speaks of old-fashioned values, it is also said to exemplify them in its daily commercial recording and manufacturing practices, portrayed, for example, in the ethnographic scene described above. Although I am not suggesting that this scene is unique to enka, it fits well with the ways in which enka is discussed within the music industry. Here, even the young are made to "persevere." The talk during Junko's evening session does not suggest that she is a bad or poorly trained singer, but rather that she, like everyone else, including those at the top of the profession, must try harder, must *gambaru* (persevere) to get it right. It does not matter that perseverance pushes the session beyond the bounds of efficiency or that it sacrifices, however slightly, the quality of the final aesthetic product. What matters is the singer's toughness, a value well supported by her family and the production team.

The industry processes of production and promotion rely heavily on *kata* (patterning). Kata-as-patterning whets an acceptance of, and even an appetite for, repetition: composing new, "old-sounding" songs, saturating the media with repeated air play, singing a song over and over, first to "get it right" and then to "get it into the ears of listeners" (*mimi ni hairu*). This is national culture validating itself through redundancy, made clear through repeated iterations.

The Enka Industry: Metaphors for the Nation

In Japan, music is big business nationally but also internationally, although primarily in Asia. Japan's recording industry and recording market in the 1990s were second only to the United States in worldwide gross sales (Kawabata 1991: 328–29). At the time of my fieldwork, every major record company in Japan had an enka subdivision (see Appendix A). Although today this is no longer true,[1] a few record companies still specialize in enka. According to the 1990 edition of *Japanese Record Industry*, published by the Japan Phonograph Record Association, approximately 28.6 percent of all new Japanese popular music releases are enka (cited in Kawabata 1991: 331). This is well out of proportion to enka's sales (see Table 3.1),[2] indicating a possible smaller initial pressing and the expectation that a greater percentage of enka releases will lose money.

Folk and rock—defined, respectively, as those Japanese songs influenced by American urban folk music of the 1960s and those influenced by past and present Euro-American rock music—garner the great majority of record

Table 3.1
Recording Sales by Genre and Format, 1992

Genre	Single (%)	CD (%)	Cassette (%)	Total (%)
Folk, rock	74.9	78.8	60.5	76.4
Enka	7.0	0.0	24.6	4.0
"Pops"	17.3	8.8	13.2	13.1
Other	1.2	1.2	0.4	0.6
Yōgaku	0.8	11.3	1.3	5.9

SOURCE: *Orikon Nenkan 1993 Nenban* (1993 Oricon Yearbook)

sales. "Pops," Japan's "middle-of-the-road" popular music influenced in part by Euro-American forms such as light rock, is second; *yōgaku*, music performed by Euro-American artists, is third; and enka is fourth. Of the major music genres, then, enka, with the lowest sales, is the industry underdog.

Moreover, as record producers repeatedly pointed out to me, enka, unlike other music genres in the 1990s, is generally sold in audiocassette rather than in compact disc (CD) form, a trend that reflects the older age of typical enka consumers and their reliance on older technology.[3] Even in its physical package, then, enka represents not cutting-edge culture but a technological backwater.

Enka as Underdog in the Japanese Music Industry

Within the Japanese music industry, enka is distinct from other genres in several ways. One difference is in what defines an enka "hit." According to several producers with whom I spoke, enka does not sell as well as other popular music genres primarily because its fans, and thus its potential buyers, are older people who do not buy recordings in the large quantities that younger people do. While this holds true in general worldwide, in Japan the enka generation is especially noted for its fiscal conservatism. As a result, an enka song can become a hit with fewer sales, comparatively, than a "pops" hit.[4]

Offsetting relatively low enka record[5] sales is the longevity of its popularity. For "pops" hits, the pattern is one of sharp peaks and deep valleys: a record ascends the sales charts quickly, stays on top briefly, and descends quickly, soon replaced by the next hit. An enka hit, on the other hand, typically rises in the charts very slowly, sometimes over several months, stays on or near the top for a year or more, and then descends slowly.[6] According to a composer of both "pops" and enka, production costs in the "pops" industry run high because so many songs have to be generated to keep up with the high turnover of hits. One can profit from a single enka song, however, for far longer, so that producing enka actually becomes more profitable over time. The saying, according to several music industry people, is that one enka hit is all a person (that is, a singer, composer, lyricist, or producer) needs to be financially secure.[7]

The music industry valorizes enka's sales pattern—a slow but steady rise, a leveling off, and a gradual decline—in sometimes nationalistic terms. Enka becomes the "handicapped" genre, the underdog, surmounting difficulties and winning through sheer effort and a strong spirit, as in this excerpt from a music industry journal: "Enka is like a marathon [runner]. It may not have the flashiness of sprinter Carl Lewis . . . , but it sends reverberations throughout Japan with a gold medal . . . in the crowning glory of competitions, the marathon. . . . Japan, too, impresses one as a 'marathon country.' . . . The marathon is a sporting event on which Japanese can pin their hopes [to win internationally]. The *konjō* [spirit] and *doryoku* [effort] [elements important in winning a marathon] which Japanese value, find parallels in enka" (Anonymous 1992c: 37). This article pits enka, the sober little guy with a mighty spirit, against the showy, facile, heavily Western-influenced "pops," whose popularity looms large. As a microcosm of Japan, enka wins the spiritual battle against the (Euro-American) world. In the discourse surrounding enka, low record sales, when combined with the spirit, effort, and perseverance necessary to withstand its particular hardships, become a virtue.

Enka as Valuable Redundancy: Repetition and Cover Versions

Another characteristic that makes enka profitable for record companies is audience willingness to purchase and listen to the same song again and again. A rule of thumb in the enka world is *"ki o terawazu ni"* (without showing off anything new); in other words, in both concerts and recordings, enka fans like to hear songs they already know (Anonymous 1992c: 31). An appetite for the familiar governs the consumption of goods in various cultural settings to a certain extent,[8] yet familiarity guides the enka industry more than most. Record companies regularly release repackaged enka, often as "Zen-Kyoku-

Shū" (Song Collection), a compilation of "greatest hits." Because production costs are minimal, these collections do not need to sell many copies to turn a profit. One record producer at Toshiba-EMI told me he spends much of his time thinking up new ways to repackage old material.[9] In fact, very few enka albums contain entirely new material. Most mix previously released songs with a few new ones. As a result, the same song in the same recorded version can be found unchanged, except for the packaging, on any number of different albums. Yet consumers' appetite for redundancy seems barely whetted by these rereleases.[10]

Another element of redundancy in the enka world is the ubiquitous "cover version," a song that is composed or given a "breakthrough" performance by one singer which is then performed (and sometimes also recorded) by another singer. Cover versions become a kind of kata of a song's performance. Although they are not unique to Japan or to enka, the general Japanese attitude toward enka cover versions is distinctive. Aside from their quantity, their most striking features are how closely they adhere to the musical style of the original song—in orchestral arrangement, tempo, and even in details of vocal stylization—and the timing of their release, within a year or two of the original. Imitation here becomes a mark of flattery rather than a measure of artistic weakness. An entertainment industry trade journal claims that "An enka song must not only be sung by the original person [to be considered truly popular], but also by other [professional] singers and in karaoke [by thousands of amateurs]" (Anonymous 1992c: 24). In other words, cover versions, whether recorded by professionals or performed in karaoke by amateurs, are barometers of a song's success. Redundancy indicates and generates popularity.

Imitation and repetition, however, introduce the problem of the listener's perception of difference. To my American ear, for example, there is little difference between an original enka version and various cover versions, primarily because I am listening for text, melody, tempo, musical arrangement, and vocalization, the elements I consider meaningful. But Japanese listeners with whom I have spoken evaluate cover versions from a very different perspective. The targets of their perception—the minute details of phrasing and vocal intonation—are far more subtle.

Any perception of redundancy also depends on one's notion of "song." According to Euro-American standards, a song is identified by the contributions of both the lyricist and the composer, who are listed in the credits in any songbook. In enka, however, credit is also given to the musical arranger, which suggests that a song, by definition, includes a particular instrumental accompaniment.[11]

As one record producer explained to me, cover versions are "popular in enka because enka fans like to hear songs that are familiar," a reflection of the "*ki o terawazu ni*" philosophy. An enka singer went further, explaining that cover versions are also a way to evaluate a new singer. Listeners can judge the merit of the new singer by his or her closeness to the established singer's performance.[12] The new singer's rendition of the song becomes a measure of proficiency.

Cover versions are also a sign of ranking, another characteristic that links enka to stereotypes of Japaneseness. The enka world is a well-defined hierarchy, one determined in part by the performance of cover versions. A newer singer performs more of them, especially in the process of putting together an album. To a certain extent, this is also true in other popular music worlds such as the United States, but in Japan even well-established, high-ranking enka singers sing cover versions in their concerts and recordings.

Enka as Confucian Hierarchy: A Place for Everyone

Ranking and hierarchy in fact structure the entire music industry in Japan, especially the enka segment. Determined primarily by popularity (as evidenced in record sales, song requests, and karaoke), but also by longevity in the entertainment world, ranking serves as a gauge in the conduct of business.[13] Ranking extends not only to singers but also to lyricists, composers, arrangers, directors, record companies, production companies, and publishing companies, each of which earns a place in a numerically ordered listing in industry publications such as the annual *Oricon Yearbook*.

Rank is expressed in several ways. As noted earlier, singing cover versions is only a partial indicator. Another is one's slot in the order of performance during certain events. The most important event in the enka world is the annual broadcast of the New Year's Eve song contest, the NHK Kōhaku Uta Gassen, in which enka plays a central role, although the contest includes various genres of Japanese popular music. Rank determines the order of the performers on the program, and enka singers generally dominate the latter, more prestigious half.

Rank, which is determined by the date of a singer's debut, or "birth," into the enka world, can require a particular kind of behavior between singers as an extension of *senpai-kōhai* (senior-junior) relations. According to these rules of etiquette, all senior singers—that is, anyone who debuted before a junior singer—should be accorded respectful behavior by that junior. Although these rules may not be observed as strictly today as in the past, the enka *geinō-kai* (entertainment world) continues to acknowledge them, if only as a fading institution. In a published conversation between the composer Ichikawa Shōsuke and the singer Miyako Harumi, the two discuss *senpai-kōhai* relations at the time of Miyako's debut in 1964, when she was sixteen years old.

Ichikawa: Harumi, your generation is about the last to experience the harshness of the entertainment world, isn't it?

Miyako: Yes, that's right. There was a fair amount of adherence to *senpai-kōhai* rules; such as, even upon entering the dressing room, you would never sit down before a *senpai*, or you would never sit in front of a mirror blocking your *senpai*. Yes, there were these kinds of things that went on. . . . However, I wouldn't have called these rules a hardship or things that I disliked, because I considered them to be just the way things were. In the end, I think that these were good things. (Ichikawa 1992a: 5)

An important element of a singer's training, at least thirty years ago, was the protocol of rank as determined by seniority.

Rank also gives singers a certain amount of creative license to individualize their performance. Some of the most candid assessments of hierarchy come from newcomers to the profession who are themselves in the process of learning the rules. As one young male enka singer preparing for his debut told me, he was taught that lower-ranked singers should perform in a straightforward manner, singing approximately thirty to forty songs in a recital or concert and doing them all as prescribed, without personal flourishes. As singers rise in rank, they can more acceptably bend the rules. One high-ranking enka singer usually sings only fifteen songs in concert, and only one of the three verses of some of them. He spends the rest of the time bantering with the audience, telling personal anecdotes, and even having guest singers of lower rank sing on stage. In this case, the higher the rank, the less one has to sing on stage and the more one may simply "be." Another singer has been known to adopt more theatrical gestures and staging in her performances as she has risen to become one of the top enka singers. Rank lets her do more, if still within the limits of the genre.

Rank gives everyone a place, including those in the lower echelons. One record producer cites the example of a talented female enka singer: she has been in the business for twenty-five years, releasing fifty-four records (over twice as many as the established singer's usual one new release per year), although only one ever came close to being a hit. The point here is that in the enka world, this singer is not a failure, merely a low-ranked figure. Rank is both a stage and a position: theoretically, lower-ranked singers can move higher as their careers progress, but this model of progress is not always realized. Moreover, in the enka world, being a lower-ranked singer means at least maintaining a position of some kind, however low. The system accommodates the entire spectrum of singers, and most manage to continue in the profession without rising, or in some cases, rising only after many years.

Enka and the Spiritual Value of Perseverance

Striving to rise in rank is important throughout a singer's career, as the following excerpt from an entertainment industry publication illustrates:

There are many [enka] singers who go for twenty or thirty years without a big hit. For example, K.Y., who has been in the business now for twenty years, continues along in her career doggedly promoting her songs as if on a small, local train bound for the provinces [i.e., on a slow train going nowhere]. Another example is F.T., who is giving a full recital [a mark of prestige] for the first time after twenty-eight years in the business. These singers never take a rest. They persevere, and never get that big break. However, their perseverance itself becomes an aspect that eventually wins the support of the public. Indeed, singers want to feel that persevering gives them a kind of audience appeal. (Anonymous 1992c: 23–24)

In giving value to the striving and the perseverance of lower-ranked singers, this publication in effect equates these singers with the enka music industry as a whole, which must likewise work hard and persevere despite drooping record sales. This emphasis on perseverance (*gambaru*) rewards effort alone rather than innate ability (Singleton 1995).[14] Singers may gain audience support not only for their singing ability but also for their inner qualities and sheer effort. The brother of a low-ranked veteran singer relates the present conditions of his brother's career in these terms: "Twenty-three years since his debut and he doesn't have a hit yet. But my brother manages to keep going. Now the staff is down to five people, including me." Optimistically, he says that his brother's popularity is gradually growing ("*dandan dandan hirogatte iru*"). The sense of perseverance remains especially strong in the careers of lower-ranked singers, who, even without a hit, manage to maintain a sense of optimism and a place within the industry over many years.

In fact, persevering purportedly gives singers of all ranks audience appeal: effort knows no hierarchy within this cultural ethic. Those at the top, like those in the middle and at the bottom, must express their commitment to trying their best, even if their effort has no large goal in sight. There may be small goals along the way: achieving record sales of so many thousand, completing a grueling concert tour, being selected to perform in the Kōhaku Uta Gassen (see Chapter 4), and sometimes yet smaller goals: pleasing an audience, completing a concert, singing a song with sincerity. This sense of striving pervades a singer's discourse throughout an entire career.

Enka songs themselves are also credited with perseverance. For example, an article in the fan magazine *Enka Jānaru* (Enka Journal) describes one song as "*shūnen no sakuhin*" (a tenacious work), because it has survived release and rerelease by different singers (Anonymous 1994b: 28). In its first incarnation, it was sung by its male composer; next it was recorded by a male *tarento* (literally, "talent"; a show business personality)[15] and then by an established male enka singer; most recently, it has been reformulated to be sung by a female singer.[16] Described as "*yonkai-me no X*" (fourth-time over song X), the song is being promoted as a "*ribaibaru hitto*" (revival hit). Here, the rhetoric of perseverance makes of this song's history a moral victory rather than a songwriting failure. In fact, according to this ideology, there are no failures, only songs and singers waiting to make the extra effort to secure success.

Record Companies and Their Images

Record companies maintain a particular image. One record producer at Nippon Columbia says that in the past, each record company had its own identifiable sound, in part because of the composers and singers who were under exclusive contract with that company and in part because the company's recording engineers developed their own mixing techniques. Nowadays, however, with freelance composers, production companies, and standardized recording equipment and techniques, the enka songs produced by different companies tend to sound alike.

These days, a record company's image is derived in part from the place it gives to enka. In the 1990s no record companies produced enka exclusively, and most only specialized in enka, or in a particular type of enka, in varying degrees.[17] The record companies in which enka plays a large role in proportion to the company's size (as indicated by the number of new record releases and of enka *shinjin*, or newcomers) are Teichiku and Crown Records, the same ones that project the most conservative "Japanese" image.[18] For these companies, enka is the main focus of production and contributes to their nationalistic, almost furusato image. Large international companies such as Nippon Columbia, Victor Music Entertainment Corporation, and Sony Records, on the other hand, regard enka as only a small segment of their enterprise and maintain a more polished, cosmopolitan image.

The image of a company also extends to its singers. When I visited two well-known record companies to meet one of their shinjin, I was struck by the difference between these singers. The fifteen-year-old female singer from the high-prestige, cosmopolitan company (Columbia) was picture-perfect, with every hair in place, flawless skin, and an expensive-looking outfit. The nineteen-year-old female singer from the more *nihon-teki* (Japanese-y) company (Crown) looked comparatively unpolished, her hair in slight disarray and her dress less expensive. Of course, comparative budgets play a large role in how singers are groomed, but aesthetic and marketing decisions also take competing definitions of "Japan" into account.

The Making of a Singer: Imaging the Imaginary

The belief in *tsukutta mono* (things made) is nowhere more evident than in the making of an enka singer. As a Nippon Columbia director rather bluntly states it, a singer is *"mawari no tsukutta mono,"* something created by those around him or her. This is a simple, professional fact. A newcomer enters the enka world on its terms, and there is little room for assertions of individual will. Singers have little control over their products, including the songs they sing and the image they project. According to the same Nippon Columbia director, a singer is a voice, and only sometimes a face; if the singer does not like the way business is conducted in the enka world, then he or she should leave.

Some singers actually claim a "natural" predilection for enka. It is almost as if enka had chosen them rather than the other way around. This view parallels some of the explanations of enka's appeal I heard, as if liking the music were a part of nature, race, or blood. A nineteen-year-old singer training to make his debut said, "I much prefer Japanese 'pops,' but somehow enka comes 'naturally' to me," so his manager was having him sing it. He further explained that he had an "enka look," by which he meant that he was not very tall, that his build was slightly stocky, and that his craggy face belied

Table 3.2
Japanese Popular Music: Solo Singers, 1991

	Enka	Non-enka	Total
Male	45*	219	264
Female	79**	317	396
TOTAL			660

SOURCE: *Orikon 1992 Nenkan* (1992 Oricon Yearbook).
*17% of total male singers. **19.9% of total female singers.

his youth. His look was rough rather than smooth. Naturalizing enka in this way, within a singer's body, voice, and spirit, lends its performance and its consumption a natal inevitability.

One way a singer can gain control over the production process is by "going independent," by establishing his or her own production company. The *Orikon 1992 Nenkan* (1992 Oricon Yearbook) lists 21 enka singers, including many, but not all, of the top-ranked stars as well as several lower-ranking singers, who have done so. (Unfortunately, no statistics are available on the number of years between a singer's debut and "going independent.") Of these 21, twice as many are male (14) as female (7), although in general more enka singers are female. In fact, as of 1991, 27.0 percent of male enka singers had set up their own production companies, while only 11.3 percent of female enka singers had done so.

Besides "going independent," various singers have also asserted themselves during the course of their career by changing record companies. This action, however, has usually been met with disapproval by the original record company and often by the general public. A record store employee told me that enka fans and music industry people alike tend to regard singers who change from one company to another as disloyal. Clearly, singers experience both internal and external pressure to adhere to the ways of the industry.

One way to understand the enka world today is to look at the statistics on singers given in the annual Oricon Yearbooks. Table 3.2 lists the number of enka singers in relation to all popular music solo singers in Japan according to the 1992 Oricon Yearbook.[19] Of 264 male singers, 45 (17.0 percent) are enka; of 396 female singers, 79 (19.9 percent) are enka. The ratio of female enka singers to male enka singers is almost two to one (79:45, or 63.7 percent).

Table 3.3
Japanese Popular Music: Solo *Shinjin*, 1991

	Enka	Non-enka	Total
Male	4*	41	45
Female	26**	54	80
TOTAL			125

SOURCE: *Orikon 1992 Nenkan* (1992 Oricon Yearbook).
*8.9% of total male *shinjin*. **32.5% of total female *shinjin*.

This compares with a ratio of female non-enka singers to male non-enka singers of about three to two (317:219, or 59.1 percent). Of the 79 female solo enka singers, 6 are foreign (from Korea, Taiwan, and Brazil); among the 45 male solo enka singers, one is foreign (from Korea). In the entertainment industry as a whole, but especially in the enka segment, females (including foreign-born) outnumber males. These figures accord with the general impression of several record producers that the trend is toward more female singers, songs, and listeners (which I discuss in greater detail later in this chapter).

In addition to these statistics, one can also look at the number of newcomers (*shinjin*) to determine where the field is headed (see Table 3.3). In 1991 the number of solo shinjin totaled 125, of whom 30 (24.0 percent) were enka singers. Of the 45 males, 4 (8.9 percent) sang enka, while of the 80 females, 26 (32.5 percent) sang enka. Among solo shinjin in all music genres, there were almost twice as many female as male singers (80:45, or 64.0 percent of the total); if one looks at enka alone, however, that figure jumps dramatically, to almost seven times as many females (26:4, or 86.7 percent of the total). Of the 26 female enka shinjin, 3 were foreign (one each from Korea, Taiwan, and the People's Republic of China). The predominance of female shinjin suggests that the feminization of the enka world will continue.

The public and the music industry view enka shinjin with great interest. The annual Oricon Yearbook lists them separately and provides more detailed information about them than about established singers.[20] Both *Karaoke Fan*, a glossy monthly magazine published in Osaka that focuses primarily on enka, and *Enka Jānaru* featured articles with photographs on the year's crop of 36 shinjin in their spring 1993 issue.[21] With the exception of two male shinjin, all were female. Shinjin vie for various prizes unique to their shinjin status, the most prestigious of which is the annual Kayō Gōruden Taishō Shinjin Guran Puri (Popular Song Golden Award Newcomer Grand Prix). This intense interest in the newest members of the staged enka imaginary suggests that this is not pure "museum nostalgia," but a living, dynamic, if nostalgically mixed, version of new and old.

The numbers also suggest that, increasingly, the "heart/soul of Japan" the music industry places on stage is a woman's heart. Women have become the cultural transmitters, the mouthpieces of this form of national culture. This is not to suggest, however, that female subjectivity is necessarily expressed or enhanced by these songs. Female singers and songs may project the genre's image, but not often in women's own words and music. In general, men, not women, control what is bought and sold. Women provide the voices and the faces, but men determine what those voices and faces will say. This is national culture produced by men, although it is consumed by both men and women.

Recruitment: Peopling the Imaginary

The enka world recruits its singers into an industry geared to selling voices, faces, and images for the highest possible profit. The most costly (and thus least common) way to enter this world is for a singer to make a recording at the singer's (or the singer's parents') own expense and then peddle it independently. I was told of a young female singer who followed this procedure at her father's expense, a cost estimated to be ¥100,000,000 ($90,909). Independence gives the singer the greatest amount of freedom and control, but it obviously requires prohibitive sums of money. At the same time, because independent singers do not have established nationwide contacts for booking engagements, they tend to perform within a circumscribed local area. In general, this method of entering the enka world is regarded negatively as outside the established recruitment channels.

Another route into the industry is through an introduction from an enka composer or lyricist, typically the singer's teacher. A singer in training for his debut and under contract with a production company explained that being recruited by a teacher, who then introduces the young singer into the industry, can be expensive. Under contract to no one, the student pays all expenses. Several current enka singers began as *uchi-deshi* (live-in apprentices) of well-known composers or lyricists, following the *iemoto* (headmaster) system of teaching and learning.[22] This practice resembles those common in the traditional arts, thus signifying the place of "Japan" and "tradition" in the enka world. Typically, the uchi-deshi lives in the teacher's household and performs menial chores without pay. The types of duties and length of service vary. Sakamoto Fuyumi, a top young (b. 1967) female singer with whom I spoke, served as uchi-deshi to Inomata Kōshō, a veteran male composer, for eight months, cleaning the house, cooking, and performing other duties along stereotypical housewifely lines, while taking singing lessons from him. In contrast, Toba Ichirō, a male singer with whom I also spoke, served as uchi-deshi to the composer Funamura Tōru for three years, during which he scrubbed floors, took care of the garden, and did other household chores, but never had a music lesson. The basic philosophy behind the uchi-deshi practice is that there is value in simply being with the teacher, absorbing his way of life, and learning by observing (*mi-narai*, literally, learning by looking; apprenticeship). In spite of a learning experience that might bewilder someone unfamiliar with the system, Toba says he learned a lot, most of which, nonetheless, was unspoken. This continuing link between enka and the traditional arts becomes a mark of the genre's historicity: it infuses feudalistic apprenticeship practices into the big business, high-tech world of the recording industry.

Another method by which enka singers are now recruited with increasing frequency is through the countless amateur song and karaoke contests held throughout Japan. These contests bring the glossy imaginary into the lives of everyday people, proffering to amateurs the possibility of professional advancement. The larger, more prestigious contests are judged by enka lyricists and composers, and attended by record company and production company personnel, who may use them to scout for new singers. Many enka singers have at least one or two prizes from these contests to their credit.

A fourth method of entering the field is through active scouting on the part of record and production company producers. Most talent searches take place in Japan; however, some scouts also travel overseas, especially to places with *nikkei* (Japanese-American) populations, like Hawai'i, Brazil, and Peru, in search of untapped talent. Among well-known enka singers of the 1990s, one was a *nikkei* woman from Brazil. The talent search extends to other Asian countries as well, in particular, Korea and Taiwan.

A fifth method takes singers from another musical genre and recasts them as enka singers. The most notable example of this process during the period of my fieldwork was Nagayama Yōko (b. 1968). She debuted under

Victor Entertainment in 1984 as a sixteen-year-old "pops *aidoru* (idol)" singer[23] and achieved limited but not spectacular success before turning briefly to television drama. Then, in 1993, she reemerged on the same record label as an enka singer.[24] A comparison of photos from her days as an *aidoru* singer and now as an enka singer reveals a complete physical transformation—from bangs and tousled hair to an upswept hairdo; from a mischievous grin or a full, cheerful smile to a subdued, distant look of reserve; from a short, brightly colored modern dress to a kimono in subdued shades. It is as if she has grown older (which she has, but not that much), leapfrogging generations while also moving backward in time. Since becoming an enka singer, Nagayama has found far greater success than she ever attained as an *aidoru* in the "pops" world.

A sixth method for recruiting enka singers is through the audition, a process that provides some details on how the industry structures its recruiting and screens its future investments. On December 6, 1992, between one and four in the afternoon, I attended the privately held 1992 Korombia Kayōkyoku Shinjin Kashu Ōdishon (1992 Columbia Popular Song Newcomer Singer Audition) at the Roppongi Art Forum in Tokyo. Of the eighteen singers who had already passed the preliminary auditions, seventeen were females ranging in age from 14 to 25. This audition thus clearly signaled the desirability of *shōjo* (premarital females) as potential major record company investments. Two of those auditioning were trying out for the second consecutive year.

Each of the seven judges and the several dozen audience members received a booklet containing photos of the contestants and information about them—birthdate, birthplace, residence, employment or school, blood type, height, weight, measurements (for females, bust, waist, hips), clothing sizes, nuclear family members, hobbies, and sports.[25] The entire audition process, both the singing and the brief interviews, was videotaped and simultaneously transmitted to the judges. While we waited for their decision, the previous year's winner performed her upcoming debut song and was interviewed about the rigors of her past year of enka training. In addition, Marushia ("Marcia," a stage name), a guest enka singer, also made an appearance. A currently successful enka singer originally from Brazil (nikkei), Marushia was herself a product of Columbia auditions (having won only after trying more than once, as the emcee emphasized). After deliberating, the judges

Nippon Columbia Auditions, 1992

announced four winners, all of them female. At this particular audition, eight of the eighteen contestants sang enka, and of the winners, three of the four sang enka. These winners could expect to debut, after extensive training, within the next few years. The two successes—last year's winner and the professional singer Marushia—were also enka singers.

As this audition demonstrates, enka continues to command a place within a major record company such as Nippon Columbia. Despite lagging sales and what is bemoaned as a general decline, the genre still garners industry attention and corporate investment. Clearly, record companies are looking to young debuting singers to continue the genre, even as the majority of its listeners are aging. Through these auditions, moreover, the industry places its greatest emphasis on *shojo* (young female singers) as a marketable commodity. Perseverance, a common trope of the audition process, was displayed by the two repeat-auditioners (even if neither won this time around) and further exemplified by Marushia herself. But the judges are looking for more than a voice and a look: they are seeking raw material for molding, packaging, and selling.

Selection: Entering the Imaginary

From the singer's point of view, the choice of which production or record company to join may be a strategic one. One male singer in training told me about the pros and cons of signing up with companies of various sizes: larger, more prestigious companies may have more contacts and money, but they can also more easily ignore you, whereas smaller companies can be more attentive to molding and promoting you.

Scouts, judges, teachers, directors, and producers likewise choose their future investments carefully. In enka, the base criterion is that the person must be able to sing or communicate through singing. More important than a beautiful voice, according to one composer, are *settoku-ryoku* (power to persuade, to communicate) and *hyōgen nōryoku* (ability to express). A second general criterion mentioned to me by another producer was *yaruki* (inner drive). This intangible element can be recognized by "knowing the person." A person must have the spiritual qualities—in particular, perseverance—to go through the various hardships required in the making of an enka singer.

Beyond these criteria, desirable attributes split along gender lines. Male singers are usually described in terms of intangibles. One manager said that a male singer must be *"otokorashii"* (masculine, manly), meaning strong and stalwart. Other industry people I spoke with gave no explicit qualifications for a male enka singer, but when I asked about female enka singers, several directors and producers listed specific physical and nonphysical attributes. One composer said that the key to bodily expressivity (in enka, more important for females than for males) is in the eyes. A female enka singer need not have a beautiful face, but if she has eyes that can express emotion, she will be successful on stage. According to a producer with Century Records, the ideal age for a female *shinjin* is eighteen to twenty-five, and the ideal female form is that best suited to a kimono (*"kimono ga ni atte"*): an oval face that looks good with hair up, eyes not too round, long neck, sloping shoulders, small breasts, narrow hips, slight to medium build, and medium height.[26] This female kimono form he considers particularly Japanese (*"nihonjin-teki"*). Television has also focused more attention on appearance, especially for female singers. In the 1990s, a whole flock of young female singers became known as "kimono *bijin*" (kimono beauties) or *"enka bijin"* (enka beauties). As one popular magazine article proclaimed, "This year as well, young beauties/singers are debuting one after the other!!" (*Kotoshi mo wakate bijin kashu ga tsugi-tsugi debyū!!*) (Anonymous 1993b: 25).

According to the manager of a lower-ranking singer, an additional requirement, especially for female enka singers, is the ability to speak with composure in public. Given the current dearth of televised enka shows, singers have turned to nonmusical talk shows. In order to make a favorable impression on these shows, he explains, they must be able to chat intelligently. Because females are assumed to be "more talkative" than males, female enka singers must be able to hold their own in conversation. An article in a music industry publication concurs: "In the past, one could sing without speaking much, but recently it has become important to be able to chatter on [on stage] to make a hit song" (Anonymous 1992c: 24).

Criteria like these reveal the gendered definition of what enka represents (Herd 1984), a femininity co-opted from the past: desirable, of marriageable age, physically attractive in the traditional clothing of Japan, and able to encourage the flow of social discourse. To the older men and women who consume these images, these singers become the ultimate, phantasmic "Japanese girl-next-door." Through her, the actual young people who walk down the street, ride on the train, and shop in the local convenience store, whose consumerism dominates the marketplace, who seem threatening because of their new ways of doing things, find active rebuttal. In their place, the audience sees women who adhere unquestioningly to established gender roles, who become victims to the vicissitudes of men and society in general, and who make of their emotions a small but aesthetic public display.

Having said this, I would point out one anomalous characteristic of enka as a genre: the range of female and male bodies, faces, and ages considered acceptable. In fact, enka puts less emphasis on youth and physical beauty than other pop genres do (e.g., *aidoru* singers), but there is still some disagreement about the relative importance of good looks on the enka stage. A beautiful female singer with musical ability is also an aesthetic object; her looks may not be absolutely essential to hit-making, but they certainly help her popular appeal.

But there is another, more subtle aspect to this question. Although pleasing physical attributes can help a singer, too much perfection distances the audience. What Hideyoshi Aizawa, the president of Sun Music Productions, says of *aidoru* singers holds true for enka singers as well: "To be life-sized (*tōshindai*) is to publicly confirm that idols are not living in this world on their own, but together with people [i.e., fans] who are there to support them and whom they are expected to support.... Human relations are what hold idols in their place" (quoted in Aoyagi 2000: 311). The enka audience wants to see and hear real people—*tōshindai*—not goddesses and gods. A performer's "ordinariness" (real or constructed) is always allowed to show through. Blemishes, facial moles, even crooked teeth become badges of ordinariness for performers who lead otherwise extraordinary lives. A performer's approachability is important to audience members, whose devoted fandom relies in part on how well a singer can generate an empathetic response.

IMAGE-MAKING: SHAPING THE PRODUCT TO THE MOLD

What follows recruitment and selection is training, the *tsukuru* (making) of the *tsukutta-mono*, and here, the kata of the genre and its values can be seen most clearly. In the language of the *geinō-kai* (entertainment world), a singer undergoing training before his or her debut is called "*ko*" (child), and the process of training and preparation is referred to as "*sodateru*" (raising or bringing up a child).

According to a pamphlet handed out at the 1992 Nippon Columbia auditions, once a singer has won the auditions and signed a contract with the company, a two-phase process, or "*suteppu-appu sukejūru*" (step-up schedule), prepares the singer to debut under the Nippon Columbia label. The first phase is "*sutaffu-zukuri*" (creating a staff), which includes a director, a manager, and a promoter that together become the "*mawari*" (surroundings) or key decisionmakers in the training that follows. The second phase is "*imēji-zukuri*" (creating an image for the singer), which refers to both "*shin-kyoku konseputo*" (concept for a new song) and "*bijuaru konseputo*" ("visual concept" of how the singer should look). According to one music producer, female singers often need to be taught not only the proper way to wear a kimono but also how to move when wearing one.[27] Although music and looks are both important to a singer's image, the singer has no control over these matters. Decisions are made by the recording company staff, who, while they take the singer's talents and appearance into account, are ultimately guided by their own predictions of market demand. Their fundamental goal is to create an image that will sell. To them, the image is pure commodity.

The record company also decides the type of song a singer will sing. A singer may audition as a pop singer but be told to sing enka, or vice versa.

When I investigated a list of shinjin, calling record companies to inquire about the genres in which they sang, I was told, in a few instances, "We haven't decided yet." One singer in training for his debut said, "Now, they're preparing me for an image. I don't know what it is yet." The company, as final arbiter, tells the singer what to sing, how to sing it, and how to look while singing it. According to a record producer from Century Records, shinjin accept image-making as a way to sell records: "From the start, a shinjin is told, 'You will sell well with this kind of image' ['*Anata wa kō iu imēji de urimasu yo' tte iu*]."

The more outspoken among the new singers may offer some resistance to this heavy-handed manipulation, but they soon learn the ropes. For example, a female shinjin in her twenties described trying to carve out her own path in the enka world: "The image of enka singers is very fixed [*seiritsu shite iru*]. In the beginning, I thought I would break the rules. In other words, I would not wear a kimono, I would sing wearing a short dress, etc. I thought I would try that, but it was all wrong. In the end, wearing a ribbon in my hair and a dress just didn't work. I was scolded [and told] that an enka singer has to be graceful [*shittori-to*] and adultlike [*otonappoku*] in a kimono, and if I tried to buck the system, I wouldn't sell any recordings. That's how it was." This singer's attempts at individuality did not fit audience expectations; they did not conform to the kata of the genre.

In many cases a singer's image is derived directly from his or her own physical appearance or character. Sometimes, however, managers deliberately contrive an image that runs counter to what would be expected. One example is Sakamoto Fuyumi (the former uchi-deshi of an enka composer). Her manager explained to me that, before her debut in 1987, decisionmakers in the production and record companies to which she was under contract regarded her as someone with unique potential. Petite and charming, with a pretty face and a sweet but powerful voice, she was very "feminine," and her voice graceful ("*shittori shita*"). Her manager concluded that if a young woman with her looks and voice sang men's songs, going counter to her "natural" image, it would be extremely "fresh" ("*furesshu*"), even "sexy" ("*sekushii*"). For her debut, she sang a men's song, "Abare-Daiko" (Wild Drums), and many of her subsequent hits have also been men's songs.

Another example is a twenty-year-old nikkei (Japanese-American) male singer recruited from Hawai'i, who in 1993 was training for his enka debut. He told me that his manager was having him sing do-enka, the most traditional of the enka subgenres. Those who hold to the uniqueness of Japanese song and its performance (nihonjinron), however, doubt that a young person, especially a nonnative singer, could sing do-enka properly. But presumably, the singer's manager thinks a Japanese audience would find it "charming" to hear a foreigner (even a Japanese-American) sing these songs "from and of the Japanese heart," a construction of "charm," however, that is based on ethnocentric condescension toward non-Japanese (cf. Miller 1995).

In both cases, the music industry has manipulated fundamental cultural assumptions about gender, age, and nationality with an eye to potential consumption. Novelty, charm, and desire play on the juxtaposition of fundamental assumptions with their obverse; we see both the pattern and its negation, kata and its breach. Desire, however, is a tenuous thing. Once satisfied, it disappears. As is true of nostalgia or the souvenir (S. Stewart 1993), to remain effective these contradictory elements must maintain their distance. The charm of someone like Sakamoto Fuyumi lies not in becoming increasingly "manlike" but in retaining her "feminine" look and manner, especially when singing men's songs. The novelty of a Japanese-American singing do-enka will only sell if the singer keeps reminding his audience that he is not Japanese. It is difference that presumably piques curiosity and generates sales.

A singer's name becomes another easily manipulated element. As an article in a fan magazine says, "A name is a person's signboard" ("*Namae wa sono hito no kanban*") (Anonymous 1994d: 46). Very few enka singers go by their given name. One of the more important aspects of image-making, therefore, is the *gei-mei* (stage name). A stage name may be used to connect a singer to a particular place, especially if that place is distant from Tokyo, thereby evoking furusato. For example, the surname of the singer Kitajima Saburō means "northern island," which refers to Hokkaido, where he was born. Other stage names might have historical associations. The singer Ōkawa Eisaku took his stage name from Ōkawa in Fukuoka prefecture, the city of his birth, and from Satō Eisaku, the prime minister at the time of his debut. A stage name can also be a way to pay tribute to those to whom one is indebted, following the practice of the iemoto (headmaster) system in the traditional Japanese arts, which identifies the singer as one who understands the old-fashioned Confucian values of hierarchy, loyalty, duty, and obligation. The singer Mori Shin'ichi, for example, has borrowed part of his stage name from Watanabe Shin, the head of the production company to which he was originally under contract, and part from his own natal name of Moriuchi. Stage names can also be considered gifts, as in the case of the singer Kanmuri Jirō, who was given his stage name by his mentor, the composer Mifune Kōshō. Other names are selected for their meaning. Kanmuri's mentor selected his name because of its unusual ideographs and pronunciation, but also because it means "reaching a peak," in this case, reaching for success in the enka world.

A stage name makes it all the more possible for a performer to separate his personal self from his stage self. Many singers, especially those who have changed stage names several times, refer to this stage self as if to a separate person. The singer Itsuki Hiroshi, for example, has debuted four times, each time under a different stage name. His current success he partially attributes to his current name. In discussing the six different stage names he has used over his thirty-year career,[28] Itsuki speaks objectively about each, and about the singer he was at the time, including his present persona:

[My] thirty years include six years when I changed record companies and names and when I was at the bottom career-wise. . . . It was just as I was wondering whether to quit or not that I entered the Zen-Nihon Kayō Senshuken [All-Japan Song Contest]. I won for ten consecutive weeks, and then I started as Itsuki Hiroshi. . . . Without those years, Itsuki Hiroshi could not have existed. . . .
When I was singing and playing the guitar at clubs, I established my basic style. That was the time I prepared most to be Itsuki Hiroshi. . . .
In fact, my voice has changed three times even after I became Itsuki Hiroshi. . . .
   [My voice] sounds mild but powerful, when necessary, and modest, when necessary. This is the way Itsuki Hiroshi sings. (Quoted in Wilson 1995: 19–22)

In the image-making process, the singer becomes a product to be made and remade according to the requirements of the market. Just as an automobile manufacturer might redesign and rename a car model in response to the desires of buyers, so too, an enka singer reinvents and renames him or herself. Such gestures can actually enhance a singer's reputation: they are regarded not as failures of past names or incarnations but as the triumph of perseverance.

Musical Training: Sounding the Imaginary

While record and production companies are busy creating the singer's image, the singer is undergoing vocal training and making a demonstration tape. The training includes lessons in vocal production and vocal expression.

One record producer commented that new singers, who are often very young, have little in the way of life experience to draw on in order to sing enka convincingly. Instead, they rely on their teachers to tell them how to impart some sense of life experience and lived emotion to their singing. Thus, behind what is meant to sound like heartfelt emotion is the discipline of a patterned and practiced technique.

Lessons consist of intense sessions of vocal warm-ups and careful phrase-by-phrase instruction. At the one professional lesson I observed, the teacher first spoke a phrase of the song as poetry and then asked the singer to repeat it before singing it. As he put it, "What's best is if you have a sense of the feeling of the song; then your voice will come forth naturally [*Kimochi o te ni ireba, shizen ni koe o dashita hō ga ii*]." This kind of teaching reinforces the importance of the lyrics, the narrative, and emotion over the music itself.

Amateur lessons demonstrate how emotional and gendered expression is molded. I compared four different lessons on singing the 1992 enka hit, "Kokoro-zake" (*Sake* of the Heart), two in printed versions with unnamed authors, one by composer Miki Takashi, and one by composer Ichikawa Shōsuke.[29] It is structurally stereotypical that the two teachers who are identified are men.

The first verse of "Kokoro-zake" is as follows:

naite amaeru anata ga itara	When I am with you, with whom I whimper and am indulged,
taete yukemasu tsuraku tomo	I can endure the pain.
sonna onna no hitori-goto	This is the soliloquy of the kind of woman that I am.
yotte samishisa wasureru yō ni	In drunken loneliness, in order to forget my pain,
nomi-hoshimashō ka	Shall we drink up?
nomi-hoshimashō ka kokoro-zake	Shall we drink this *sake* of the heart?

All four lessons include a *wan-pointo* [*adobaisu*] (one-point advice), a brief, summarizing pedagogical statement. Lesson 1 instructs singers to "pay close attention to *ko-bushi* [ornamentation] and expression, which indicates convulsive sobbing [*shakuri-ageru hyōgen*], while singing gently/moistly [*shittori*] and femininely [*josei-rashiku*]." Lesson 2 cautions, "Sing without sounding too somber/dark [*kuraku naranai yō ni*]." Lesson 3 warns, "Sing *ko-bushi* not too heavily/strongly [*kitsuku naranai yō ni*]. Try to sing with the intention of expressing only true feelings [*hon no kimochi dake*]." Lessons 4a and 4b emphasize the way in which words are articulated (*hatsuon no shikata*) as they express feelings (*kanjō no hyōjō*). The two common points are the expression of feelings and conveying femininity in one's singing. Here, femaleness is constructed by both affirmation—"*shittori*" (gently; "moistly"), "*josei-rashiku*" (femininely)—and negation—not "*kurai*" (somber; dark), not "*kitsui*" (heavy, strong).

All four lessons take a similar approach to the first line of the song, "*Naite amaeru, anata ga itara.*" Lesson 1 instructs, "*Yasashiku*" (gently, tenderly). Lesson 2 cautions, "Without putting in too much force [*rikimazu ni yawarakaku*], sing sweetly [*sunao ni*] . . . Little by little put in more feeling, but take care not to express it too strongly [*tsuyoku narisuginai yō chūi*]." Lessons 3 and 4 (a, b) stress the importance of the text as well as the attitude of *amaeru*, of actively seeking the man's indulgence through the kind of expression that feels cloyingly passive. In Lesson 3, Miki feels that *amaeru* imparts the full meaning of the entire song (*kashi no imi o jūbu ni rikai*) and suggests singing the word "*anata*" (you; darling) as if appealing to one's lover (*aite ni uttai-kakeru yō ni*). Ichikawa, throughout the televised lesson (4b), both describes and demonstrates how to express *amaeru*—singing sweetly with a little-girl (or little-boy) smile to convey a feeling of intimacy (*shitashimi yō na kanji*). His approach to *amaeru* involves not languor (*darari to shinai yō ni*), but a continuing, if restrained energy that makes each note ring. Watching his demonstrations during the televised lesson, one would conclude that singing a note involves directing as much energy out as in, effecting a highly controlled, mannered kind of charm. In fact, he asks the nineteen-year-old female pupil he is instructing to sing with "charm" (*aikyō*). At one point during the lesson, she giggles in embarrassment at mimicking his demonstration. Ichikawa quickly but gently admonishes her and the members of the studio audience who have been laughing along with her, reminding them that Miyako Harumi, the famous singer he trained for a time, constantly uses this technique, and that it is one of the ways she gives her songs their sense of intimacy (*shitashimi*).

In the third line, "*Sonna onna no, hitori-goto,*" the climax of the song, the lessons all suggest ways to convey the sense of climax. Lesson 1 says to sing rhythmically. Lesson 2 suggests that the singer emphasize each syllable by singing each one with a different vocal expression. Lesson 3 recommends clear articulation (*hatsuon o shikkari to*) and imbuing each phrase with strong emotion (*shikkari to kimochi o komete*). Lesson 4 instructs singers to sing strongly (*tsuyoku*), but not too strongly (*utai-komu*), so that the singing is always tender (*yasashiku*). To do otherwise, says Ichikawa, would be to make the song force itself on its listeners (*rikinde kikasō to suru to oshitsuke-gamashii uta ni narimasu*).

In the line immediately following, "*Yotte sabishisa, wasureru yō ni*" (In drunken loneliness, in order to forget my pain), singers are instructed in all lessons to pull back, to make this section "*shittori to*" (gentle/moist, i.e., feminine). Miki suggests singing with feminine "*amaeru*" (*josei-rashiku sukoshi amaeru*) and offers a way to achieve it by adding a kind of breathiness (*iki no fukidashi-kata de*). A whispered breathiness, characteristic of many female enka songs, gives the performance a sense of intimacy and helpless pleading. Ichikawa further cautions, however, that because the song's line can flow along so easily, it is important that the singer express a sense of caring empathy to avoid sounding glib (*Nagare-yasui desu kara, taisetsu ni omoiyari o motte utatte kudasai*).

The last two lines, "*nomi-hoshimashō ka / nomi-hoshimashō ka, kokoro-zake*," include notes in the lowest and the highest registers of the song. All the lessons comment on the rhythmic execution of these lines. Miki (Lesson 3) cautions that the lower register should be sung moderately (*hikaeme ni*), so that it does not sound too strong (*amari tsuyoku naranai*). In the televised lesson (4b), Ichikawa asks his pupil to sing the line as if it were a true invitation directed to a real person (in this case, to him). What he is in fact asking is nothing less than that the singer flirt with him but in a specific manner—with bright smiles, sweet rounded tones, and the little-girl affectations of a broken heart.

In general, these teachers agree on a fairly narrow definition of the best way to sing this song, or, in other words, on the kata for this song. The point in these lessons is not so much how to sing "Kokoro-zake" but how to sing it as Fuji Ayako sings it: through sweet begging, cloying smiles, and *amaeru*. The vocabulary used in all four lessons—*shittori shita* (gentle; "moist"), *josei-rashii* (feminine), *aikyō ga aru* (charming), *yasashii* (gentle, tender), *sunao* (mild, gentle)—itself forms a kind of kata for this song and for the particular construction of femaleness upon which it is built. Just as the teachers who are identified here are male, we may assume that the teacher who trained Fuji Ayako to sing this song in this manner is also male. These men define the kata of femaleness for professional singers as well as for the countless amateurs who aspire to sound like them.

Personal Training: Lessons in Hardship

Along with various forms of company-based preparation, enka singers also cite personal processes that help them in readying themselves for their debut. Most involve the importance of hardship and suffering. Biographies of enka singers, and often the singers themselves when they grant interviews, never fail to mention the hardship of their early days. Some who today own luxury homes in several countries talk of early days spent as a penniless *nagashi* (strolling musician), going from bar to bar singing songs for meager pay much like the prewar enkashi. As one aspiring singer told me, to be a good enka singer he has to experience some hardship (*kurō*), so his nightly work as a server and host at a bar is helpful to him. He does not get paid much and lives frugally. He talks with customers and listens to their stories of hardship. Living far from home and working at the bar, he is learning firsthand (or at least at close range) the meaning of some of the expressions he encounters in enka—*hitori-zake* (drinking sake alone), *kaeritai* (longing to return home), *sabishii* (lonely). These kinds of experiences, he says, will give him the *aji* (flavor) he can impart in his singing.

Waiting is one hardship experienced by many aspiring singers. What seems to be important in the enka world—whether for the singer in training for a debut or one hoping her next release will be a hit—is perseverance, patience, diligence, and hard work. The process of striving is in some ways more important than the goal, and the ethic of gambaru, a trope of the industry as a whole, permeates the training process. According to one trainee, it doesn't matter how long the training takes as long as he does it in the best way he can. In each of our interviews, I asked when his debut would be, but I was expressing my own impatience rather than his. He seemed willing simply to do the bidding of his manager, trainers, and teacher.

Debut: The Birth of a Singer

A singer's debut marks the end of one process and the beginning of another. In objective terms, it is merely the date on which the singer's debut recording is released,[30] but because the term *shinjin* (newcomer) is used only during the year following the debut, the debut day takes on symbolic importance as the actual date of the singer's initiation and formal "birth" into the enka world of business, promotion, and commerce (and is thus noted in, for example, Oricon's annual compendium of the popular song world).[31] The rate of success for enka shinjin and songs is not high. As one record producer estimates, of the 22 shinjin that debut through his company in a year, only one or two will succeed.[32]

A debut might go completely unremarked, or it might become a media event. When one young female singer made her debut, on May 21, 1993, Crown Records, the company to which she was under contract, created such an event (a "*tai-appu*," "tie-up" or promotional collaboration) for the occasion by chartering a train to the rural town depicted in her debut song; the company also arranged for her to sing during the trip.

Other singers may mark the occasion of their debut with a party. As one of approximately 350 guests, I attended a party for a sixteen-year-old singer, debuting with Century Records, at a banquet hall in Ōmiya, on the outskirts of Tokyo. The gift-giving (including its costs) and the ceremony provided an explicit display of the socioeconomic obligations that make such a debut possible. Most guests sent or brought gifts, usually in the form of envelopes of money and flowers. In return, they received a shopping bag of gifts, including the singer's debut cassette (¥1000/$9), a commemorative towel (¥500/$5), and a seven-inch commemorative desk clock inscribed with the singer's name and debut date (estimated cost, ¥5000/$45). The entrance to the banquet hall and the hall itself were lined with large floral displays, including arrangements from the composer, the lyricist, the record company, family members, the local popular song club, and a *kōenkai* (support organization, fan club) that had already been established for her. Guests were treated to a six-course meal, speeches by record company officials and local politicians, the ceremonial breaking of a sake barrel, toasts, performances by the debuting singer during which she received further presents of money (typically ¥10,000/$91 or ¥20,000/$182, handed over or stuffed into her kimono) and flowers,[33] and karaoke, during which various members of the audience sang duets with her.[34] In one of the last segments of the program, volunteers among the guests each sang one verse of the debut song, and then the debut singer again sang the song. By the end of the program, audience members had heard the song any number of times, and, with cassette in hand, could also listen to it at home. Finally, using a "lucky number" process, the announcer and the singer's mother handed out further gifts to approximately twenty-five guests. At the end of the party, as several guests— including the composer, the lyricist, the record company producer, and me (a guest of the composer)—were waiting to leave, the singer's mother hastily

Singer at Her Debut Party

handed each of us an *o-rei* (honorarium) of ¥20,000 ($182) in an envelope and some leftover flowers. Overwhelmed, I staggered out of the hall carrying the original shopping bag of gifts from the singer's family to guests, the envelope of money, and a dozen red roses.

Two features of this debut party stand out: the flow of gifts and money and the prominent role of the singer's mother. Even by my conservative estimate, the event must have cost around ¥4,070,000 ($37,000). Exactly who paid for it is not entirely clear, although gifts of money also flowed in from the guests, most of whom brought envelopes containing at least ¥10,000 ($91) or ¥20,000 ($182),[35] often accompanied by bouquets of flowers.[36]

Moreover, the hub of the event seemed to be not the singer but the singer's mother, who greeted the guests, saw to their needs, showered them with gifts, and thanked them at the end. Many of those present seemed to be her friends and business acquaintances, not the singer's. As much as the singer's image may have been a product of the production and record companies, in this setting, the singer was clearly her mother's product.

The Making of a Hit Song

As several composers, lyricists, and producers have repeatedly told me, enka is first and foremost a genre of words rather than of music. As one might expect, a song usually begins as a set of lyrics in a 7–5 syllabic structure similar to that used in *waka* (Japanese vernacular poetry), to which music is added.[37] The lyricist Kudoh Tadayoshi says that in conceiving of a song, he begins with the emotions evoked by a scene or a situation and writes a poem about it. The poem is subsequently set to music by a composer. The well-known male composer Yoshioka Osamu, according to popular lore, likes to go to a *ryokan* (Japanese-style inn) and write his songs while half-reclining on *tatami* (Japanese straw flooring) instead of sitting at a table. Here, even the making of a song enacts its reputed ties to tradition.

The record industry refers to the entire promotional enterprise surrounding a song as waging a *"kyanpein"* (campaign), and the effort put forth in these campaigns is responsible for a song's success (theoretically, if a campaign is waged long enough and hard enough, the song will become a hit). The goal of the publicists is to have the song *"mimi ni hairu"* (enter people's ears) and become a part of the listeners through sheer repetition. In many cases, the campaign begins even before a song is released for sale. Such was the case for "Kokoro-zake" discussed earlier, one of the biggest hits of 1992. Its release followed months of repeat performances on radio and television as well as sales of sheet music. Through this kind of orchestrated publicity campaign, the actual release of the recording becomes a much-anticipated event.[38] A music industry article cites the adage "If enough dust accumulates, it will become a mountain" (*Chiri mo tsumoreba yama to naru*). In other words, by making many small, repeated efforts, one will accomplish a big feat: produce a hit (Anonymous 1992c: 24).

The primary form of promotion in the enka world has always been the personal appearance. Frequent exposure in personal or broadcast appearances is considered the best way to increase a singer's popularity. This approach upholds enka's reputation as a conservative, old-fashioned genre that embodies the traditional face-to-face society of Japan's past. A singer waging a campaign must perform as often as possible and in as many places as possible (typically rural areas first, then big cities), singing, shaking hands, and meeting the public. This *dōsa-mawari* (performing place-to-place) finds precedent in other itinerant performances by individuals and troupes, ranging from premodern kabuki to contemporary *taishū engeki* (theater of the masses). In enka, face-to-face performance is especially important because it represents effort and hard work. According to an article in a music industry publication, "Enka fans are older adults who are not as subject to pushy [mass media] ways. They are very discerning as to which singers are truly trying their best" (Anonymous 1992c: 22). Sheer effort, in the promotional process as much as in the music itself, is considered more important than singing ability. This combination of the premodern and the electronic is aimed less at music-making that at hit-making.

These promotional methods conveniently take advantage of the enka listening public's tolerance—even appetite—for repetition. At a media publicity event, for example, a singer will sing the song not once but two or even three times. In concert, a singer will often sing his or her newest song twice, once at the beginning of the concert and once at the end. At a two-day *matsuri* (festival) I attended in 1993, an enka singer was promoting her newest song.[39] At each of her three fifteen-minute appearances each day, the singer sang side-A of her new release twice, side-B once, and an old hit once, with the same joking banter in between. Within less than three hours, she had sung the same song no less than six times. "This song is easy to learn [*oboeyasui*]," the singer cheerfully exhorted us, "and easy to sing [*utaiyasui*]. Please learn it![*Oboete kudasai!*]." Sheets containing the lyrics were passed out, and at each appearance, when the singer asked audience members to join her on the final song, several always did. Given the close scheduling of her appearances—at 1:00, 2:00, and 3:00 P.M.—chances were good that the audience for one might easily become the audience for the following one. In addition, in between the singer's live appearances, the new release was played repeatedly over the loudspeakers.

Other ways a song might "enter one's ears" include repeated radio, television, and cable broadcasts, and karaoke. As one record producer puts it, "By having a song sung at karaoke by amateurs, everyone is made to hear it [*Honnin no kawari ni utatte, minna kikasetari*]." To get more "ear time" for a song through these forms of media, production companies wage a vigorous publicity campaign to encourage fans to request the song by phone, postcard, letter, or fax, and fans use all these methods massively and efficiently.

Some of the best campaigners are members of the singer's kōenkai/fan club, which are usually operated by the record companies (see Chapter 6).

Another very effective way to promote a song is through a *"tai-appu"* ("tie-up") with some other form of media, especially television. As in the early days of film-music industry mutual promotions, arranging for a song to be the theme music in a television series or a commercial has been considered a coup for a record company.[40] In the early 1990s, however, a magazine published an article decrying the dwindling opportunities for promotion in the enka world. According to this article, with the "bursting of the [Japanese] economic bubble" in 1991, opportunities for music industry tie-ups with films or commercial products were decreasing, making promotion more difficult (Anonymous 1992c: 21). The number of televised music programs has also decreased, and enka singers must resort to talk shows, game shows, and cooking shows to keep their faces before the public. But here, a singer's image may actually be enhanced by its obverse: a female singer who performs in a kimono may wear Western dress; a male singer who usually wears a tuxedo may appear in a sweater. The notion that a singer might emerge from behind his or her stage persona and appear as an everyday person makes these shows an enticement for fans, who hope to see another side of their star.

Enka singers also appear in advertisements for various products, places, and organizations, especially those that draw on themes of furusato, tradition, and "Japan."[41] The pictures of enka singers on post office informational posters are a good example, as are their personal appearances at local post offices to promote new songs and tourism to furusato-rural areas. Horiuchi Takao, for example, a young male enka singer, appeared in Tokyo on March 23, 1993, in a concert sponsored in part by the national postal service to commemorate the one hundredth anniversary of its parcel service. Here, Japan's internal ambassadors of song invoke "the people's" past and promote domestic tourism, in effect sanctifying enka, while glamorizing a staid national institution.

The effect of the current economic recession in Japan further reinforces enka's underdog image. At any given moment, the enka world can survive by relying on gambaru and individual human effort, by, as the adage recommends, "making mountains out of dust." For some but not for all, the promotional "dust" of handshakes, of singing to audiences large and small, of traveling to out-of-the-way places in order to sing one more time, of wearing outlandish costumes on game shows, of appearing on every radio show that offers a booking (whether at 2:00 A.M. or, worse, 6:00 A.M.) pays off. For those whose efforts do not produce a hit this time, there is always the next song, which they will promote with even greater effort. The rate of success in the enka world, like that for other commercial music, is not high. Far more singers and songs remain in obscurity than gain nationwide fame. Although the same kata guide every step, the industry knows full well that in the end, there is no magic formula that can guarantee success. The most that can be said with any assurance is that human effort, portrayed in enka lyrics as well as in the commercial processes of producing stars and hits, will always find a place in the enka world.

Nearly every step in the production and marketing process is embedded in the enka imaginary. From its underdog status to its persevering singers, songs, and managers, to its face-to-face promotional campaigns, enka presents itself as an oasis in the high-tech, big business world of the music industry. The enka industry itself (setting aside, for the moment, its music and lyrics) has become synonymous with preindustrial "Japan," where business was conducted on a human scale. In the end, according to this construct, bureaucratic structures and decision-making come down to hard-working individuals who meet heart-to-heart. This is not nostalgia. It is a national cultural industry that takes its patterned practices from a reconfigured past and heroicizes them.

CHAPTER FOUR

Enka on Stage

Patterning the Practices of Intimacy

Tokyo, September 26, 1991, 6:45 P.M. I am sitting at a table in a tiny, exclusive restaurant that features kaiseki ryōri *(elegant Japanese cuisine originally served in conjunction with the tea ceremony), the guest of an executive at Terebi Tokyo (TV Tokyo), one of the major broadcasters of enka shows. A composer himself and a producer of enka television shows and recordings, he is indeed "Mr. Enka." An animated raconteur, he explains his philosophy about performances: "In my mind, a good enka performance should ask the audience to meet the singer some of the way. If a performer gives too much, goes one hundred percent of the way, then the audience is exhausted. It's like sex. I prefer a performer who goes seventy percent of the way, which makes the audience meet them thirty percent. That way, both the singer and audience contribute something to the performance, and they're both satisfied."*

Performance—"the most directly social of all the arts," as Joseph Bensman says (1983: 7)—first presumes a distance between the performer and the audience and then attempts to bridge that distance in various ways. In analyzing the dynamics of American country and western music, the ethnomusicologist Aaron Fox considers what he calls "de-naturalizing" or distancing conventions (e.g., proscenium stage, out-of-the-ordinary costuming) and "re-naturalizing" or bridging conventions (e.g., shaking hands with the audience, engaging in stage patter, speaking in local dialect) (1992: 55–56).[1] Both processes highlight the social nature of the performer-audience interaction, the seventy-thirty relationship of which "Mr. Enka" speaks, or what Renee Shield calls "resonance" (1980: 106).

How far a performer goes has as much to do with the context and with that individual performer as with cultural expectations. The variables of the meeting ground (e.g., stage size, related activities, frequency of performance, number of performers, gender of performers, cultural expectations) constitute a kind of "slide-rule of performer-audience interaction," on which seventy-thirty is only one setting. Given a different set of cultural expectations or conditions, a performer might be required to "do" more or "do" less. A female singer, for example, might be expected to perform more theatrically than a male. Whether the give-and-take between performer and audience is seventy-thirty, ninety-ten, or fifty-fifty, the enka performer attempts to produce and reproduce the sociality that lies at the heart of this genre. This chapter and the next focus on enka performance, analyzing the creation of "resonance" through the kata (patterning), both formulaic and nonformulaic, that structure this national spectacle of patterned intimacy.

Live Performances: Creating a Display of Patterned Intimacy

The work of intimacy-making, of "re-naturalizing" the performance,[2] involves creating the façade of a social relationship and making it believable. For an enka fan, seeing a singer perform in the flesh is tantamount to "meeting" him or her. When I ask enka fans whether they have ever met (verb "*au*") a particular singer, they answer yes, even if they have in fact only attended a concert.

An enka singer communicates to listeners through patterned words, music, gestures, and staged effects. Listeners likewise respond with patterned iterations of encouragement and approval in the form of applause, shouts, or actual gifts. The *kakegoe* (shouts) most commonly consist of the singer's name or nickname coupled with a term of endearment, such as "Sabu-chan!" for singer Kitajima Saburō (see Prologue), but they might also include "*Umai!*" (Well done!) for vocal bravura—a long-held note, a broad vibrato, or a dramatically rendered serifu (recitative). These patterned responses have their historical roots in "traditional" Japanese theater forms such as kabuki and taishū engeki (theater of the masses) (Shively 1978: 20–21; Ivy 1995: 227–30, 233–39). An enka concert, then, becomes an important venue not only for the singer but also for the listeners, who perform the "traditional" role of audience member.

The patterned ways in which an audience expresses itself are of two types, "spontaneous" and "planned." Spontaneous expressions render performer-audience resonance immediate, dynamic, and vibrant. Audience members may break out in enthusiastic applause or kakegoe in response to a particularly rousing moment. In lieu of (or in addition to) these spontaneous expressions, planned reactions also contribute to the resonance of the interaction. Hand-waving, especially at the end of a concert, serves as a gesture of farewell: the singer waves to audience members and they wave back. A variation, waving "penlights" (small, purse-sized flashlights), is done in a more organized fashion, usually by fan club members who have purchased these flashlights in advance. They might wave them from side to side in unison, swaying back and forth in their seats, during particular songs or in a small circle during a singer's held note.

Gift-giving is another common form of planned audience response to enka performers. At almost all the enka concerts I attended, members of the audience gave the singer presents, which ranged from floral bouquets, money (tucked in an envelope or handed to the singer directly), or shopping bags filled with an assortment of items, to more humble gifts, such as *manjū* (bean-jam buns), canned juice, or potato chips, to personal or handmade gifts, such as a glass-encased Japanese doll made by the giver's mother, a pillow embroidered with the star's name, or *shiitake* (dried mushrooms) brought back as *o-miyage* (souvenir gift) from a trip to the countryside. The very humbleness of some of the gifts as well as their personal nature suggest that fans regard these enka stars as friends and intimates, as indeed *tōshindai* (life-sized). Sometimes the gift-giving is staged: when I sat in the fan club section during one concert, a leader of the kōenkai handed me a bouquet of flowers to give the singer.

At several of the concerts I attended, a special time called a *"fuan purezento kōnā"* (fan present "corner") was set aside for this gift-giving.[3] Fans lined up, often directly below the stage, awaiting their turn to hand a present to the performer in exchange for a handshake and a few words of thanks. For fans, the perquisites of such close proximity carry untold meaning. On a warm September afternoon during one of these "corners," more than one female fan was thrilled when a male enka star took her handkerchief, wiped his brow with it, and handed it back to her laden with his sweat, if not his tears.

Women far outnumber men at enka concerts, and audience response generally follows gendered lines. Although both men and women applaud, more men shout kakegoe, more women give gifts, and far more women participate in fan-club-derived activities such as penlight-waving. It is important to remember, however, that this kind of response is neither uniform nor obligatory. At any given concert, the audience might be engaged in a range of simultaneous activities, from enthusiastic penlight-waving to dozing. In the newer concert halls, food and drink are not permitted, but in the older venues, such as Shinjuku Koma Gekijō (see Prologue), especially when the program is a long one combining period drama and a song show,[4] concert-going follows a more "traditional" format that can include eating, drinking, and even sleeping.

In the lobby, a booth run by members of the singer's kōenkai, who also hand out membership application forms, displays goods bearing the singer's name and likeness (see Prologue). What they are actually selling is a form of commodified intimacy. A separate booth staffed by record company employees sells the singer's CDs, cassette tapes, videotapes, and posters. Souvenirs offered at these booths help to prolong the concert experience: an audience member can symbolically purchase a small piece of the singer to take home.

On the enka stage (as on the American country and western stage), chatting between numbers becomes a patterned means through which the singer emerges from behind the kata of song into the kata of talk, which reaches out to the audience on a more personal "folk" level. The kata of talk mingles self-deprecating humor with stories of early hardship to create a bond of intimacy between performer and listener.[5] If shared tears are the medium of resonance in songs, then shared laughter is the preferred medium of resonance in stage patter.

Some singers bridge the gap between the stage and the audience by moving closer to their listeners. In many cases these moves seem spontaneous: in fact, however, they are highly choreographed. According to one pattern, the singer first positions herself where one would expect, at center stage, then moves downstage on one side to sing a verse to that half of the theater, and finally, crosses the stage to sing the next verse to the other half. By ensuring that each corner of the theater receives an equal amount of performance time, the singer creates a kind of orchestrated democratization among the audience. At some enka concerts, singers actually leave the stage to shake hands with audience members. Mori Shin'ichi, a well-known enka singer, makes a point of doing this at nearly every concert and, in many cases, during the same song. The move is well prepared for by his staff, who crouch around him, opening his way, holding his microphone cord, and controlling enthusiastic fans. At other enka concerts, handshaking is the privilege of fan club members only, who line up after the performance to greet their star.

Some performances include an opportunity for selected audience members to sing with the star on stage in a prescheduled "*duetto kōnā*" ("duet corner" or segment). At one concert I attended, the singer went downstage and asked two elderly audience members to sing the chorus of her well-known song with her; at another, the singer asked audience members to come up to the stage to sing a duet with him.[6] Opportunities to perform with the singer, whether live on stage or by simply mouthing the words in a "silent" private duet from one's seat, bring the audience into the spectacle. The sing-along "re-naturalizes" the performer as one of the "folk," as tōshindai (life-sized), and turns the stage into something closer to a living room, a karaoke "box," or a private party.

What singers sing also follows a kata from one concert to the next. Quite often singers will sing their debut song no matter how many years have elapsed. They are also likely to sing all or almost all of their biggest hits, even if there is time for only one or two or three verses of each. According to the manager of one top singer, enka fans pay money to hear the songs they know and love, not something new, so the concert program becomes as predictable as a cassette rerelease of old hits. The kata goes like this: if the performer is singer X, chances are that the audience will hear songs A, B, and C, and that song A will most likely come at or near the same spot in the program. Fans who attend a concert expecting to hear singer X sing song A in the same time slot (near the end, for example, if it is a tear-jerking hit) find comfort in having their expectations met. Kata creates and then fulfills expectations.

The final song of a concert, dubbed "*rasto nambā*" ("last number"), is imbued with poignancy, as are endings in general. As if they are lovers parting, the performer often remarks wistfully to the audience that their time together must come to an end. To my surprise, however, the audience does not always sit spellbound, carried away by matching emotion. Whether the last song is part of the regular program or an encore, some audience members very pragmatically gather their belongings and prepare to leave. The last song, then, is marked by the re-naturalizing of audience members into their everyday worlds: the rustling of bags, the donning of coats, and the gradual filling of exit aisles. Japan is a densely populated country. Trains must be caught, and crowds fought. The rush of contemporary life resumes even before the performer can sing the last note.

Mediated Performances: Broadcasting Intimacy

In contrast to live performances, mass-mediated performances bring the immediacy of the performer-audience relationship from the concert hall into one's own home.[7] For those living at a distance from urban concert venues and those who cannot afford the high ticket prices, broadcasts of enka performances over radio, television, and cable make singers and their songs accessible. In addition, the widespread use of video and other recording technologies means that a broadcast can be replayed and savored over and over, to one's heart's content.

And yet, the singer-audience relationship afforded through mass media is qualitatively different from the relationship cultivated in live performance. As Andrew Painter puts it, "Everyone can share in the close and informal relationships represented on Japanese [radio and] TV precisely because those relationships are largely imaginary. . . . It is experienced as both public (produced and circulated in society) and private (viewed inside the home)" (1996: 227). Here the fiction of intimacy is even more exaggerated than on the live stage. An electronically mediated relationship not only lacks the immediacy of a live one, it also suspends belief in some basic premises. A performer has no immediate sense of a listener's response, only the delayed tally of sales and media requests. A listener cannot respond to an actual moment of performance, only to the prerecorded broadcast. A social relationship between singer and audience that is based on radio or television broadcasts is necessarily held together by the suspended sense of time and place: it is an asynchronous, disembodied intimacy.

Radio: National Nostalgia on the Airwaves

Radio is a primary means of disseminating new enka songs and giving older songs renewed exposure. Listeners can also request their favorites. Lacking television's visual element, radio presents enka as a purely aural phenomenon. But radio is more likely than television to retain a "live" element, since radio programming often features studio disc jockeys (albeit playing prerecorded numbers). Moreover, radio is eminently transportable, allowing listeners to bring enka along as an intimate companion at home, on the road, or almost anywhere.

In the Kantō area (Tokyo and its environs), some radio stations broadcast specialized enka programming as well as popular music shows that sometimes play enka.[8] Of particular interest are the late-night enka shows broadcast between 1:00 A.M. and 5:00 A.M. on various radio stations. According to one radio show producer, these shows are aimed at truck drivers, who form a large segment of male enka listeners. Driving alone in the middle of the night, truck drivers tune in to these radio shows, usually hosted by young, mid-to-lower-ranked female enka singers. The female hosts tend to be cheerful and informal, and their amiable chattiness draws these listeners in. These shows take requests for enka songs by mail, phone, or fax (fax machines can be found at many truck stops). When songs are aired, the requester's name, age, and prefecture are given. Not only does this personalize the request, but it also brings the listening truck drivers together into an electronic "community." Between enka songs, the announcers give information about current road conditions and sports news.

The only completely live enka radio show on the air today is *Hatsuratsu Sutajio 505* (Lively Studio 505) of NHK, which is broadcast nationwide from Tokyo on Wednesday nights. Begun in 1985, it was a deliberate attempt to create a nostalgic radio program that harkened back to an era of live music with an orchestra and singers. According to the program's producer, "*hatsuratsu*" (lively, animated, fresh) was chosen to impart a feeling of vitality and liveliness, especially to the older people who would most likely compose the program's audience; studio 505 is the NHK studio from which the program is broadcast. According to one of the program's original directors, NHK felt a particular responsibility to serve the older segment of the population by providing a show that emulated the radio broadcasts of the past.

I attended several rehearsals and broadcasts of the show and obtained copies of several scripts. Admission to the broadcast is free, but seating is limited to about 200. In general, those who attend are members of the fan clubs of the singers who appear. But there are also some weekly regulars I came to recognize, such as a small, wiry man in his sixties wearing a jacket autographed by various enka singers and carrying a photo album of singers' pictures he has taken over the years; an overweight, glazed-eyed man in his thirties, often accompanied by his mother, who snapped photographs of him with different singers after the show; and a large, greasy-haired man in his forties with missing teeth and dark glasses, who yelled the singers' names loudly during the show. These are some of the "groupies" of the program and the genre.

For studio and home audience alike, the program deliberately, even blatantly, evokes a sense of nostalgia for the past. With that nostalgia comes a sense of finding a comforting place within the tumult of the present and the future. The announcer's introduction emphasizes a balance between looking back and looking ahead. One script reads: "Yesterday's memories become tomorrow's dreams—today's happiness becomes life's sustenance—songs are always life's friends. Singing nostalgic songs to that person and new songs to this person—wholeheartedly [*kokoro o komete*], we send you live popular song radio, *Hatsuratsu Sutajio 505*!" (Nowada 1992: 2). Another script claimed that "Nostalgic songs bind days long gone with today. And new songs tie today with tomorrow. Piecing together the span of experiences of a person's heart [*hito no kokoro no saigetsu o tsuzutte*], we send you live popular song radio, *Hatsuratsu Sutajio 505*!" (Marubashi 1993: 2)

In this discourse, enka binds together yesterday, today, and tomorrow. It also binds hearts, led by its music, into its imaginary. The repeated invocation of *kokoro* (heart) as the means by which the program is sent forth to a national audience is essential to its tone of sincerity.

Television: Three Examples of Televisual Intimacy

The primacy of television in Japanese life has transformed enka into a visual entertainment form. As broadcasts increasingly focus on young female singers, the camera's close-ups magnify subtle gestures—a glance, a trembling lip, a slight heave of the shoulders. Like the microphone, which allows singers to whisper where they previously had to project (and has made possible the rise of singers who can *only* whisper) (Hamm and Lamb 1980: 93), the television camera creates its own intimacy, or what Andrew Painter calls "televisual *uchi*" (insidedness; in-groups) (1996; cf. Abt 1987).

Fewer television shows today include enka than in the heyday of the 1970s and 1980s. However, enka continues to be a part of regular programming, and weekly television guides list it as a separate category. In the Kantō area, enka is broadcast primarily in the form of specialized regular programming, although a few general popular music shows also include it.⁹ The balance of this chapter looks more closely at three contemporary examples: a typical enka show, through which the genre has been defined, a late-night show demonstrating the extremes to which the genre is being stretched as a cultural practice, and a yearly special that features enka prominently in its construction of nationhood.

The only long-running popular music show dedicated exclusively to enka is Terebi Tokyo's *Enka no Hanamichi* (literally, "Flower Way"/Stage Passage of Enka).¹⁰ This half-hour program went on the air in October 1978, and over twenty years later, it continues its deliberate evocation of *furusato* (hometown) and nostalgia. The show takes a standard-bearer approach to the genre and thus provides a good index of the current state of enka. It is self-defining and self-limiting. According to the show's producer, Hashiyama Atsushi, the rule of thumb is that no *shinjin* are allowed, so that appearing on the program is one indicator of success in the enka world.¹¹

One male fan of the show, in his eighties, explained to me that the narrator is meant to sound like an older female bar owner who has had her own share of life's hardships, someone to whom a male patron could tell his troubles. In reality, however, she is Kinomiya Ryōko, a professional voice actress, who has narrated the show since its inception. According to Hashiyama, before Kinomiya records the narration for a show, she purposely goes to bars to drink and sing in order to achieve her characteristic husky voice (Wilson 1993a: 19–20).

Every show begins with a similarly phrased voiceover introduction by Kinomiya to a non-enka orchestral theme. The ponderous music and the husky-voiced narration of the handwritten script immediately set the mood: "*Ukiyo butai no hanamichi wa omote mo areba ura mo aru*" (If the *hanamichi* of the stage of the floating world has a surface, it also has an underside).¹² In many ways, *Enka no Hanamichi* serves as the arbiter of the genre. The songs are a mix of old and new. The singers are not newcomers but familiar, established faces. The mostly nighttime sets help fans visualize the enka imaginary: its snowy inns, empty wharves, and forlorn-looking bars. Here, one can see the performer in a melodramatic context enacting the story, "living" the song. *Enka no Hanamichi* brings the genre, wrapped in past scenes and emotions, into the viewers' living room. Watching the show transports viewers back not only to past times and distant places, but to feelings far removed from the daily bustle.

If *Enka no Hanamichi* is intentionally dark and moody, the late night *Enka TV* is just the opposite: light, irreverent, and zany.[13] It looks and feels more like some neo-enka pastiche. Launched in 1987 by producers at Terebi Asahi (TV Asahi), *Enka TV* was conceived as a way to attract the young disco crowd into the enka fold. As Kawashima Yukio, the producer of the show, explained to me:

> The general public has this very dark, somber image [*kurai imēji*] of "enka people." However, when you meet these enka people, you find that they are not really dark and somber, but up-to-date people [*gendai-jin*] who go to discos, go drinking, and say crazy things. So you say to yourself, "So these kinds of people sing enka! They live in the regular, modern world." Our program is one that began with the idea of trying to place enka in this milieu [*enka o kō oite miyō*]. . . . We are creating a show that places enka in the farthest imaginable spot [*ichiban tōi tokoro*], where we thought we would have fun with it, where we thought it would be enjoyable. . . . Song is a phenomenon of the present, so we had the idea of creating a listening venue that would relate to the current times.

To project a more up-to-date image, the show's creators have combined a hodgepodge of elements, and the craziness of the mix is entirely deliberate. During the one-minute span of the opening credits, various images flash one after another on the TV screen: discotheque spotlights; a seagull flying low over the ocean as the letter "E" tumbles by; a couple walking by a docked ocean liner as a ship's horn sounds; images of young people screaming and waving their arms at a rock music concert; another letter "E," larger than the first, floating by; a close-up of a shotglass on a bar counter; waves crashing over rocks and the title "Enka TV"; and finally, as the music switches abruptly from disco to shamisen, a dissolve to a silkscreen of Mt. Fuji with the rising sun behind it. This is a world far removed from the somber atmosphere of *Enka no Hanamichi*.

Originally, the time slot for the program was 1:15 A.M. Gradually, however, the time was pushed later and later, until by 1992, the broadcast began at 5:00 A.M., in time to catch early risers. According to the producers of the show, the mixed audience includes young people who have stayed out most of the night, those who work in the music industry, and older people who wake early. The cohosts for the program have been selected for their youthful, "hip" image. One is Sasaki Masatoshi, a young male pony-tailed "pops" composer; the other, Sone Yoshiaki, is an older male composer who has himself sung and written in various genres, including enka. The singers who appear on the show are generally low- to mid-ranking male and female singers, including shinjin. A few top singers also appear, primarily to perform and promote their latest record, and there is usually at least one young female singer in a short, low-cut dress.

The format of the show is primarily music interspersed with loose, joking banter and several unique features. Each week, in a segment entitled "Midnight Enka Best 10" (written in English), the cohosts review the latest Oricon enka charts of predicted top record sales.[14] Each show also has a loose theme, about which the cohosts take delight in bantering with guests. The theme of a show broadcast on January 16, 1993, for example, was *furo* (Japanese bath). The cohosts leeringly asked the bosomy young guest singer questions, such as How long do you stay in the furo? In what order do you wash your body? Do you ever take a bubble bath? The camera, meanwhile, was focused on the singer's cleavage.

One of the most characteristic aspects of the show is the camerawork. Unlike other enka shows, which use two or three cameras in steady shots, with little movement, *Enka TV* uses a *wan-kame* ("one-camera") technique. The camera revolves around the singer (a technique called *"guru-guru,"* revolving), zooms in and out quickly, and sometimes shoots from exaggeratedly low and tilted angles.[15] After watching several clips from various *Enka TV* broadcasts, I concluded that the revolving camera technique is most often used when a singer is being most expressive through extra-musical growls or ko-bushi ornamentation. Kawashima explains, "Enka singers don't move around much when they sing. They usually stand in one spot. So to give a livelier feeling, we decided to have the cameras move." It is a technique also seen in music videos in the United States. According to Kawashima, using the one-camera technique creates a sense of immediacy around, for example, becoming a lover, and raises it to an erotic pitch. This combination of song and sex derives in part from the conventions of late-night television and in part from the genre itself, which alludes to a veiled eroticism. Here, the camera achieves what the enka performer sings about but does not enact.

Musically, one of the most fascinating parts of *Enka TV* is a segment called "Music Academy" with "Professor" Sone, one of the cohosts. Preceded by a shot of a statue with a raised clenched fist and the words "Enka Have to Knuckle Power" (in Japanese-fashioned English, or "Japlish"), the segment takes an example of Western popular music, such as rhythm and blues, and attempts to convert it into enka (see Chapter 5). The use of "knuckle power" in the fractured English phrase is a play on words, and refers to ko-bushi ornamentation, which the producers consider an essential characteristic of enka. The literal meaning of *ko-bushi* is a fist, hence the clenched fist statue, which in the United States is associated with power and minority rights. However, when written with different ideographs, *ko-bushi* is a vocal ornament, a small *fushi* (joint, knuckle; knot, node; melody). Sone reports that he coined the phrase "knuckle power" as a playful expression of the power of enka, here symbolized by its ko-bushi. The frequent attempts to insert English into the program reflect the producers' sense of what it means to be up-to-date in contemporary Japan. The title of the show is in English and various print signs, such as the segment introduction "Enka Have to Knuckle Power," are in "Japlish." All the songs, however, are sung in Japanese, and Japanese is the language of conversation.

Ultimately, the success of *Enka TV* was short-lived, but at least from 1987 through 1993 it made an attempt to span the gap between the older generation of enka listeners and a younger generation, between enka's reputed rural audience and the urban crowd, between enka's working-class image and a "classless" middle-class society. While the music remained intact, everything surrounding it was charged to entice this broader spectrum of listeners, especially the young. Enka's older audience members became eavesdroppers on their own music in a show geared to those fifty years younger. *Enka TV* stretched the genre to its limits: it presented enka primarily as a sound canvas upon which to sketch a pastiche of old and new. Its aim was not so much to shape emotions as to throw them into the mix of what it perceived as contemporary Japan.

Older listeners receive their due, however, in what is considered the most important yearly broadcast special for enka singers and for the general public in Japan, *NHK Kōhaku Uta Gassen* (NHK Red and White Song Contest), held every New Year's Eve (December 31) since 1951. Begun as a radio show but televised since 1958, the contest pits teams of singers, one white (male) and one red (female), against each other. In 1992, eighty-five singers competed over a period of two-and-a-half hours for the team trophy. Although reputedly not as popular as in the past, the Kōhaku is still a national institution, and watching it to welcome in the New Year is a ritualized activity for many Japanese families. Moreover, being selected to participate in the contest is still regarded as a significant benchmark of official acceptance and success in the enka world. In the months leading up to the announcement, many enka singers talk about being chosen to sing in the Kōhaku as their goal for the year. For example, in September 1993, the singer Kanmuri Jirō was quoted as saying, "This year with my song . . . my target is to make it three years in a row of Kōhaku participation [*san-nen renzoku no kōhaku*]" (Anonymous 1993e: 44).

Although the Kōhaku is not, strictly speaking, an enka event, enka singers dominate. In the 1993 program, for example, twenty-four of the fifty-two singers and groups, or almost half, performed enka. Moreover, the order in which singers perform in the program is also important, since the higher-ranked singers sing later: in 1993, nine of the last ten singers sang enka. The most prestigious spot of the evening, that of the final singer (*tori*), generally goes to an enka star.

Created by NHK, a state institution, the annual Kōhaku has become an index of official popular entertainment in Japan, and it continues to place enka in the limelight of Japanese popular music, where it plays a central role. Enka singers share the stage with rock singers and others; a kimono is as electronically enhanced as a sequined jacket. The hierarchy of songs suggests that enka still occupies the top position in the popular music world, at least as defined and promoted by NHK. Moreover, the Kōhaku has increasingly focused on themes of nostalgia and cultural nationalism—in 1992, family and childhood; in 1993, unchanging Japan ("*kawaranu Nippon*"). Such nationally broadcast mass media programs inextricably link song and emotion to nationhood. Enka retains a vital part in the cultural presentation of Japan to itself.

CHAPTER FIVE
Clichés of Excess
Words, Music, Bodies, and Beyond

> "In a lesson, the teacher will say to do it in a particular way, but as a professional, you have to find your own way to sing the song. If you don't have a bit of kosei [individuality, originality], then you cannot really sing well."
>
> —Female *shinjin* in her twenties

The spectacle of enka is meant to affirm, not to unsettle, and affirmation relies on recurring patterns of expression, emotion, interaction, and movement. Here, familiarity breeds a sense of national intimacy, even as enka's critics challenge its national status. Chapter 4 discussed the patterning of the presentation in live and mediated enka performances. This chapter examines three basic components of the genre itself—the text, the music, and the singer's physical movement—which comprise its *kata*, or patterned forms. Not only do the kata provide a language for expressing emotion, they also embody that emotion, sensually wrought and theatrically staged. The practices of enka are grounded in artifice, whose clichés become formulaic expressions of intimacy.

What the clichés of enka deliver is excess. Its melodramatic forms express convention through an overwrought style (cf. Frye 1976), what Kathleen Stewart, in relation to American country and western music, has called "an *excess* of sensation that overwhelms 'the senses' (or ordinary sensibilities); there is too much pain, too much longing, too many memories" (1993: 222).

This sense of "too much," implicated in what Bourdieu calls "the facile" (1984: 486), stamps enka as a kind of class expression that overflows the emotional containers of middle-class society.

Listening to the plethora of new enka releases every year, few of which will ever become hits, one hears cliché after cliché. The song titles alone—"Sakaba" (A Bar), "Sakaba Hitori" (Alone at a Bar), "Ame Sakaba" (Rainy Night at a Bar), "Ame Yo-zake" (Sake on a Rainy Night), "Sake Kizuna" (Bonds of Sake), "Sake Yo!" (Sake!), "Kokoro-zake" (Sake of the Heart), "Kanashii Sake" (Sorrowful Sake), "Tejaku-zake" (Pouring Myself Sake), for example—repeat a limited set of key words, expressions, and themes. Each song also relies on a ghostly recombination of musical forms and phrases drawn from older songs. In a similar way, new singers adopt the images and gestures of their predecessors, not wholly but selectively, conceiving of and structuring the present in relation to the patterns of the past.

Redundancy and cliché are one reason for enka's directness. The music of enka is imprinted bodily (mimi ni hairu, entering one's ears): listeners do not necessarily hear one particular song repeatedly, they overhear a whole corpus of songs with overlapping phrases, melodies, and tonal arrangements. The repetitiveness of the genre creates its own kind of "musical habitus" (cf. Bourdieu 1977), a "structured and structuring structure," bodily imprinting a set of musical expectations and familiarities over time. This musical habitus allows the listener to consume the song at a primal level, through direct emotional, even bodily, appeal.[1] The aim of the following analysis, then, is to recognize the patterning or kata in enka as critical elements of that appeal. They are not mechanical triggers of emotion but rather the ground where industry, singer, song, performance, and listener interact.

Yet, as the singer quoted at the beginning of this chapter notes, kata is never all there is. For a singer to succeed in the professional enka world, kata, although necessary, is only the first step. A performer must go beyond kata and give the buying public something new, even if within familiar patterns. One has to project some kind of kosei, an individualism that is as important to the genre and its consumption as kata. The concept of kosei, and the degree to which teachers and singers mention it, provides a rejoinder to the patterns discussed in this chapter.

To probe the kata of enka, I have analyzed the texts of 115 songs dating from the 1950s through the 1990s as well as the music of 28 of these 115. I chose these songs as representative of consumption in the 1990s (see

Appendix C for a full list).[2] Despite the sociopolitical changes during that period, I discuss the songs as one corpus, because my purpose is to analyze the contemporary uses to which these still-popular songs are put.

Textual Kata: A Modern Musical Recasting of Waka

Enka songs, which usually consist of three verses of five to eight lines each, follow the poetic features of *waka*, a traditional form of Japanese secular poetry and Japanese folk song.[3] Robert Brower lists the following elements as central to waka, and they characterize enka song texts as well: 1) lines of five or seven syllables; 2) an emotional lyricism expressing beauty and sadness, particularly through images of nature; 3) content that is occasioned by an event or a natural scene; 4) a xenophobic sense of Japanese linguistic and cultural purity; 5) a simple structure combined with sophisticated rhetoric; and 6) a reliance on conventional patterns we might here call kata (1983: 201–2). Enka-as-waka exploits limited resources through word play, imagery, and repetition. Enka may, in fact, be considered a modern commercial recasting of waka set to Western instruments and transmitted electronically.

Serifu: Talking Emotions

A form particularly common to the traditional do-enka subgenre of enka is the *serifu* (recitative), a brief spoken section between verses similar to the "talking" section of many American country and western songs and often serving the same function. An expression of the song's most dramatic highlights, the serifu makes the greatest demands on the singer's acting ability.[4] On stage, the serifu invokes a different kind of framing and evokes a separate response. In anticipation, a hush falls on the audience, and the instrumental accompaniment becomes softer or falls altogether silent. A spotlight singles out the performer on stage, who may prepare by shifting his or her bodily presentation. These stage conventions convey the impression that the singer is temporarily dropping the kata of song to speak from the heart, although in fact, the serifu—written and well rehearsed beforehand—is itself a form of kata. A comparison of the same singer's performances of the same serifu (or, to make the point even clearer, of *different* singers' performances of the same serifu) reveals far greater similarities than differences in, for example, breath pauses, speed, and emphasis. Following a particularly moving serifu performance, the audience might applaud or call out the performer's name, as the singer continues with the song.

The language of the serifu is conversational. It abandons the orderly rhythms of the five- and seven-syllable verse form in a flood of words and emotions. In print, most serifu suggest the tumbling rush of words and the comparative messiness of speech. A singer is more likely to cry while performing the serifu than while singing the verses. The vocal delivery might include exaggerated whispering, begging, pleading, imploring, or plaintive shouting. For example, the last "Kāchan [Mama]!!" in the final serifu of "Miso Shiru no Uta" (Song of Miso Soup) (1980) is delivered as a wail. Some serifu actually shift from the third-person narrator to a first-person main character, so that a different voice is heard. In "Ganpeki no Haha" (Mother at the Wharf) (1954), for example, the verses, which tell about a mother and her plight, are in the third person, but in the serifu section, the mother herself speaks. Other serifu may reveal new information, casting a completely different light on the drama in the sung verse. In "Ringo Oiwake" (Apple Folk Song/Packhorse Driver's Song) (1952), for example, a girl sings plaintively of a painful parting (*tsurai wakare*); only in the serifu, however, is it revealed that she has been parted from her mother, who died in Tokyo. Only here, that is, is the girl identified as an orphan.[5] As a narrative device, then, the serifu acts as a revelatory tool that conveys peaks of emotion as well as critical details of fact.

Key Words: The Poetics of Emotion

An analysis of the key words—the clichés—common to this version of Japan's national emotional culture inevitably requires some discussion of their semantic content. Although many would regard the study of meaning in isolation from its particular sociohistorical context or reception as problematic (e.g., Hall 1985, De Certeau 1984, Jenkins 1992), meaning is not purely context-driven, nor is it entirely in the hands of its interpreters. It derives from a broadly agreed-on range of designations, even when these are intended ironically or as a form of resistance. The following discussion addresses some of the main themes enunciated in the words of enka songs (acknowledging, of course, that different audiences may respond to these themes in different ways). Table 5.1 is a list of words that occur in 22 or more (19.1 percent) of the 115 enka songs in the corpus. I take Mita Munesuke's (1992) historical

Table 5.1
Word Frequency in Song Texts

Word	English	Number of songs	Number of Occurrences
Yume	dream	59	93
Kokoro	heart/soul	57	92
Anata	you	55	68
Sake	rice wine	41	149
Namida	tears	53	68
Naku	cry; weep	45	85
Onna	woman	41	81
Hito	person	41	72
Koi	love	37	70
Hana	flower	35	46
Hitori	person alone	34	49
Mune	chest; heart; breast	35	38
Watashi	I; me	33	63
Ame	rain	30	56
Futari	couple	29	42
Inochi	life	29	37
Saku	bloom	25	31
Kaze	wind	25	30
Otoko	man	24	45
Yuki	snow	24	42
Nomu	to drink	23	36
Fune	boat; ship	22	29
Kanashii	sorrowful; sad	22	28
Shiawase	happy	22	28

study of key words in Japanese popular songs as an important reference and point of departure.[6] The point of this analysis is not simply to outline the occurrence of these words—here restricted to *dream, heart/soul,* and *tears*—in enka songs but to highlight them as the delimited, stereotyped vocabulary of a past poetics that has been reconfigured in the present.

The word that occurs in the largest number of enka songs and is among the highest in frequency is *yume* (dream). In Mita's study, yume has the second highest frequency after *namida* (tears). In enka, dreams dwell on past loves, on mother, and on furusato. They do not goad the dreamer into action but encapsulate the dreamer in a state of inaction and resignation:

aa yume hagure koi hagure	Ah, my dreams are lost, my love is lost.

"Koi Uta Tsuzuri" (Love Song Spelling) (1989)

Dreaming becomes a state of being cut adrift from the everyday world. Instead of working toward fulfillment, the dreamer waits:

anata ni yume de aetara ii to	Wishing I could meet you in my dreams
kon'ya mo omou ame no yado	Is something I ponder tonight in this house of rain.
itsu-ka soeru to shinjite matte	I wait, believing that someday I will be with you.

"Nakase Ame" (Rain Which Makes One Cry)(1991)

Waiting becomes an activity unto itself (not unlike training for one's debut).

Dreams occupy a central place in the life of the dreamer. But these are not the dreams encountered through happenstance during a typical night's sleep; they are laden with hopes and promises. In everyday life, opportunities are limited, but in the imagined life of dreams the possibilities for fulfillment are limitless. Through dreams, life is given meaning and made endurable:

yume o kokoro no tsue ni shite	Dreams have become the staff of my heart
noboru jinsei tsuzura-zaka	As I climb the winding slope of life.

"Jinsei Tsuzura-zaka" (The Winding Slope of Life) (1991)

Without dreams life would seem pointless and formless; in dreams it gains focus and shape. Dreams carry the dreamer out of the past and into the future:

kurō o kasaneta namida nara	Since these tears are laden with hardship,
yume o ashita ni tsunaida mune o	My heart is bound with dreams of tomorrow.

"Kokoro-zake" (Sake of the Heart) (1991)

A common enka metaphor links *dreams*, *boats*, and *floating*:

yume o tsumi ni no inochi-bune	This boat of life carries our load of dreams.

"Kaji" (Rudder) (1992)

mizu ni nagashita yume ikutsu	My many dreams have drifted away in the water.

"Koi Momiji" (Autumn Leaves of Love) (1992)

Their association with a floating world (*ukiyo*), with wandering, transitoriness, and rootlessness, imbues dreams with an otherworldly quality that is separate from but coexistent with the everyday world. This emphasis on a floating world parallels the narrative introduction to the television show *Enka no Hanamichi* (see Chapter 4)

The second most frequently occurring word is *kokoro* (heart/soul). In conjunction with *mune* (breast, chest), which shares some of the meaning of *kokoro* as its physical seat, the concept heart/soul is central to enka. It is the core of the self, where truth, purity, and emotion reside. The further one goes from that core, the further removed one is from truth and purity. What one says, even how one looks, becomes a social mask that hides the core of how one feels:

hitori-potchi ga suki da yo to	I said that I liked being alone,
itta kokoro no ura de naku	But in my heart, I cry.

"Kanashii Sake" (Sorrowful Sake) (1966)

According to these songs, one's emotions live most truly in one's *kokoro*, and in enka, that *kokoro* is always in turmoil—throbbing, yearning, reeling:

kagami no naka de aitai kokoro	In the mirror, my heart, which wants to be
ga tokimeku	with you, throbs.

"Ma-yonaka no Shawā" (A Shower in the Middle of the Night) (1990)

kokoro mo mune mo boroboro de	My spirit, my heart are in tatters

"Shiroi Kaikyō" (White Straits) (1992)

Heartache is a theme also common to many Euro-American popular songs, but the assumption in at least some of those songs is that wounds will heal, that the protagonist will see a brighter day. In enka, the pain continues as a condition of life, as of art. Life without pain may be comfortable, but it is not necessarily worth singing about; it is a life lived in pain that inspires song.

And the heart in pain may burn or freeze. In enka, the ultimate tragedy is a heart so cold it can no longer feel:

yagate kokoro wa fuyu-geshō	Soon my heart will be frozen over in winter make-up.

"Fuyu-geshō" (Winter Make-up) (1991)

fuyu de nakute mo kokoro wa samui	Even if it is not winter, my heart is cold.

"Nakase Ame" (Rain Which Makes One Cry) (1991)

The remedy for a cold heart is human warmth, especially in the form of a lover's embrace.

Clichés of Excess

aa samui mune ni	Oh! In my barren heart
namida ga kōru kokoro ga moeru...	My tears freeze and my passion burns...
aa daite kudasai	Oh! Please embrace me.
aa samui mune o	Oh! Please embrace my barren heart.

"Hagureso" (Drifter) (1991)

futari no kokoro atatame-atta	To heat up each other's hearts
nukumori ga aa nukumori ga	There is warmth, yes warmth,
aru ja nai ka	Isn't there?
yasuragu negura o omae no mune ni	At last I have found a comforting nest in your breast.
yatto mitsukete kono ore wa	I will not let you go; I draw you close to me.

"Nukumori" (Warmth) (1992)

But the peaceful warmth and the "comforting nest" described in "Nukumori" are fleeting. What remains far longer than warmth itself is the memory of warmth, and the seat of memory is the kokoro.

The concept of kokoro in enka is highly gendered: although men's songs sing of kokoro, far more women's songs dwell on the affairs of the heart. "A woman's heart" is such a common phrase, it has become a single word, *onna-gokoro*, which occurs seven times in four of the analyzed songs. For example,

onna-gokoro no yarusenasa...	The impossibility of a woman's heart...
onna-gokoro no nokori-bi wa	The embers of a woman's heart
moete mi o yaku...	Sets my burning self aflame...

"Minato Machi Burūsu" (Harbor Town Blues) (1980)

The parallel expression *otoko-gokoro* (man's heart) occurs only once, and then, only in contrast to *onna-gokoro*:

baka yo baka baka baka na no	I was a fool! A fool, a fool!
ne baka deshita	What a fool I have been!
onna-gokoro no kizu-ato ni...	The scars of a woman's heart...
otoko-gokoro mo shiranai de	A man's heart is something I
shiranai de	don't understand, don't understand.

"Tejaku-zake" (Pouring Myself Sake) (1992)

A woman's heart loves foolishly. She commits herself to one person only to suffer painful longing thereafter. A man's heart, on the other hand, may or may not love, or love long; romantic liaisons seem to play a lesser role in defining who a man is. Men's songs sing instead of *otoko-michi*, the "path of a man," and of his longing for furusato (hometown). This tension between onna-gokoro and otoko-michi defines the gendering of enka (see Chapter 7).

Tears (*namida*) and crying (*naku*) are also among the most common words in enka songs. Singly or together, they appear in 75 of the 115 songs in the corpus (65.2 percent). In Mita's study, *namida* was the most common noun among all songs, and its occurrence increased steadily over time, to a high of 36.7 percent in the postwar years 1946–63 (1992: 31). If tears in enka are a sign of intense emotion, that emotion is rarely happy, since it arises from heartache, parting, and sorrow. To examine the gender dynamics of enka, I will consider several defining criteria: who cries, when, where, why, how, and for how long.

In enka, both men and women cry, but women cry more often and for slightly different reasons. Among the 33 men's songs in the corpus, for example, 15 (45.4 percent) include words for crying and/or tears; among the 76 women's songs, 53 (69.7 percent) include references to crying. Clearly also, men and women cry in different ways. The following examples describe men:

omoi-dasu tabi ni, kono mune	When I recall [my furusato],
ga kyū' to itaku naru n desu.	my heart aches terribly.
omowazu namida ga dete	Without my realizing it,
kuru n da nā.[7]	tears well up in my eyes.

"Miso Shiru no Uta" (Song of Miso Soup) (1980)

ase to namida o wake-atta	We shared both sweat and tears
ikutose no kibō no michi ni	For many years on this road of hopes.

"Kita no Daichi" (The Land of the North) (1991)

. . . *namida to ase koso*	. . . The life of a man is one
otoko no roman	of sweat and tears.

"Matsuri" (Festival) (1984)

tsurai namida ya kuyashisa o	I will store my bitter tears and regrets
hara ni osamete niō-dachi	In my gut, standing firm with feet apart.

"Otoko-michi" (The Path of a Man) (1991)

kimeta michi nara otoko nara	If you are a man and have decided upon a path,
naku na nurasu na yoru no ame	Then do not cry, do not get drenched in the evening rain.

"Otoko no Jōwa" (A Man's Love Story) (1989)

Men may sometimes cry for lost loves, but they cry more often for their furusato (including their mother) (see Chapter 7). Crying is part of life's struggle, and tears intermingle with sweat. More interesting, however, is the discovery that men try not to cry. They hold back their tears, which are obstructions to a higher principle, and suppress their sobs for the sake of their chosen path.

For women, on the other hand, crying is an essential part of onna-gokoro, a woman's heart:

> nurete setsunai onna no namida — I am drenched with sadness—
> the tears of a woman.
>
> "Fuyu no Eki" (Winter Train Station) (1993)

> namida namida namida namida — Tears, tears, tears, tears!
> namida karete mo kareru na koi yo — Even if my tears run dry, it won't mean that my love has withered.
>
> "Onna no Defune" (Woman of the Sailing Ship) (1983)

In addition, women's songs contain far less about public issues, such as furusato and life's path. Instead, women cry copiously over men. Their tears flow because of broken hearts, private affairs, and failed romance.

Mita (1992: 37–38) refers to the "pearling of sadness" in Japanese popular songs dating from the beginning of the Shōwa period (1926) to the present. By this he means that sadness, enveloped in layer on layer of beauty, is valued in and of itself. In enka too, tears aestheticize sadness. One does not simply cry, one waits, allowing sadness to mount until one perfect teardrop (or more) forms and falls.

> namida ga porori to koboretara — When a teardrop wells up and spills over,
> utai-dasu no sa funa-uta o — I begin to sing the sailor's song.
>
> "Funa-uta" (Sailor's Song) (1979)

> ochiru namida wa miren desu — My falling tears are tears of lingering
> tsurai kedo — affection, painful as they are.
>
> "Koi Momiji" (Autumn Leaves of Love) (1992)

Crying includes the welling, pooling, and falling of tears, each one a stage to be cherished. One does not wipe tears away: in enka's aesthetic of hardship, suffering, and pain, they are a mark of beauty.

Tears in enka arise not willfully but "naturally." They appear "in spite of oneself, unaware" (*omowazu ni*):

> namida ga omowazu waite kite — My tears are flowing, in spite of myself.
>
> "Ginza no Koi no Monogatari" (Ginza Love Story) (1966)

shirazu-shirazu ni afureta namida   Before I knew it, tears welled up in my eyes.
          "Haha-goyomi" (Calendar of Memories of Mother) (1988)

According to this view, tears tap into that part of a person that is outside human control, an elemental quality of tears that accounts for some of their beauty. In theory, that is, tears spring not from the social face but from the kokoro/mune, which does the actual crying:

ano hito koishi to mune ga naku   My heart sobs with longing for him.
          "Airenka" (Song of Pity) (1992)

mune ga shin-shin naitemasu   My heart overflows with tears.
          "Kita no Yado kara" (From an Inn in the North Country) (1975)

kokoro ga susuri- naite iru   My heart sobs a bit.
          "Funa-uta" (Sailor's Song) (1979)

Tears play honne (private feelings) to a smile's tatemae (public face). In fact, although the structure of enka songs frequently portrays the protagonist in confrontation with the social world, the tears he or she cries are usually "secret tears" ("*sotto namida*"), hidden from the outer world that has caused them. Private tears, of and from the heart, belie the public face:

hito-me o shinonde kakurete naita   We cried, hiding from the eyes of the world.
          "Inochi Kurenai" (Crimson Life of Passion) (1986)

Sotto namida no ko-yubi kamu   With secret tears, I bit down on my finger.
          "Omoide-zake" (Sake of Memories) (1979)

Like dreams, tears come more often at night than during the day:

aa yanagase no yoru ni naite iru   Ah, I cry at night in Yanagase.
          "Yanagase Burūsu" (Blues of Yanagase [in Fukuoka]) (1966)

aitakute koishikute nakitaku naru yoru   I want to see you and love you on this night when I want to cry.
          "Yuki-guni" (Snow Country) (1986)

Like dreams, crying is also associated with drinking. Alcohol allows one to let down one's social guard, exposing a more "natural" self; the exposed kokoro finds expression in tears. Oftentimes, the drinking and the tears come together in a synesthetic merging of the senses:

sake ga namida o sasō no ka	Doesn't sake make you cry?
namida ga fuka-zake nedaru no ka	Doesn't crying make you drink?

"Airenka" (Song of Pity) (1992)

o-choko ni o-sake tsugu tabi ni	Every time I pour sake in my glass,
namida ga ochiru oto ga suru	It sounds like tears falling.

"Ame Sakaba" (Rainy Night at a Bar) (1988)

yoeba kanashiku naru sake o	I drink the sake which makes me sad,
nonde naku no mo koi no tame	And cry for the sake of love.

"Kanashii Sake" (Sorrowful Sake) (1966)

naite ii yo to iu sake ni	To the sake which seemed to say that it was all right to cry,
namida bakari o misete iru	I showed nothing but tears.

"Ame Yo-zake" (Sake on a Rainy Night) (1988)

o-sake no shizuku wa	This drop of sake
watashi no namida yo	Is my teardrop.

"Yoi-gokoro" (Drunken Heart) (1992)

nagasu namida no tejaku-zake	I serve myself sake of flowing tears.

"Tejaku-zake" (Pouring Myself Sake) (1992)

namida sakazuki eee sake	My sake cup fills with tears—yes
kizuna	—the bonds of sake.

"Sake Kizuna" (Bonds of Sake) (1993)

The merging of sake and tears makes every drink a cup of sorrow. Sometimes tears are linked to other liquids, such as rain and rivers:

sore to mo namida ga kareru made	Will [this late autumn shower] rain until my tears run dry,
makura nurashite kazoe-uta	Drenching my pillow?

"Koi Uta Tsuzuri" (Love Song Spelling) (1989)

tomedo naku hoho tsutau	A river of tears down my cheeks
namida no ato o	
oikakete oikakete	Runs endlessly, runs endlessly.

"Yuki-guni" (Snow Country) (1986)

... ā kawa mo naku	... even the river cries.

"Omoide no Yado" (Inn of Memories) (1992)

umi ni namida no ā guchi bakari	The ocean is filled with nothing but tears of lament.

"Minato Machi Burūsu" (Harbor Town Blues) (1980)

kokoro ga naki-nurete	My heart is soaked with tears.
hitori de naki-nurete	Alone, I cry soaked with tears.

"Tokai no Tenshi-tachi" (Angels of the City) (1992)

In this national discourse of song, one may become drenched in sentiment. Tears provide an emotional "wetness," in sharp contrast to one's unemotional public "dryness."

Enka's emphasis on tears endows even nonhuman, inanimate objects with the ability to cry. The deliberate use of one homonym (*naku*, to cry) for another (*naku*, to cry out, to roar, to shout) calls attention to the tearfulness of the crying. In these songs we hear the wailing of the shamisen, or plucked lute ("*naki-jamisen*," "Bōkyō Jonkara" [Song of Homesickness] 1985), crying nights ("*naku yoru*," "Michinoku Yuki Akari" [The Gleam of Snow in the North Hinterlands] 1992), howling north winds ("*kita kaze ga naite fuku*," "Yagiri no Watashi" [Yagiri Crossing] 1976), even blizzards that, together with the low moaning whistle of a train, sound like sobs ("Kita no Yado Kara" [From an Inn in the North Country] 1975: "*fubuki majiri ni kisha no oto / susuri-naku yō ni kikoemasu*"). In enka, everything, from shamisen to storms, has the potential to cry; everything possesses a kokoro that can feel pain. This projection of emotion onto objects and elements of nature makes for a kind of "environmental" empathy: the jilted lover does not cry alone but in concert with everything around her.

The crying lasts a long time, until it becomes less a passing condition than a state of being:

naite urande yo ga fukeru	I cry and cry, and the night wears on.

"Kanashii Sake" (Sorrowful Sake) (1966)

naite miru wa kon'ya mo	I will cry and cry tonight
namida kareru made	Until my tears run dry.

"Midare-bana" (Strewn Flowers) (1988)

If the attachment lingers and the conditions that thwart a successful union remain unchanged, the crying continues, even many years later.

These keywords (dreams, heart/soul, tears) and others form one aspect of the textual kata of enka. In their use of allusion and their predilection for ambiguity, enka songs turn the spotlight on emotion, offering a vocabulary of redundancy and excess through which emotions are shaped and expressed. This kind of emotive language shares a common past with premodern Japanese poetry, waka in particular, whose tears have for centuries gone unwiped. In these songs, the line between states of consciousness is constantly slipping, and the slippage itself is aestheticized. At the same time, nature's seasonal ephemerality becomes the metaphoric topos for human society. The ever-flowing tears of enka have been enculturated as enshrined national idiomatic expression.

Musical Kata: Aural Processes of the Past

Enka is a vocal performance (usually a solo but sometimes a duet) accompanied by Western instruments in some combination of guitar, violin, mandolin, saxophone, clarinet, oboe, and accordion.[8] Several enka songs also feature a male or female chorus singing wordless vocables. Japanese instruments, such as the *shakuhachi* (end-blown flute), *koto* (zither), *shamisen* (plucked lute), and *taiko* (drum), play a limited role, often serving merely to impart a traditional Japanese "flavor" to the music.

The great majority of enka songs are written in duple meter with a slow to medium tempo (the median tempo of my 115-song corpus is 74 beats per minute). Most enka songs use one of two pentatonic scales, known as yonanuki major and yonanuki minor (*yonanuki* means "without the fourth and seventh degrees of the scale"), which were popularized through Meiji-era school songs.[9] Of the 28 song melodies I analyzed, 27 are written in a yonanuki scale: 8 in yonanuki major, and 19 in yonanuki minor. The melodic movement within a song tends to follow the conjunct intervals of the yonanuki scales; melodic leaps often signal an emotional highpoint. The melodic range is generally wide and exploits both the upper and lower vocal registers. Among the songs I analyzed, it varied from an octave to a fourteenth (minor), six notes wider than an octave, with a median of an eleventh.[10]

I divide musical kata, or patterning, into two types: compositional and performative. Compositional kata (CK) are those patterns that can be recognized by looking at a musical score. Because enka is primarily a vocal genre, however, I examine singing more closely through what I call "performative kata" (PK)—patternings of vocal expression in the actual performance of a song that are discerned only through listening.

Although these performative kata are not indicated in the score, they constitute an important aspect of the musical language of enka. In theory, a singer who had never heard a particular enka song could sing it "straight" by reading the score note for note as written. The result would be recognizable as enka, but few fans of the genre would savor the listening experience, since it would lack the real flavor ("*aji*") of enka. A skilled enka performer embellishes the score in codified ways, playing with the rhythm (Okada 1991) and sometimes the notes, and adding appropriate vocal ornaments. Through these embellishments, the performer conveys the sense that the song springs from the heart rather than from a composer's dictate. The real flavor of enka, then, lies in the conventions of heartfelt expression, and these, at least in theory, are as individual as a person's kokoro. In practice, however, and this is critical to enka's appeal, even individual expression follows set patterns (see Chapter 3), implying that all hearts (or at least the hearts of all enka fans) beat as one.

Both compositional and performative kata are essential to the aural definition of the genre. For example, when composer Sone Yoshiaki "enka-fies" non-enka pop songs during the "Musical Academy" segment of *Enka TV*, a regular feature of this late-night show (see note 8), he basically does two things. First he adds the compositional kata of rhythm to the pop song's chordal accompaniment, as shown in Example 1.[11]

Rhythmic Chordal Accompaniment
Example 1 (*top*): Sone Yoshiaki. Example 2 (*bottom*): Kawai Personal Keyboard.

This accompaniment pattern is in fact almost identical to the one produced by the Kawai Personal Keyboard's "enka" selection shown in Example 2, which is notable for being so unremarkable (not unlike that of various genres of "middle-of-the-road" Western pop music). It is not particularly significant in other Japanese musics, nor does it serve to propel the music forward rhythmically. Its blandness, however, serves as a steady ground that highlights the more expressive figure of the melody. But then Sone adds performative kata—vocal ornaments and inflections appropriate to enka. He nasalizes his singing and adopts a wide, slow vibrato. Most significantly, he adds ko-bushi—quick melodic ornaments—especially on the penultimate notes of a phrase. By Sone's definition, these performative kata are enough to "enka-fy" any pop song.

The reaction of the co-host and the guest singer to Sone's adaptation is typically one of amazement. When Sone first adds rhythmic chords, the listeners nod cautiously, as if to say, "Yes, this is beginning to sound a little like enka." However, when Sone begins to sing in the enka style, listeners express surprise bordering on disbelief. They seem totally astonished that something as supposedly foreign to "Japanese sensibilities" (e.g., a rhythm-and-blues song sung by an African American) could be made to sound so indigenously familiar. The performative kata of singing clinches Sone's magic act.

Compositional Kata (CK)

Table 5.2 is a listing of compositional musical kata in enka, musical elements that the composers with whom I spoke interpret as conveying particular affective expression. The yonanuki minor key (CK-1) is, as mentioned earlier, more prevalent in enka than the yonanuki major key (CK-2). Several composers say that CK-1 imparts a sadder quality and is used more often in women's songs. CK-2, on the other hand, is said to impart a more positive, energetic quality and is used more often in men's songs. That said, however, I would point out that two of the biggest commercial hits of the early 1990s, "Kokoro-zake" (Sake of the Heart; see Chapter 3) and "Settchūka" (Flowers in the Snow), both women's songs, were written in yonanuki major, suggesting a possible trend toward enka songs in this key.

The acoustic guitar (including the mandolin) (CK-3), one of the instruments that defined enka in the 1930s Koga merodii (see Chapter 2), still does so. Its portability suggests intimacy, as does its soft-to-medium dynamic range. As a plucked instrument, it cannot sustain a pitch for long before it must be plucked again, and the repetition, in its tremolo, gives a fine-grained texture. Textured sound is clearly an important element in enka, one that will reappear in the discussion of performative kata.

Table 5.2
Compositional Kata (CK)

CK-1	Yonanuki minor
CK-2	Yonanuki major
CK-3	Guitar/mandolin
CK-4	Saxophone
CK-5	Chorus
CK-6	Low vocal register for female singers
CK-7	"Conversation" with instrument(s)
CK-8	Accented repeated notes (instrumental)
CK-9	Syllabic text setting
CK-10	Even note values
CK-11	Repeated notes (vocal)
CK-12	Melodic ornamentation preceding end of phrase
CK-13	Phrase ending with long held note
CK-14	Leaps

By contrast, the saxophone (CK-4) sustains a pitch as easily as a singer and does so within a more extensive soft-to-loud dynamic range. The instrument is closely associated with *mūdo enka* (mood enka), popularized in the 1960s and the most common subgenre in the 1990s. In its ability to bend pitches, undulate between notes, and swell in volume, the saxophone transmits a kind of aural sensuality. Furthermore, its distinctive timbre can easily cut through a typical stringed instrument background to produce a wail-like sound.

In several enka songs, a male and/or female chorus (CK-5) intermittently sings wordless syllables, becoming a kind of human instrument in the ensemble. In fact, the chorus acts much like an aural *miuchi* (fellow insiders), sanctifying the emotions expressed by the individual singer as those of the in-group/support group as well (cf. Lebra 1992: 108–11).

A significant number of women's enka songs are sung in a low vocal register (CK-6),[12] in sharp contrast to the high-pitched voice that is the socially sanctioned speaking voice for women in Japan. To a certain extent, the more highly pitched the voice, the more socially elevated the person, since pitch indicates levels of politeness as well as social class (cf. Kinsella 1995). One explanation for the low register here may be that in enka, the female protagonists—typically barmaids, mistresses, or jilted lovers—often come from the lower classes, and a low voice indicates their social position.[13]

Clichés of Excess   107

In many enka songs, one or more instruments (often a guitar) engage in a "conversation" with the singing voice, filling in between sung phrases (CK-7). This kind of voice-instrument dialogue is found in premodern Japanese popular song, in particular in the *ai no te* (light shamisen accompaniment) to narrative genres such as *kiyomoto* (narrative music for kabuki) and *gidayū-bushi* (narrative song in *bunraku* puppet theater). In these musical conversations, the plucked instrument supports the voice with short iterations and figures that resemble Japanese conversational patterns: one person does most of the speaking, while the listener supplies intermittent but essential support in the form of *aizuchi* (listener utterances) (cf. Smith 1983: 76–77; Lebra 1987: 344).[14] In enka, as in the premodern genres, instrumental "aizuchi" comment on and empathetically support the emotions expressed by the singer.

The instrumental accompaniment to some enka songs includes accented repeated notes (CK-8), as shown in Examples 3 and 4. Taken by themselves, these instrumental accents do not necessarily convey any particular meaning, but they are noteworthy as illustrations of the kind of formulaic artifice, bordering on musical triteness, found in enka songwriting.

Accented Repeated Notes
Example 3 (*top*): Excerpt from "Kokoro-zake" (Sake of the Heart).
Example 4 (*bottom*): Excerpt from "Settchūka" (Flowers in the Snow).

During my fieldwork, teachers, composers, and singers repeatedly reminded me that enka is above all a verbal art form intended to tell a story or convey an emotion. The next series of compositional kata (see Table 5.2) all demonstrate this belief. The text setting of songs is primarily syllabic (CK-9), and the rhythmic note values of these syllabic settings are even (CK-10), reflecting the rhythms of spoken Japanese. Also emulating speech, the pitch of these even notes tends to be repeated (CK-11) or to occur in a narrow range within one phrase. In addition, after a flurry of repeated notes, a phrase usually comes to a brief rest before circling above and/or below the final note (CK-12) to end on a held note (CK-13). Examples 5 and 6 demonstrate this kind of phrase structure, as well as other compositional kata.[15] To a certain extent, this kind of structuring, which combines repeated notes and melodic ornamentation before the held end note, mirrors Japanese sentence patterns,

Example 5 (*top*): Sung Repeated Notes: Excerpt from "Funa-uta" (Sailor's Song).
Example 6 (*bottom*): Melodic Ornamentation Preceding End of Phrase: Excerpt from "Hi no Kuni no Onna" (A Woman of Volcanic Land).

whose semantic force is shaped by the end of the sentence rather than the beginning. Here, too, melodic interest focuses on the end of phrases.[16] Although most melodic movement within a yonanuki scale is stepwise, many enka songs include an occasional musical "leap" (CK-14) that often parallels an emotional leap in the text. These leaps occur in conjunction with higher pitches (approached by the leap), rhythmically denser phrases, and/or increased volume.

Examples 7 and 8 illustrate this kind of musical-emotional leap. The text in Example 7 is "A-na-*ta* [octave leap from C to C] ko-i-shi-*i* [major sixth leap to an even higher D]" (I long for you). The sentence is the confessional centerpiece of the entire song, but each word also carries its own emotional force. In combination with the musical setting—within an otherwise smooth, stepwise melody, two consecutive spiky leaps to the highest notes of the song, each leap jumping from *jigoe* (chest voice; "natural voice") to *uragoe* (head voice; falsetto), discussed below as PK-1 and PK-2, respectively—the effect is one of an agonized musical scream. This agony is echoed in Example 8. Here also the musical leap evokes a cry on the wordless syllable "A-a" to express an emotion that is beyond words.

Musical-Emotional Leaps
Example 7 (*top*): Excerpt from "Kita no Yado kara" (From an Inn in the North Country).
Example 8 (*bottom*): Excerpt from "Tsugaru Kaikyō Fuyu-geshiki" (Winterscape of the Tsugaru Straits).

Performative Kata (PK)

Table 5.3 lists performative musical kata, which, although not notated in the score, are as important to the emotional expression of an enka song as the compositional kata, if not more so.

Table 5.3
Performative Kata (PK)

PK-1	*Jigoe* (chest voice; "natural" voice)
PK-2	*Uragoe* (head voice; falsetto)
PK-3	*Hanagoe* (nasal voice)
PK-4	*Rubato* (rhythmic playing with melody); lag
PK-5	Gliding between pitches
PK-6	*Ko-bushi* (ornamentation)
PK-7	*Yuri* ("vibrato"), including delayed *yuri*
PK-8	Exploiting voice breaks
PK-9	Extreme and variable dynamics
PK-10	Whisper
PK-11	Sigh, breathy pitch
PK-12	Groan
PK-13	Sobbing pitch
PK-14	Guttural rasp
PK-15	Grunt; pre-pitch and post-pitch
PK-16	Gasp
PK-17	Husky, exaggerated low register
PK-18	Thinned, exaggerated high register
PK-19	"Digging" emphasis at beginning of syllables
PK-20	Prolonged initial consonants
PK-21	Glottal stops before vowels
PK-22	Rolled "r"

One of the most basic elements of singing is the question of which "voice" to use, or rather, where in the body vocal sound resonates. In Japanese vocal theory, the three main voices are *jigoe* (chest voice; "natural" voice; PK-1), *uragoe* (head voice; falsetto; PK-2), and *hanagoe* (nasal voice; PK-3). Of the three, the chest voice (PK-1) and the nasal voice (PK-3) are used most frequently in enka and may be considered characteristic of the genre. The nasal voice in particular is farthest from the Western *bel canto* ideal, and so becomes an even more distinctive cultural marker. However, according to enka composers and voice teachers, the mark of a truly skilled enka singer is the ability to use each of the three voices as the song requires. The choice is determined to a certain extent by pitch (PK-1 vs. PK-2), as shown in the "leap" discussed above, but to a larger extent by expressivity: a singer may sing three same-note pitches in a row, but each will have a different expressive quality in relation to the voice the singer uses. What is important is not whether the singer achieves a smooth, seamless whole but whether he or she can change timbres, even within the same pitch, to produce a textured sensuality.

An expressive element that can be heard in every enka performance is rubato (PK-4), the rhythmic manipulation of the melody. Instead of singing the melody exactly as written, the singer alters the rhythm slightly, speeding up here, slowing down there, to impart a sense of personal expression to the song. Even this personal expressiveness, however, is a codified part of the song's kata. In enka, rubato is most often achieved through a vocal lag within, rather than between, phrases. A singer may drag a melody throughout a phrase yet preserve the rhythmic unit of the phrase and start again in time with every new phrase, so that each remains a discrete unit of measure. The practice of rubato also sets up a degree of tension between the vocal melody and the instrumental accompaniment. While the melody takes rhythmic liberties, the accompaniment keeps strict time, juxtaposing what sounds like individual expression with a controlled ground beat. This kind of opposition between voice and accompaniment is also apparent in other aspects of performative kata.

Melodic movement is generally stepwise also, but even within these steps singers elide notes, especially by gliding up to pitches from below (PK-5), effectively dissolving the beat. Instead of attacking a note straight on the beat, the singer begins with either a quick or a prolonged build-up to the pitch and reaches it off the beat, thus creating a sense of vocal lag (rubato). The sometimes sliding pitches of the vocal melody contrast with the crisp notes of the instrumental accompaniment.

One of enka's main vocal characteristics is its use of ornamentation, or *ko-bushi* (PK-6). These quick-turn ornaments most often occur on or near the penultimate note of a phrase and build up to the phrase's end. Slower, ko-bushi-like musical gestures may be written into the score as part of the melody (as in CK-12), but true ko-bushi is a decorative vocal addition. In theory, ko-bushi is optional, and some singers use it more than others. In practice, however, as Sone Yoshiaki demonstrates, it is as important to the genre and as essential to a good performance as the composer's melody. Some singers are, in fact, known for their skillful ko-bushi.

Another important vocal characteristic of enka is *yuri* (PK-7), a distinctive "swinging" of the voice that is similar to vibrato, but slower and broader than that common to Western song.[17] Within yuri there are subpatterns. Sometimes the yuri is so slow as to be "rhythmicized"—set to a rhythm of repeated eighth or sixteenth notes. At other times, it is performed faster, on notes of shorter duration, or delayed on a long, held note. The singer sings the note straight, and only midway through introduces a narrow yuri, which widens as the singer holds the note.[18] The yuri may also serve to adjust a singer's pitch. One top female enka singer is known for her technique of singing a long, held, slightly flattened note, then resolving the tension by gradually rising through yuri to the correct pitch. In the enka context, yuri is an affective tool for building and resolving tension and for expressing the primal emotions associated with a quavering voice, a tremulous sigh, or a racking sob.[19] Yuri gives aural expression to the tears of enka.

In moving from one voice to another, especially between the chest voice (PK-1) and falsetto (PK-2), and shifting vocal register, a singer's voice "breaks" in a slight cracking sound (PK-8). This effect is heard especially in performances by female singers, who sing in falsetto more often than male singers do. This sound effect gives further texture to the singing, further flavor to the expression. The singer manipulates the result, deliberately choosing to use falsetto here and not there, guided in part by the anatomy of the throat and vocal chords and by the conventions of cultural expression.

Some of the best-known enka singers, especially those who perform the "traditional" do-enka, make use of highly variable vocal dynamics (PK-9), going from very soft to very loud not only within a single song but within a single phrase or subphrase. This technique reinforces the notion that enka is a verbal art form more akin to dramatic storytelling than to ear-pleasing song. In some performances I have attended, the enka singer at times sings inaudibly, her head turned away from the microphone, a mode of performance that comes very close to speech-song.

Related to but distinct from the dynamics of volume (PK-9) are the vocal techniques of the whisper (PK-10) and the breathy sigh (PK-11). Female singers use these "soft-touch" kata more often, and in a pleading fashion that suggests feminine vulnerability and passivity (see, for example, the enka lessons in Chapter 3). These techniques, which rely on electronic amplification for their effect, re-create the emotional bond between lovers by suggesting an aurally enhanced one between the singer and the listener(s). The effect is one of staged intimacy.

When pleas fail, the resulting pain is often expressed in groans (PK-12). This is not pain externalized in a loud outcry, but self-reflexive pain internalized in moans. An expressive technique more characteristic of female singers, it is subtle and sensual, suggesting a mix of pleasure and pain. It effects a kind of aural seduction built upon intimacy, empathy, and vulnerability. A more overt expression of pain is the sobbing quality added at the beginning of a pitch through a brief vocal glide from a higher note (PK-13). Heard in non-Japanese genres, such as American country and western music, this kata of pain is also the more usual provenance of female enka singers. It gives the songs a staged crying sound.

A characteristically male expression of pain is the guttural rasp (PK-14). This grating, scraping vocal sound is almost amusical: the melodic pitch of the song is thrown over in favor of timbre and texture. Another kata more often associated with males is the grunt (PK-15), which usually occurs before a pitch as an extra, nonmelodic utterance, but also at times after a pitch as an emphatic finale. In contrast to the pain-centered kata associated with helplessness and passive resignation, the grunt is associated with strength and active resolve. It is the kind of abdomen-centered sound that requires physical exertion even as it metaphorically expresses such exertion.[20]

Both male and female singers also sometimes gasp (PK-16) during singing, especially as they approach or reach a musical climax. The gasp conveys a feeling of breathlessness, a build-up of emotional intensity. An inhaled gasp may also precede an exhaled sigh (PK-11) in a natural pairing of breathed expressions.

In singing, both female and male performers may exaggerate low (PK-17) and high (PK-18) extremes of the vocal register to intensify the emotions they convey. In PK-17, the singer exaggerates low notes with a throaty huskiness. In PK-18, the singer exaggerates high notes with a thin, edgy reediness. In both cases, the point is not beauty but sheer artifice: these deliberately applied techniques give the singer greater expressive range.

Enka singers might elaborate in various ways on the sounds within a word to add texture, create another kind of rubato (cf. PK-4), or dramatize the story. For example, some singers give dynamic and melodic emphasis to the beginning of a phrase through what I call "digging" (PK-19). Approached by way of a gliding lower pitch, initial sounds swell before the actual pitch is sung. The use of prolonged initial consonants (PK-20), another kind of elaboration, almost makes one syllable into two (e.g., *no* becomes *n- o-*). Still another inserts glottal stops before vowels (PK-21) or rolled "r" sounds within a word (PK-22) to add texture.[21] Yet not all vowels are glottalized and not all r's are rolled. The point here is that the singer inserts these elaborations selectively to emphasize an emotion or to highlight a regional or subcultural display. The rolled "r" (PK-22) marks enka's expression as polysemically atmospheric.

Bodily Kata: Gendered Display

Making sense of enka's imaginary also requires attending to the visual display of the enka singer, in particular, to the spectacle of the body.[22] As Richard Leppert points out, "The semantic content of music . . . is never solely about its sound. . . . It is especially to be understood as the result of mediations between the ear and the eye" (1993: 18). These mediations become all the more important in commercial music-making, whose success depends on the trade in bodily images. The body—amplified by the power of the stage, captured and reproduced in glossy advertisements, and electronically transmitted via television into homes throughout the nation—somaticizes identities that are at one and the same time gendered, racialized, and nationalized.

THE BODY IN SPACE: POSES

The singer's pose, captured in the cartoon figures and promotional photographs of record albums, is an important aspect of the enka performance. Like the dancers of *nihon buyō* (Japanese classical dance) and kabuki, whose movements have been likened to a series of poses (Brandon 1978: 84–86), enka singers, especially female enka singers, dramatize their presence on stage and the emotional crystallization of their songs through posing—before, during, and after their actual singing. Table 5.4 summarizes the kata or patterns of posing.

In general, the singer's pose and how it is framed are a reflection of gender constructions, which physicalize the dichotomy between onna-gokoro (woman's heart) and otoko-michi (path of a man). In photographs, female singers tend to be viewed at an acute angle to the camera, their bodies sometimes in a curved or bent position. Raised camera angles and views shot from above allow the viewer to look down at the singer. A female singer's head, especially when isolated in a close-up, is often tilted to one side at about a thirty-degree angle from the frontal plane of her body and slightly lowered. Male singers, on the other hand, tend to be photographed straight on or at only a slight angle. Still shots of male singers are sometimes taken from below, giving an impression of greater physical stature. They are also more likely to be depicted with head straight, or even slightly raised, rather than tilted.

Clichés of Excess

Table 5.4
Male and Female Poses

	Male Kata	Female Kata
HEAD:	Straight	Cocked to one side Tilted to the side and slightly down
EYES:	Direct gaze Frontally directed gaze	Some direct gaze, but if head is down, eyes must be looking up Looking down and to the side
MOUTH:	Little smiling	Some smiling
SHOULDERS	Straight	Slight twist to form S-shape
ARMS:	Down at sides Elbows out	Down at sides Elbows in Elbows bent
HANDS:	At sides On hips In pockets	Touching collar of kimono Touching front of obi Holding sleeve Clasped together low in front of body Clasped together loosely at chest level, fingertips touching in prayer gesture
FINGERS:	Fist Loosely curved	Fingers held together Loose grouping of fourth and fifth fingers (together and bent in), second and third fingers (together and stretched out), thumb cocked straight up
CHEST:	Upright	Slightly concave
HIPS:	Weight evenly distributed	Weight unevenly distributed
LEGS:	Straight or spread out in shoulder-wide stance	Together
KNEES:	Straight	Bent; slightly knock-kneed
FEET:	Straight or pointing out, heels at 90-degree angle	Pigeon-toed

As might be expected, in the majority of photographs the singer gazes at the camera, addressing and engaging the audience by looking directly at them, selling recordings by locking potential buyers in a mutual gaze.

Depending on the position of her head, the female singer's gaze may be directed slightly upward or shown as downcast. Male singers, on the other hand, are often shown gazing directly at the camera or, if photographed from a low camera angle, looking slightly upward.

Both males and females smile, but their smiles are those of promotional pleasantry rather than sincere emotion: they are controlled and social rather than broad and exuberant. When I spoke to enka fans, they explained that it is acceptable, even admirable, for a male singer to smile very little on stage: it demonstrates a seriousness of intent, a kind of male sincerity. There is a notable gender difference, too, in the cultural interpretation of an unsmiling face. A woman's normal social face is a smiling face. She shows that she is accommodating herself to others, putting their needs before hers, and encouraging a pleasantly sociable atmosphere by providing a visually appealing environment. When a woman does not smile, therefore, the typical interpretation is that something is out of place. She may be sad, lonely, or angry. What is worse, by not smiling she also commits the social sin of imposing her unhappiness on others. When a man does not smile, however, the interpretation is that he is serious, thoughtful, weighing things in his mind. He is sincere.

The kimono-clad female body is often posed in an S-shape—head to one side, shoulders slightly twisted, hips counterbalancing shoulders, knees together and bent, and feet in a distinctive pigeon-toed stance—to emphasize graceful angles and curves rather than straight lines. The female body thus becomes a series of planes, intersecting at subtle angles, which are revealed as the eye moves from one plane to the next (see Chapter 7). In television and video performances, the camera, serving as the viewer's eye, often captures the female singer in kimono in a slow upward pan: from toes to knees to hips to chest to face. In Western dress, the female body still tends toward curves and angles, but it does not in general assume this S-shaped pose. The pose of the male body, by contrast, whether attired in Japanese or Western dress, is one of well-defined parallel lines: shoulders straight, chest upright, weight evenly distributed at the hips, knees unbent. And, unlike the female body, which curves in upon itself trying to take up ever less space, the male body—hands on hips, elbows outspread, legs a shoulder-width apart, feet splayed at a ninety-degree angle—constantly enlarges its claimed space.

The positioning of a singer's hands (including fingers) is also gender-specific. The hands of a female singer can almost be said to "contain" the female body during a performance: they touch each other and the singer's upper body, fondling the kimono collar or the edge of a sleeve; they are clasped together in her lap or held loosely at chest level in a praying gesture. They also move asymmetrically, one hand gesturing, the other motionless at the singer's side. The fingers of the hand, sometimes the fourth and the little finger, sometimes the index and the middle finger, are often held together, or nearly so.

Male hands, by contrast, appear stiff and graceless during performance. If they are not down at the singer's sides, they are resting on his hips (arms akimbo) or hidden in his pockets. In one common variation, the singer stands, one arm down at his side, the other held stiffly at almost a ninety-degree angle, as if waiting for someone to catch hold of it or cling to it, the hand at waist level in a loose fist. In actuality, however, this is a standard male portrait pose, an alternative to standing at attention, arms down at sides. Male hands might be clenched in a fist or rest loosely curved and separate, but they seldom hold onto anything, whether collar, sleeve, or the other hand.

The male and female poses represented in record advertisements, I would contend, suggest that women are the main dramatic and emotional focus in enka (cf. Gledhill 1987). Both male and female singers are presented according to the stock clichés of portraiture, but female singers are also shown in unusual, dramatic, or colorful poses—vivid bodily representations of onna-gokoro. Their faces, lit dramatically, are caught in frame-filling close-ups. Wearing or surrounded by reds, pinks, mauves, oranges, and purples, they are shown crouching, kneeling, or lying down. In one photograph, a woman, her back to the camera, turns, her mauve kimono loose and low around her back, her hair down. In another, a woman in a rose-colored kimono, resting on one arm and with one tabi-clad foot showing, crouches against a swirled background of rust and green and stares up at the camera.

These and other, similar depictions visually situate women at the heart of the drama, the emotional ground zero. In contrast to men's stillness and steadiness, they are eye-catching, volatile, heart-rending. In enka, the female body is an object of beauty specifically tied to emotional turmoil. Women carry the burden of the genre's tears.

The Body in Space and Time: Movements and Gestures

Photographs and drawings capture a posing body that in performance becomes a live spectacle in space and time. Although a complete kinesic analysis of the movement patterns in enka performances is beyond the scope of this study, the following overview of gestures is intended to illustrate and emphasize their patterning. My focus is on repeated movements, whether those of one singer singing one particular song or those of various singers singing different songs. The implication is that these movements are not spontaneous but rather patterned, predetermined, and sometimes even choreographed.

One group of gestures involves the use of the back, echoing songs in which the back becomes a canvas for conveying emotion.

dakareru sono tabi ni senaka	This time when you held me,
ga kanashikute	my back felt so lonely.

"Kokoro Kōrasete" (Freeze Our Hearts) (1993)

onna no senaka no samishisa	The loneliness of a woman seen
ga	from behind
naite naite ta	As she cried and cried
wasurenai	Is something I will not forget.

"Sakaba" (A Bar) (1990)

In a live performance, the singer's back can become an eloquent means of expression. Although on the Western stage it is a cardinal rule that one does not turn one's back to the audience, on the enka stage a performer may do so deliberately as an expressive gesture. Enka performers and audiences are well aware of the subtle emotional message conveyed by a turned back.[23] In their view, the back may reveal tension, disappointment, rejection, or elation more truthfully than the face (cf. Lebra 1992: 106–8). As the singer Itsuki Hiroshi comments, "In a way, it [i.e., strength as well as tenderness] is expressed by a man's back. You have to be most sexy when you turn around and show your back [on stage]" (quoted in Wilson 1995: 49). What is interesting about Itsuki's statement is the expression "show your back." The back, even fully clothed, is at once sensuous and expressive.

In enka performances, codified gestures that fall into overlapping categories—female vs. male singer/Japanese vs. Western dress—demonstrate qualitative differences. Female singers in kimono, for example, tend to use their bodies in a more dancelike manner, and with more aestheticized elements of control, energy flow, and grace, than male singers in Western dress. The contrast between the aestheticized movements of female singers and the physical restraint of male singers suggests a gendered approach to both quality (what men and women do on stage) and quantity (where, on the "slide-rule" of performer-audience interaction, one performs; see Chapter 4).

Table 5.5
Female Enka Singer's Patterned Body Movements

HEAD:	Singing with face turned away from camera Singing with face turned into shoulder, head slightly lowered Fast or slow shaking of head at moments of emotional intensity Small movement of the head from side to side, led by the jaw, like a doll with its head on a spring
EYES:	Turned upward Turned downward Closed during moments of emotional intensity
MOUTH:	Small, random movements of mouth and lips, as if preparing to speak
SHOULDERS:	Shrugging of shoulders, head turned upward, chest sunken in
ARMS:	Reaching forward at chest level (gesture of longing) Slowly lowered from raised position while undulating wrist and fingers (flame gesture)
HANDS:	Holding microphone with both hands at upper chest level Clenching end of sleeve with same hand (e.g., right sleeve with right hand) Clenched fist, sometimes with light punching in air or at obi-level for emphasis Touching hand to cheek Resting hand on top of obi
FINGERS:	Rhythmic flicking of fingers to emphasize particular beats or ends of phrases
LEGS/KNEES:	Bending of knees, twisting of torso into S-shape Sudden slight bending of knees, as if they are buckling Slight bouncing, knees bent
FEET:	Asymmetric pigeon-toed stance, including small kick to the side and back with inward-turned foot Asymmetric pigeon-toed stance, with the inward-turned foot on tiptoe, bearing no weight
WHOLE BODY:	Turning around completely, back to audience, contrasted with turning to face audience (also performed by males, but more common among females) Tense to the point of quivering, in contrast to drooping limply between verses or collapsing into a bow at the end of the song

Table 5.5 lists some of the patterned gestures and body movements used by female enka singers (the order within each category is from more frequent to less frequent). In most instances, the list does not include gestures discussed previously under poses or those related directly to producing sound (e.g., the jaw movement necessary to produce a wide vibrato or hand clapping). These female body movements express two main themes: emotional intensity and emotional intimacy. Female singers mark peaks of emotion by shaking their head, closing their eyes, making small soundless motions with their mouth and lips, flicking their fingers, buckling their knees in a slumping posture, and tensing and untensing their body. One pattern involves shrugging the shoulders, raising the chin, and caving in the chest to suggest a body shrinking in pain. Other, smaller movements suggest a quivering intensity. In portraying intimacy, female singers occasionally lower their head or turn away from the audience ("showing one's back"), as if they sing within a private space defined by their shoulder. Their eyes gaze above or below the audience, or even into the distance, conveying a sense of detached intimacy, as if audience members are eavesdropping on the singer singing to herself.

One gesture that is ubiquitous among female singers but less common among male singers is what I call the "gesture of longing": the singer extends an arm out in front of her body slowly, at chest level, often as she is singing the long-held note at the end of a verse. Through her outstretched arm and her voice, the singer expresses her yearning for her absent lover. In an exaggerated version, the singer's chest, chin, and hips follow her outstretched arm, a gesture that throws her body off balance, in tune with her emotional state. Other gestures serve for the most part as rhythmic time-keepers, accentuating a particular beat or the end of a phrase. This rhythmic emphasis increases the emotional intensity, infusing the female body with a sense of dramatic tension.

Both male and female enka singers cry, but female singers do so with greater frequency. Tears, a hallmark of sincerity, and on stage one of the most effective and primal kata, testify to the singer's intense engagement with the song. In a kind of "emotional contagion" (Hatfield, Cacioppo, and Rapson 1994), the singer's tears also induce tears in audience members, who have come to empathize and perhaps to experience their own emotional catharsis. As a singer performs on stage, the audience may watch at a distance and with a certain degree of detachment, but when audience members sense that the singer is actually crying, her tears draw them into the drama, erasing the divide between spectator and participant. Tears transform the stage into a platform of authenticity.

Like other body movements, crying also has its own kata. The most unabashed example is that of Misora Hibari, the late (but still reigning) "queen of enka" and to my mind the "queen of tears." Misora's tears are profuse, unchecked and unwiped. As the camera follows her in close-up during a performance, her eyes fill with tears that well, pool, and finally spill over. The viewer is caught in the moment's dramatic tension, some of which dissipates once the first tear falls. The unsettling question, Where will her tears flow?—down her cheek? along her jawline to her neck? off her face?—remains. The crying of other singers is not as profuse or overt. A common pattern is what might actually be called "near-crying": as the singer looks up, tears well in her eyes but are not allowed to fall. Instead, she withdraws, sometimes biting her trembling lower lip, the song, or at least this episode of near-crying, ended.

In certain cases, the audience is aware of the singer's tears because of the gulping that has preceded them. In others, the singer waits until she is bowing to audience applause to cry: the audience discovers her tears only when she wipes them away with her hand. In both cases, the audience's awareness of the performer's crying enhances its perception of her. This ultimate embodiment of emotion becomes proof of her merit, involvement, and vulnerability. As she reaches within, to a personal reservoir of pain and tears, she also reaches out to tap that common reservoir within members of the audience. Tears, and the suffering they display, become an irresistible link between singer and audience.

In enka performances, posing, gesturing, and crying serve to further dichotomize the human body, already differentiated by sex, according to the culture's constructions of gender. The body becomes a canvas upon which the kata of sexuality are painted in giant strokes. Embodiment becomes engenderment. At the same time, and with equally grave results, the body parades emotion even as it evokes emotion: it becomes the medium through which pain, longing, and resignation are conveyed, eliciting in turn an empathic, cathartic response in audience members. In enka, this "song of Japan," sexuality and emotion come together in a visual display made comprehensible by a shared sense of national desire.

Brian Moeran argues that the construction of femaleness in Japan's glossy monthly women's magazines is unrelated to sexuality (1995: 117), by which, however, he means overt depictions of sexuality, such as an open mouth and exposed breasts and thighs. Yet sexuality is revealed not only through mere embodiment; it is also revealed through highly enculturated modes of expression. I would argue that the construction of Japanese femaleness in enka is entirely about sexuality on its own terms. Here, covertness is essential to desire. Just as social interaction encompasses the well-practiced, controlled public face, so desire (male) is constructed from a public mastery of modesty and vulnerability (female). Modesty plays upon sexual subtlety in a strand of hair or a wayward tear.

This kind of desire is in some ways the direct opposite of what Anne Allison (1996: xv) has dubbed "the infantilization of female sex objects," exemplified in the "Lolita-complex"/schoolgirl fetishes found in *manga* (Japanese comics), pornography, and other forms of popular culture (Schodt 1996: 37; Clammer 1995; cf. Kinsella 1995). Enka is "mature," heterosexual desire, racialized as "Japanese" by this "song of Japan." And yet, both "Lolita-desire" and "enka-desire" share a common definition of femaleness that is based on passivity, helplessness, and vulnerability. In enka, female subjectivity is physicalized in the body's stereotyped performance of pain and longing. Desire becomes a volatile commodity "in heat" for the nation, the culture, the race. The connections between the body, the past, and the nation may be complex, but that complexity only serves to tie them more firmly together.

Beyond Kata: Cliché and Its Limits

Although enka is defined in part by the written score (notes, tempo, words, and so on), it is defined in even greater part by what happens in performance. Musically, the instrumental accompaniment easily comes across as trite and clichéd. It proceeds in an even rhythm and according to formulaic phrases that on electronic keyboards are actually preprogrammed. The songs themselves are also highly clichéd, yet their familiarity is seen as a positive quality that makes deeper, more direct communication possible. The singer's performance, in contrast, is dramatic and emotional, bending rhythms and melodies, adding colorful vocal texture, and breaking down in the near sobs of emotional suffering. The staid background music foregrounds the dramatic vocal theatrics. Yet what may surprise those unfamiliar with enka is that many of these vocal techniques of gendered emotional expression are as unspontaneous and formulaic as the instrumental accompaniment.

In the enka world, bodies and voices communicate through a language of patterning. In fact, the formulaic nature of kata allows what might almost be considered anomalies to proliferate: young performers sing of hard life experience; singers of Korean ancestry perform songs considered to be "the heart/soul of Japan"; female singers perform men's songs (and vice versa). These crossovers—of age, ethnicity, and gender—are made plausible by the kata of performance: the elements of performance have been broken down into well-rehearsed units of expression, from a breathy whisper to an outstretched arm.

Actual performances by top singers, however, demonstrate the power of kosei (individuality, originality), of going beyond the conventions. In other words, what puts singers at the top of the field and keeps them there is that they extend the genre even while staying within it, doing what has been done before but also, in subtle ways, what has not been done before. Originality and creativity, based firmly in kata training, are what take one to the apex of the singer hierarchy. To the untrained ear, the difference may be nearly undetectable, but to one more experienced, it is resounding.

Although kata is still the basic language of emotional expression in enka performance, breaking out of the conventions—standing apart even while standing within—is what makes a star a star. One must find and develop one's kosei, even if the goal is a recording industry product. Most singers start out singing safely, following kata closely, as they have been trained to do. But even record company scouts are looking for that little bit of something extra in a new singer. As a singer rises, she or he breaks out little by little, although never forsaking kata completely. True mastery *of* kata means mastery *over* kata. Those at the top convey the impression that no one can sing quite like them: their kata is not only distinctive, it is elusive.

CHAPTER SIX

Consuming Enka's Imaginary

Listening, Singing, Doing

Aomori, July 17, 1997, 8:20 A.M. The day is already warm. As I sit near an open window thinking about my next interview appointment, I hear, somewhere in the distance, the unmistakable sound of enka, broadcast over scratchy speakers. The voice of Misora Hibari is singing "Yawara" (Judo). As the music grows louder, so too does the sound of tires approaching slowly on the gravel road. Soon a grocery truck pulls into view, its loudspeakers blaring Hibari's song. Can one be made to salivate as well as cry at the sound of enka? I grab my wallet and rush out to buy snacks for the household.

For some in contemporary Japan, enka is the nostalgic, sentimental background music they overhear in sushi bars, public bathhouses, or taxis as they go about their everyday lives.[1] For others, such as the businessmen whose work day is punctuated by the sound of telephones and electronic beeps, enka is part of an after-work night world of *izakaya* (bars) and karaoke (Linhart 1986).[2] For still others, however, attending enka concerts, practicing enka songs, and joining enka fan clubs is a full-time avocation. This chapter examines fan clubs and karaoke clubs, two basic forms of organized public consumption of enka's imaginary. The two accompanying case studies are intended to illustrate some of the ways in which individuals "do" enka and give meaning to their activities.

What this chapter does not attempt to examine are the unorganized forms of individual consumption—listening to "Ame Sakaba" (Rainy Night at a Bar) on the radio in the middle of the night while driving a truckload of freight along the highway, watching *Enka no Hanamichi* on television after the dishes are done, or reading about the singer Sen Masao's financial woes—all of which are absolutely critical to the genre but less accessible to the researcher. Here, the focus is on the public consumption of enka, but with the proviso that this is not the whole picture; it does not address the "fandom" of the great number of people (especially men) who are not inclined to join a club or sing in public.

Enka's Appeal

The attraction of enka may be related to the connections listeners see between the situations depicted in the songs and their own lives. For example, a male government employee in his forties from the small hamlet of Shariki in Aomori (northern Honshu) speaks of a closer, more direct relationship to enka songs than does a Tokyo housewife. The lives of the songs' characters are not exactly like his, but he feels deeply connected to the sights and sounds of this "song of Japan." Furthermore, although his teenage son prefers punk rock, enka is still a more prominent part of daily life in his community than it is in Tokyo.

The reason people most often gave to explain why they liked enka is that listening to it and singing it relieves stress (*"sutoresu o kaihō suru"*). Japan's urban commuter life is by now legendary for its high level of stress, especially for men, who comprise the majority of commuters. Overwork is a way of life, as are hours of daily commuting on crowded trains. According to an architect in his sixties, listening to enka and singing it at night after work is an antidote to the cut-throat, emotionally arid daytime world of business. Enka, he says, in effect absolves businessmen of their "sins," the chief one being their own dehumanization in the "dry" world of technology and high finance. It rehumanizes them by returning them to their own "wetness"— their own humanity, their own Japaneseness—through their emotions.

Another reason for enka's continued popularity, and one cited more often by men than by women, is that enka is music of, by, and for the Japanese people (which of course overlooks the fact that many enka singers are non-Japanese and that various enka songs are popular in other Asian countries). When I asked one sushi restaurant worker, a male in his twenties, why he liked enka, the only explanation he could come up with was that he was the type of person who preferred Japanese green tea to coffee and rice to bread.

This kind of racial-cultural explanation links enka to the prevailing discourses that divide the world into two spheres, "Japan" vs. "the West," discussed in Chapter 1. As the forty-one-year-old male singer Toba Ichirō explained to me, "Every country has its music: France has its *chanson*, the United States has jazz, and Japan has enka." According to Toba, a person from one country cannot fully appreciate or sing the music of another country. Another male enka fan, this one in his seventies, also invoked the idea of "Japan," commenting that he liked a particular older female enka singer because she was kind (*yasashii*) and warm (*atatakai*); she was "Japan's mother" (*Nihon no okā-san*).

Other reasons people give for liking enka tend to be more personal and more intimately tied to the details of their lives. Fans talk about enka as a restorative. For example, a female fan in her sixties said that listening to a particular male enka singer gave her a reason for living (*ikigai*) following the death of her son and a subsequent nervous breakdown. A male fan from a rural area told singer Toba Ichirō that after hearing Toba's song "Kyōdaibune" (Ship of Brothers), he regained his health and zest. The male singer Hosokawa Takashi says that enka is part of people's lives and helps them to persevere ("gambaru"), especially through difficult times ("*kanashii toki mo, tsurai toki mo*"). These fans tend to personalize the genre: it supplies them with the stories and inspiration that help them through their daily lives. For them, enka is like an elixir.

Finally, there is the appeal of sexual attraction. As a producer at Century Records comments, if singers do not have some degree of sex appeal, their records will not sell. According to several music industry people, men "naturally" like female singers because they are female, and women like male singers because they are male. This "natural" appeal, however, can too easily become a heterosexualized generalization. Same-sex fandom, particularly of female fans for female singers, also abounds. The manager of one older female singer believes that her attraction for female fans is semi-sexual, much like that of the all-female entertainment troupe Takarazuka (cf. Robertson 1998).[3]

According to one karaoke organization head, heterosexually based patterns of consumption are changing, not because of increased recognition of same-sex practices and relationships, however, but because of the tremendous popularity of karaoke. Women want to listen to female singers whose songs they can sing in karaoke, not to male singers. Given the burgeoning karaoke industry, enka's primary appeal may soon be simply that it provides songs, offering people a way in which they themselves can perform within enka's imaginary.

Kōenkai and Fan Clubs

Strictly speaking, *kōenkai*, defined as "support groups," are distinct from *fuan kurabu* or "fan clubs"; in practice, however, the two are spoken of as one and the same. A kōenkai implies a formal relationship based on obligation and finances; a fan club implies an informal relationship based on emotion. Kōenkai can also be found in nonmusical contexts, such as politics[4] and sumō wrestling, where they function as leading financial backers. In the enka world, the two terms are used interchangeably, although kōenkai suggests an old-fashioned, "traditional" (i.e., Japanese) image, while "fan club" suggests a more "modern" one. Older fans usually refer to a singer's kōenkai, but some younger fans, as well as record industry people attempting to give a more "modern" image to the organization, use the term "fan club." On its official stationery, for example, the Mori Shin'ichi Kōenkai includes both the Japanese form of its name and the English form ("Shinichi Mori Fan Club").[5]

Whether they call themselves kōenkai or fan clubs, the organizations that support individual enka singers are run by the record company to which the singer is under contract (an arrangement that does not necessarily apply, however, to all performer fan clubs in Japan). It is record company employees, not necessarily fans, who run the organization, with the guidance, planning, and financial backing of the company. An organization's loyalty to any one singer, then, coexists with a contractual financial relationship.

Expressions of fandom differ along gender lines. In general, female fans join clubs far more often than male fans, so that every fan club, whether devoted to a male or a female singer, includes an inordinate number of female members. Proportionately higher numbers of males belong to fan clubs for female singers and often take a leadership role in these organizations. In the course of my fieldwork I interviewed the heads of eight different kōenkai, four dedicated to various male singers and four to female singers, and became a member of two of them. Six of the eight singers are at the top of the profession, while the remaining two are in the middle-upper ranks. The following case study of Mori Shin'ichi and his fan club examines the "kata of fandom" through the interactions between this singer and his fans.

CASE STUDY: Mori Shin'ichi and the Mori Shin'ichi Kōenkai

Mori Shin'ichi (b. 1947) is the epitome of the well-groomed, tuxedo-clad male enka singer. Debuting in 1966 with the song "Onna no Tameiki" (The Sigh of a Woman), he has since reached the top of the profession by singing songs written either from a woman's point of view or about the most important woman in the lives of many Japanese men: mother. Sensitive, serious, and vulnerable, he is widely considered to be a "woman's man."

To explain Mori's popularity, the ethnomusicologist Koizumi Fumio has suggested four key elements: 1) Mori expresses women's feelings (*onna no kimochi*); 2) he sings in an older, nineteenth-century narrative style called *shinnai* (a type of ballad drama), which Koizumi feels present-day Japanese still appreciate; 3) his songs combine both the Japanese pentatonic scale and Western "blues"; and 4) he is handsome yet looks as if he could be easily hurt (*hansamu de nan to naku kizutsuki-yasui*) (1984: 32–38).

Another reason for Mori's appeal is his voice, which is husky to the point of hoarseness. The Japanese musical aesthetic, far more than that of Western music, relishes texture and timbre. Even within this aesthetic, however, Mori's voice might be considered a liability rather than an asset. Indeed, according to one biography, his first efforts as a singer were repeatedly rebuffed by record companies: "'That voice is no good [*Dame da yo, ano koe wa*]'" (Asahi Shimbun Sei-bu Honsha 1992: 285). But according to some fans and critics, therein lies his strength. His voice gives sound to the melodrama of enka: rough rather than smooth, striving rather than static, *kurai* (dark) rather than *akarui* (light), filled with emotional tension rather than happily relaxed. According to one fan, the best surroundings for listening to Mori sing enka are at night in winter. In effect, his hoarse-sounding voice has become one of his greatest assets, not for itself but because of the greater effort he must constantly exert. Among his fans, this effort is itself precious. As his biographer writes, "The mystery of Mori's husky voice is that it is able to impart strong emotions in Japanese people's hearts" (ibid.). The fact that his voice allows him to express emotion with great intensity becomes cause for deep admiration.

Fans who have met Mori or seen him in person often comment on his good looks, although it is interesting that the word they use, *kawaii* (cute, endearing), is usually applied to women and children rather than to men. In 1993, at age forty-six, he seemed to evoke as many maternal as sexual feelings in his fans: he gave them a "rush" of motherhood. In fact, when Mori's fans were polled in 1987 (Mori, then forty, was younger than many of them) about his place in their lives (*dō iu sonzai ka*), over 10 percent of respondents answered that he was "like a son" (Mori Shin'ichi Kōenkai 1987). One sixty-nine-year-old woman recalls, "My mother always liked Mori Shin'ichi. She said he was a good example of *oya-kōkō* [filial piety]." Indeed, he presents the image of the perfect son—handsome, well-groomed, serious, and above all, devoted to his mother. Moreover, unlike actual sons, who often leave home, he is always available via television, radio, audiocassette, or videotape. As the mood strikes, fans can invoke Mori into their lives at will, confident that he will always be there, singing of his longing for his mother and his broken heart. His neediness is part of the draw.

Fans comment that Mori is intelligent (*atama ga ii*) and serious (*majime*). He is also known as a man of few words. Watching him for the first time, I was surprised at the absence of the kind of showmanship I would expect of an American performer or even other Japanese performers—no informal chatting between numbers, few expansive gestures, minimal "playing" to the crowd. Instead, he stood on stage soberly singing one song after another.[6] Also to my surprise, at least some fans I spoke with said that his "no-frills" performance shows how sincere he is. Instead of padding his performance with empty chatter, he sings his songs in a straightforward manner.

In the 1987 poll mentioned earlier, the most frequent responses to the question about Mori's place in his fans' lives after "like a son" were: "gives my life meaning" (*ikigai*), 18.4 percent; "soothes me" (*yasuragi*), 12.2 percent; "supports my heart/soul" (*kokoro no sasae*), 8.2 percent; and "provides me with pleasure" (*tanoshimi*), 6.1 percent. For these fans, Mori is obviously doing far more than merely singing on stage.

According to the current club head, a Mori Shin'ichi Kōenkai has been in existence since Mori's debut over twenty-five years ago. The present kōenkai, however, was organized in 1979, the year Mori went "independent" and set up his own production company. By 1992, it included approximately 10,000 members throughout Japan and a few in foreign countries. Women members far outnumber men, and although they range in age from their twenties to their nineties, the majority are in their forties and fifties.

Like the kōenkai of other enka singers, Mori's is run by the production and record companies to which he is under contract. Workers at the kōenkai, therefore, are company employees, but not necessarily fans. As one worker told me, she is not a fan but must give the impression that she is, or at least never seem to favor another singer over Mori.

The kōenkai presents itself in subtle ways as a fan-generated organization, although it is in fact a company-derived one. For example, the organization does not hold meetings per se, nor does it have officers. Two or three times a year, however, it holds a *"rikuesto shūkai"* ("request" gathering; info-meeting) in both Tokyo and Osaka. The use of the English word "request" suggests that the gathering is being held at the request of fans, but in reality it is a creation of the production and record companies behind the kōenkai. During these gatherings, fans listen while representatives of the production and record companies and the club head (a paid employee) talk about Mori's upcoming appearances and activities. Between 30 and 60 members were present at each of the two rikuesto shūkai I attended, nearly all of them women in their fifties or sixties. Each attendee was given a promotional packet containing a list of television and radio stations, program times, and station addresses, along with a stack of twenty prepaid postcards. By the time I arrived, several fans were already busy filling in these postcards, which would be mailed to a television or radio station, to request Mori's latest single.

The role of the kōenkai as an arm of the production or record company publicity department is significant. At the "request" info-meeting, Mori's manager asks fans not only to keep requesting Mori's songs by phone or postcard but also to sing Mori's songs in karaoke, to "carry" the songs, as it were, "into the ears" (mimi ni hairu) of the listening public. At one meeting, Mori's manager even rebuked fans for the paltriness of their *"seien no ryō"* (amount of cheering) at Mori's last televised concert before a live audience, especially because the fans for the program's other featured singer seemed to cheer far more loudly and enthusiastically. (To this, one fan retorted, "But I couldn't see! [*Mienai*]"). Another meeting gave fans detailed instructions for a publicity event scheduled for the following week: they were told where to be, what to do, and even how to sound in giving support to Mori.

This kata of fandom ensures a perfect fit between fans and singers, or, more accurately, between fans and singers' production and record companies. Mori needs support to be a success; his fans want to support Mori. The kōenkai guide them toward the best means of achieving both objectives—buying and promoting his records. The following excerpt from a fan letter published in *The Shinichi Mori News*, the monthly kōenkai *kaihō* (newsletter),

Consuming Enka's Imaginary 131

"Mori Shin'ichi in Asakusa," a Publicity Event

expresses the personal pleasure one fan derives when Mori's latest song (and thereby Mori) does well: "When Mori's latest song became a big hit this autumn, my heart beat fast. I hear it [Mori's latest song] a lot on the radio, and seeing it lined up with the 'Best 10' when I enter a record store makes me so happy. Fellow fans, let us all try our best to spread [shintō suru] the melody of 'Warui Hito' [Bad Person] throughout Japan" (Mori Shin'ichi Kōenkai 1993c: 3). Fans take it upon themselves to ensure Mori's success. Through omoiyari (empathy),[7] they assume Mori's goals, including his rivalries, as their own, gladly shouting and cheering for Mori, especially when he performs with a rival singer.

A worker at Mori's kōenkai office pointed out several ways in which avid fans treat Mori as if he were a kind of kamisama (god). For example, among the various "kyarakutā gudzu" (character goods) the kōenkai sells are zabuton (cushions) inscribed with Mori's signature, but many members who buy them claim they would never think of "defiling" them by actually sitting on them. The club also sells packs of facial tissues, which members collect (or give to friends as presents), yet another addition to their mounting stockpile of Mori treasure. This same principle, buying to collect, applies to telephone cards,[8] towels, handkerchiefs, chopstick holders, and other items. By collecting these "pieces" of Mori, the fans dotingly accumulate bits of Mori's persona, much like religious devotees surrounding themselves with icons of worship.

Each issue of *The Shinichi Mori News* features a front page color photograph of Mori. One month, according to a kōenkai worker, when the ten-by-fifteen-inch sheets were folded as usual to fit into the mailing envelope, the photo of Mori ended up folded in half lengthwise. Several upset fans called the office to complain: their idol should not be seen cut in half. Now the newsletter designers are more careful in their placement of the front cover photograph, so that even when folded it appropriately frames Mori's face.

Women's expressions of fandom are often motherly. If Mori does not look well during an evening television appearance, the next morning the kōenkai office is flooded with phone calls from fans anxiously inquiring about his health. At concerts, devoted fans often bring *bentō* (box lunches) to kōenkai workers. And after the concert, some members busy themselves picking up trash and cleaning up the theater. According to one club member, a messy theater after a Mori concert reflects badly on Mori himself. Another expressed her concern over the behavior of fans who leave litter under their seats or take flowers from the lobby: "In these kinds of ways, Mori's fans' manners are called into question. After a while it will be regrettable when it becomes an impediment (*shishō*) to Mori['s image]" (Mori Shin'ichi Kōenkai 1993c: 2). These fans, tightly linked by omoiyari (empathy), regard Mori as an extension of themselves.

For an initiation fee of ¥1000 ($9) and a monthly fee of ¥500 ($4.50), members receive 1) seasonal greetings at midsummer and New Year's in the form of a photo postcard of Mori; 2) the opportunity to purchase concert tickets in advance to get the best seats; 3) notices of free activities, such as the "request" info-meeting; 4) the monthly kaihō (newsletter), *The Shinichi Mori News*; 5) an invitation to purchase a ticket for the annual *fuan no tsudoi* (fan gathering, party); and 6) notice of special events, such as members-only concerts and tours with Mori himself.

The last three items effectively demonstrate how the kōenkai becomes an effective interface between the singer, the singer's image, and the singer's fans. *The Shinichi Mori News* is the most frequent and most regular point of contact between Mori's kōenkai and its members. During the two years of my membership (1992–94), the four-page format was the same each month:

front page: large color photo of Mori and formulaic seasonal greetings; second page: a philosophical "talk essay" by Mori, a *hāto tsūshin* ("heart" communication) greeting from a person in some way connected to Mori's current work, with Mori's response, and upcoming concert information; third page: *fuan no hiroba* (fans' section, including fan letters), display of Mori "character goods" for sale, a letter from the kōenkai office staff, and a two-month schedule of Mori's activities; and fourth page: glossy color photos of Mori from his recent concert and television appearances.

What is most important to members is the feeling, conveyed by the newsletter, that Mori is in direct communication with them. His greetings on the front page take the form of a personal letter. This, coupled with an enlarged photo of Mori, makes it seem that the star is looking directly at each fan and speaking to her. Here is a translated example of Mori's greetings taken from the November 1993 issue:

We are well into autumn by now, so how is everyone?

I thank you for the great cheers of support [*ōkina go-seien*] I have received everywhere on my nationwide Min'on concert tour,[9] which began in October. Thankfully, I feel very happy that the concerts have been well received.

With the rooting of all of you [*minasama no go-seien ni yotte*], my song "Warui Hito" [Bad Person] has been able to ride the crest of popularity, and I wholeheartedly [*kokoro o komete*] face the challenge of making this a song that many people hear and can sing to themselves [*kuchi-zusamu*].

From now on this is the time of year in which it gets colder by the day, so everyone, please take good care of yourselves.

[Signed,] Mori Shin'ichi (Mori 1993a: 1)

The language of the letter, written as if from an inferior to a superior, is respectful. The opening and closing paragraphs are stereotypical greetings appropriate to the month. Mori emphasizes the support (*seien*) he receives from his fans and his gratitude. Never resting on his laurels, he continues to work hard, "wholeheartedly facing the challenge" of making his newest song successful. That success is indicated by how many "ears" it has entered—how many people have heard it and are singing it. The letter gives the impression that Mori is an earnest, hard-working performer who strives to please each of his fans. The relationship is a kind of dual dependency—a rebounded *amae*—in which each serves the other: the singer depends on his fans for support, and the fans depend on the singer for emotional sustenance.

In the "talk essay" on the second page of the issue, Mori subtly switches from servant to sage. His essays range from a description of an incident at a recent concert to a reflection on the news of a friend's marriage. Each is supposed to impart a touch of wisdom, a lesson for life. In one, for example, Mori talks of losing his voice at a concert. The lesson: never take things for granted (Mori 1992c: 2). In another, he talks of evaluating personal happiness not from the perspective of one day's ups and downs but from a larger, lifelong perspective (Mori 1993b: 2).

One of the most revealing sections of the newsletter is the *fuan no hiroba* on the third page, a compilation of letters from fans selected by the kōenkai staff and Mori's responses. Each letter includes the writer's initials and city or prefecture. In reading them, kōenkai members experience a sense of community, often agreeing with the writers' sentiments. At the same time, Mori's polite responses deftly defuse the one-to-one exclusivity of the letters. He expresses his gratitude and indebtedness, but at a generalized level, effectively universalizing the interchange. Some of the most common expressions in these fan letters focus on kokoro: *kokoro ni hibiku* (resonate in one's heart); *kokoro ni nokoru* (remain in one's heart); *kokoro o tsunagu* (connect to one's heart); *kokoro o ugokasu* (moves one's heart); *kokoro no kate* (nourishment for one's heart).

In his responses, Mori also cultivates an interdependent relationship with his fans—or, at least, the image of such a relationship:

T.H. from Yamaguchi prefecture: I went to your April 18 concert in Hiroshima. Your wonderfully appealing singing voice—your humorous comments during the concert—your gentle smiling face [*yasashii egao*]. On that red stage wearing a red suit, you looked like such a young person.[10] When I see you on stage, I lose all track of time passing [*toki no tatsu no o wasurete shimaimasu*].... That night after my family had gone to bed, I was alone, so I took out the fan club bulletin with the lyrics to your latest song in it, and quietly sang the song to myself. I think I would like to master the song and sing it at karaoke places. I look forward to seeing you again in your June concert.

Mori: ... Thank you for your support at the Hiroshima concert. During my June concert, I will certainly sing my new song again. I feel that I would like my fans to sing along with me (in a quiet voice!?) at the concert. (Mori Shin'ichi Kōenkai 1992a: 3)

Mori responds to another fan letter by saying, "I have long been conscious of my responsibility as a singer to my fans, who have supported me, and from now on I will persist in meeting the expectations of my fans" (Mori 1992a: 3). In yet another reply, he reiterates his feeling of indebtedness: "Without forgetting my indebtedness to you my fans, I will persevere" (Mori 1992b: 3).

In their sense of mutual appreciation, the letters and Mori's replies sometimes verge on the intimate:

Y.E. from Kanagawa prefecture: . . . [During the concert I attended,] I got to shake your hand, and I forgot my age, and it became a wonderful memory. Your hand was amazingly soft, a hand that had the warmth that moves people's hearts [*hito no kokoro o ugokasu*]. I think that I would like to make the emotion of that day live on in my daily life as nourishment for my heart [*kokoro no kate*]. (Mori Shin'ichi Kōenkai 1992b: 3)

H.F. from Hyōgo prefecture: . . . [During the concert I attended,] I got to shake hands with you, and I grasped your soft hand with both of mine. I was greatly moved. It was a night that transported me out of the fatigue of the day.

Mori: Thank you. I feel that your appreciation of my recital also lifts me out of any fatigue that I might have. From now on, I will strive to please you all. (Mori Shin'ichi Kōenkai 1992e: 3)

M.K. from Osaka: I was thrilled to have a commemorative photo with Mori. . . . Some time later, on the train home from the fan club party, I would look at my photo [of the two of us together] and remember the warmth of Mori's cheek on mine and feel so happy. I hold the warmth of Mori in my heart [*mune*] and promise to support him all the more from now on.

Mori: Thank you. I, too, hold my fans' warmth in my heart. (Mori Shin'ichi Kōenkai 1992f:3)

Some letters speak of tears and of crying while listening to Mori's songs, especially those about mother, such as "O-fukuro-san" (Mother Dear) and "Usagi" (Rabbit).

T.H. from Tokyo: . . . I was moved to tears [by your singing in concert], but if they are tears with such a fine aftertaste, then it would be fine for them to flow any number of times [*konna ni atoaji no ii namida nara nando nagashite mo ii*]. (Mori Shin'ichi Kōenkai 1993a: 3)

H.T. from Kanagawa: [At the concert I attended,] without thinking, I found myself singing along with Mori, softly to myself. And upon hearing Mori's heartfelt rendition of "Usagi," tears came to my eyes and I was enraptured [*kiki-horemashita*]. (Mori Shin'ichi Kōenkai 1993b: 3)

K. from Tokyo: My mother was shot by a gunman and hospitalized. On the days when I went to visit her in the hospital, there was the television program *Omoide no Merodii* (Melodies of Memories). I knew of the program through the kōenkai newsletter, so I switched the television on and waited for Mori's appearance. My mother seemed to be living by drops on a truly meager liquid diet, but at that time she opened her eyes. Taking my mother's hand and stroking her face, I listened, crying, to "O-fukuro-san." With those tears in my eyes, I couldn't see Mori's face, but I listened with feelings that I hadn't felt before. My mother could hear clearly, too. Now my mother's life is just about over, but for me her life was the greatest gift. I will listen to Mori from now on treasuring her. I am eternally grateful to Mori's singing.

Mori: Thank you for your story. For me, too, when I sing "O-fukuro-san," I remember in my heart various aspects of my own mother. From now on, I would like to sing the song with all my heart as a song well-loved by everyone. (Mori Shin'ichi Kōenkai 1993d: 3)

Some letters mention ways in which Mori has made the writer's life better. In one example, a mother writes that she and her twenty-year-old daughter happily attend Mori's concerts together. "Through Mori's songs, this mother and daughter have no discord" (Mori Shin'ichi Kōenkai 1992d: 3). Another writer praises Mori's "talk essays," claiming that her life has improved by reading them: "I feel in my heart that because Mori's singing is born of such wisdom, he has an appeal altogether different from other singers" (Mori Shin'ichi Kōenkai 1992c: 3).

But the major benefit of membership in Mori's kōenkai is the opportunity to get closer—physically and emotionally—to the star. One example is the annual *fuan no tsudoi* (fan get-together) held in the fall (one in Tokyo and one in Osaka). Many fans look forward to this event with great anticipation. At the one I attended at the Shin Takanawa Prince Hotel in Shinagawa, Tokyo, in November 1992, there were approximately 450 fans, around 90 percent of whom were female. Once everyone was seated, Mori entered the room singing. He walked through every aisle, shaking hands and having his picture taken. Among the evening's activities was a quiz game. Fans were asked mundane questions about Mori, and the two with the most correct answers were given prizes. The questions included 1) What kind of tree does Mori like? a. *sakura* (cherry),[11] or b. cedar (answer: *sakura*); 2) What kind of quiet place does Mori like? a. ocean, or b. mountain (answer: ocean); 3) When Mori catches a cold, what does he do? a. go see a doctor, or b. go to bed right away (answer: go see a doctor); 4) If Mori buys a cute puppy,

Mori Shin'ichi Greeting His Fans

what does he call it? a. Mori-chan, or b. Shin-chan (answer: Mori-chan). Clearly, the game rewarded those who knew the most Mori trivia or could at least second-guess him. The fan party also featured a *karaoke taikai* (karaoke contest) that was restricted to Mori's songs. Before the party, 42 contestants were winnowed by audition down to ten, and these ten then competed for three prizes, ranging from a Mori CD or cassette to a choice of one of Mori's stage jackets. The contest rewarded those who could most closely approximate Mori in performance.

For many fans, the most important part of the event was the opportunity to have their photograph taken with Mori. This took place at the end of the evening, when fans lined up with their tickets, which entitled them to one photo. A professional photographer took the shot with an "instant-picture" camera, so that the fan could take home the treasured record of her evening with Mori. One fan told me that she always carries all the photos from previous fan parties with her, mementoes of a fantasized relationship.

Another example of kōenkai-staged intimacy was the "telephone date" in July 1993, an opportunity to speak with Mori individually by phone. Here, Mori's relationship with fans emulated a "real" [hetero]sexual one; however, participation was contingent on buying "Warui Hito" (Bad Person), Mori's newly released single. The "telephone date," in other words, was a thinly veiled promotional tactic to boost record sales. The prize offered, in the guise of Mori himself, was a few minutes of Mori's time by way of the telephone. In order to apply, kōenkai members were required to submit their name, address, phone number, times they would be available, a subject for discussion, and the record company insignia and product number cut from the CD or cassette label of "Warui Hito." From these applicants, three were selected. The August 1993 issue of *The Shinichi Mori News* included transcripts of all three conversations. The topics tended to be mundane—diet tips, golf, his song repertoire. Each woman, not unlike a young girl on a date, expressed her excitement in phrases such as, "This is like a dream!" and "Oh dear, what shall I do? This is the real thing, isn't it? Oh, my heart is pounding!" One woman confessed that she had intended to take a tranquilizer for this momentous occasion but accidentally took some fever medicine, making her feel especially intoxicated. In each case, Mori chatted awhile but invariably got to the point of asking his "date" what she thought of his newest song (Mori Shin'ichi Kōenkai 1993e: 2).

One final example of the patterned intimacy between singer and fans so carefully cultivated by the kōenkai is the occasional tour with the star. In March 1994, approximately seventy fans traveled with Mori to Honolulu, Hawai'i.[12] (Actually, star and fans traveled separately, Mori preceding his fans by a few days.) The effort Mori expended to please his fans was tremendous (I do not think an American entertainer, especially one of his stature, would go to such lengths or make himself so accessible). This suggests yet another way in which the "slide-rule" of performer-audience interaction (see Chapter 4) shifts, this time offstage. Mori greeted each of his fans from Japan with a lei. Then fans from both Japan and Hawai'i attended a luncheon, during which there was a *karaoke taikai* of Mori's songs and an opportunity to be photographed with him. Later, with fans from Japan, Mori went on a dinner cruise, during which he danced the hula, greeted everyone at each table, and posed for photos with each fan. Before the four-day tour was over, Mori had taken the time to visit each fan's hotel room and chat briefly with each one. And, perhaps most important for Mori's image, each of these activities had been photographed, and the photos were featured in the following month's newsletter.

Mori's efforts to please his fans are nearly as prodigious as theirs to please him. From this relationship of mutual dependency, a kind of "kata of interaction" arises. Mori inspires emotions, both maternal and sexual, that prompt his fans to do whatever they can to help him. When I asked members why they joined his fan club, many answered, "To support him" (ōen shiyō). At the same time, his efforts also aid them in their lives and gratify their emotional needs. These interactive processes are the basis of their felt "relationship." Although commercially generated in part, this relationship is no less real or important to his thousands of fans.

I have emphasized the relationship between Mori and his fans, but the kōenkai also encourages relationships between fans. In some cases, their mutual devotion to Mori becomes a basis for friendship. Fans see each other at concerts in part because the tickets they have bought by mail from the kōenkai office seat them together in one section. They also see each other at meetings, at parties, and sometimes on tours. With membership as their common ground, fans inevitably recognize each other's faces, and some begin to converse with one another. They have plenty to discuss: Mori's latest television appearance, Mori's newest song, Mori's photo in last week's magazine. As I caught the train after one Mori concert, a stranger recognized me as a fellow fan club member and made room for me on the seat next to hers. Our subsequent conversation, needless to say, revolved around Mori. Another woman I spoke with had traveled alone by train for two hours to attend Mori's annual dinner party. She said she didn't mind, however, because once at the party, she was surrounded by people with whom she felt comfortable, even if she did not know them well. The degree to which members who did not otherwise know each other socialized outside club activities varied from not at all to occasionally. However, concerts, meetings, and parties occur approximately eight to ten times a year, and thus become occasions for renewing friendships.

The kata of fandom demonstrated by the Mori Shin'ichi Kōenkai is grounded in an ideal of mutual dependency and support. Mori reaches out to fans in patterned ways, in patterned settings, and through the patterned expressions of enka. His gesture is institutionalized within the kōenkai through the newsletters and preprinted seasonal cards members receive, and the preset activities at club parties. In each case, Mori (aided by his staff) assumes the humble position of a good servant working hard to please his fans, his skill presumably arising from his ability to anticipate his fans' needs through omoiyari (empathy). This image of the striving servant is essential to his acceptance among fans.

Poster of Mori Shin'ichi Outside Shinjuku Koma Gekijō

Fans also reach out to Mori in patterned ways. They give him flowers and gifts at certain moments during concerts, wave their "penlights" in unison during his performance of particular songs, and become members of his kōenkai. As members, they write him letters, show up at info-meetings, attend parties, go on tours, and request and sing his songs. Most important, they reach out to him by reaching within, adopting an attitude of omoiyari (empathy) that in turn makes his needs their own. They want to serve the servant.

Omoiyari, then, is at work on both sides. Mori's omoiyari, however, deliberate and well planned, is at least in part the product of an office staff whose job is to promote him and his records. There is no realistic way Mori could empathize with every one of his fans, although he must give the impression that he does. Conveniently, in this context, kata may prove particularly efficient—one pattern can apply to a broad constituency of fans and situations. Up to a point, the more formulaic and generalized Mori's communication is, the greater the number of fans he can reach through what is perceived as appropriate expression. His fans, in contrast, speak in specific terms, even if in patterned forms. Their expressions of omoiyari focus on him alone—one night, one smile, one touch. In the end, the role of the kōenkai is to bring these practices—those of both Mori and his fans—together, thereby establishing a "kata of fan-star interaction."

Karaoke

In Japan, singing in public at formal and informal social gatherings has long been popular. As John Embree notes of prewar rural life, "During the ordinary humdrum of daily life there is scant opportunity for self-expression, but at . . . drinking parties anyone who feels the urge may display his abilities" (1939: 105). Singing at such gatherings, much like karaoke today, was a form of sharing: each person in turn became a performer to the others' applause. The well-established practice of *monomane* (mimicry) as a form of amateur and professional entertainment is another precedent.

Although the music of karaoke reflects popular local traditions, originally it was closely linked to enka.[13] In technical terms, karaoke, which in a general sense means singing to prerecorded accompaniment, might be defined as "the technological reification of kata-driven expression." That is, if music is assumed to be patterned—to have a fixed tempo, fixed dynamics, fixed embellishments, and a fixed interpretation—then karaoke is the audio-visual "hardware" of kata that makes patterned vocal expression possible.

For the enka fan, karaoke is one way in which consumption of enka can become a hobby. During the period of my fieldwork, at least two nationally distributed monthly magazines, *Karaoke Fan* and *Karaoke Taishō* (Big Prize), were devoted to karaoke hobbyists. Each gives the latest news of enka singers, shows, and songs; the text and music of new songs with brief instructions for singing some of them; listings of top songs; results of karaoke contests; and information on the newest karaoke equipment. *Karaoke Fan* also includes various lists of "*besuto 20*," the top twenty songs according to data collected from readers, *karaoke sākuru* ("circles"; informal voluntary associations), *karaoke bokkusu* ("box"; private rooms for rent by the hour), and *sunakku* ("snack"; bars). *Karaoke Taishō* includes "Karaoke Kā-san" (Karaoke Mother), a cartoon strip about the trials and tribulations of a middle-aged housewife who is also a karaoke fanatic. Since 1990, NHK (Japan Public Broadcasting) has also produced *Karaoke Enka Kashōhō* (Karaoke Enka Singing Method), a thirteen-week televised series of singing lessons taught by the well-known composer Ichikawa Shōsuke (see Chapter 3). Audience members can also buy an accompanying booklet (Ichikawa 1992a, 1992b).

Karaoke and enka hobbyists can also join any of a large number of organizations, where they will meet others who share their love of public singing. Karaoke sākuru ("circles") are generally small, geographically based groups of fifteen to thirty people who share a love of karaoke singing. Some "circles" are organized by karaoke teachers to create opportunities for their students to practice and sing for each other. In addition, there are national (and a few international) karaoke clubs, with as many as 25,000 members. The case study that concludes this chapter describes one of them.

The spread of karaoke from the night-life world of bars to private bokkusu ("boxes") since the 1980s has attracted a wider, hobbyist market that ranges from middle-aged businessmen to women and students. Once owners of karaoke boxes realized the potential of this newfound market, they quickly added daytime business hours, creating the playfully dubbed *"hiruoke"* (daytime karaoke) whose patrons are for the most part female (Anonymous 1991: 16).

The growth of karaoke as a hobby has put increasing emphasis on singing well. To this end, there are lessons, how-to books and magazines, and the previously mentioned television series. Although participation is still foremost, in many karaoke venues singing well now takes precedence. The concept of "singing well," however, rests on the assumption of a single model of proficiency, that based on professional performance kata. In the 1990s, for example, many karaoke machines came equipped with a built-in rating system. When a singer finished singing, his or her performance was electronically scored, and the score transmitted in a digital readout. These scores, however, are based solely on measurable quantities such as pitch, rhythm, and volume. According to one oft-repeated story, when a top professional enka singer sang his own hit song with one of these karaoke machines, he ended up with a poor score. The current prevalence of karaoke contests also highlights the value placed on singing well. These contests, held locally and nationally, present an interesting mix of competing ideologies: on the one hand, a contest is a contest, with winners and losers; on the other, participation is itself highly valued, and contests attract a wide array of abilities.

Of course, not all Japanese enjoy singing to karaoke in public. A significant number actually claim to despise it. According to a 1988 survey, the chief reasons respondents gave for disliking karaoke were tone-deafness, shyness, being forced to sing, and being forced to listen to others sing (Ogawa 1989: 4). A fellow anthropologist reports that one of her Japanese friends looks down on karaoke as something "declassé," which suggests that for some Japanese, karaoke (and enka) carry strong class associations. Nevertheless, most of the people I spoke to—both fans and nonfans—will sing karaoke if required to do so socially, and many know at least one song they can perform at a moment's notice.

The rise of karaoke over the past decade has fueled changes in enka songs and in the industry as a whole, foremost among them the extended life given to enka by involving the general public as singers. Karaoke hobbyists welcome each new enka hit with unbounded enthusiasm, eager to learn the latest songs and display their singing expertise. Releases of enka singles often include both a singing version and a karaoke version on the same cassette or CD. This extended life, however, has been granted on karaoke's terms: the requirements of karaoke have become the requirements of the enka industry.

As one record producer explains, "We record company people think in terms of creating songs that are easy for the average person to sing [*ippan no hito ga utatte kureyasui uta*]." Countless promotions now claim that a song is easy to learn (*oboeyasui*) and easy to sing (*utaiyasui*). But the company's notion of "singability" refers to a narrow pitch range, limited ornamentation, and predictable melodic and rhythmic lines.[14] As one enka singer explained to me, when he records a song, he cuts out a lot of ornamentation (kobushi), because it would make the song too difficult for the average person to sing. Instead, he inserts just enough to accommodate the genre, but within the limits of what he thinks the average person can imitate (*monomane dekiru yō ni*) in karaoke. Thus, karaoke has encouraged simpler patterned expression geared to the lowest common denominator of vocal ability.

More recently, a countertrend has emerged. Because the many fans of karaoke have raised the general level of amateur singing, companies are now promoting songs not for their general singability but for their level of challenge for experienced singers. Likewise, for professional singers it is a matter of pride that a song in their repertoire is somewhat difficult to sing. The singer Mikasa Yuko explains the popularity of her latest hit in these terms: "Nowadays karaoke fans skillfully handle even difficult songs well [*sekkyokuteki ni*]. I think this is related to my song becoming a hit" (Anonymous 1994e: 38).

Another result of the karaoke boom has been a shift in the object of fans' devotion from the singer to the song. According to the head of one karaoke organization, many karaoke enthusiasts now buy a recording of a new song for the song itself rather than out of loyalty to a particular singer. They choose a song because they want to sing it, not because they want to listen to it. *Konfidensu* (Confidence), an industry publication, reports on the same phenomenon: "Recently, enka fans are buying a song for its merits, rather than because of the artist. This may be an . . . effect of karaoke, such that fans now prefer songs they themselves can perform" (Anonymous 1992c: 24).

The current female domination of karaoke through the introduction of hiru-oke (daytime karaoke) has feminized enka (see Chapter 3) by increasing the number of female singers and women's songs. In many karaoke "circles" and clubs, women far outnumber men. Karaoke fan magazines feature humorous items, such as the comic strip "Karaoke Kā-san" (Karoake Mother) mentioned earlier, and articles on topics geared to women, such as make-up tips for karaoke performances (Anonymous 1993b: 14–17). In a few instances, a male enka singer has even rerecorded a song in a key more suited to a female vocal range, hoping to appeal specifically to female karaoke fans (Anonymous 1994c: 39).

The intertwining of karaoke and enka is no more evident than in the numerous karaoke taikai (contests) that have proliferated in contemporary Japan. At all the karaoke contests I have attended or read about, enka—sung by young and old, male and female—is by far the most common genre. The judges at these contests also tend to be connected in some way to the enka world, whether as composers, lyricists, producers, or even singers.[15] Some contests feature a guest performance by an enka singer, and the more prestigious the contest, the more highly ranked the singer.

Contests are an important way to promote an enka song, especially if that song is the contest's designated *kadai-kyoku* ("theme" song; obligatory repertoire song). These kadai-kyoku—purchased on cassette or CD, listened to repeatedly, and practiced by contestants—"enter one's ears" forcibly, through sheer repetition. If hit-making in enka relies to a large extent on repetition (see Chapter 3), then kadai-kyoku status becomes a singularly efficient means of ensuring the success of the process: these songs "enter the ears" of the contestants who practice them, but they also "enter the ears" of audience members, who hear the same song sung by each contestant. In 1994, as part of his twentieth-year career celebration, the enka singer Kadokawa Hiroshi held a national karaoke contest featuring his hit song "Ichiya-bune" (Boat of One Night) as the kadai-kyoku. Of the 4,800 applicants (all of whom presumably listened to and practiced Kadokawa's song), 30 traveled to Tokyo to compete in the finals, and one woman was ultimately selected as the winner (Anonymous 1994c: 39). Other singers (and their managing staff), including those at the top of the singing hierarchy, use karaoke contests to promote new songs through what is called a *"karaoke kyanpein"* (karaoke promotional campaign). In 1994, for example, the veteran stars Mori Shin'ichi, Itsuki Hiroshi, and Kitajima Saburō all embarked on separate karaoke campaigns to promote their new songs.

Case Study: Nihon Amachua Kayō Renmei (NAK)

The following case study charts the complex development of organized karaoke in Japan, but it also shows the vital place of karaoke—and thereby of enka—in the lives of some of its most ardent fans. For many of these fans, karaoke (and, by extension, enka) has become a way of life.

The Nihon Amachua Kayō Renmei (Japan Amateur Popular Song Federation), more commonly known as NAK, was established in 1982. By 1991, with a membership of around 25,000 organized into 124 branches primarily in Japan but also in Hawai'i, Los Angeles, and Brazil, it claimed to be the largest worldwide karaoke organization. The statistical information on NAK members made available to me was from 1988, and over ten years later, membership has changed considerably. In 1988, 8 percent were in their twenties, 24 percent in their thirties, 31 percent in their forties, 27 percent in their fifties, and 10 percent in their sixties and older. The majority, then, were middle-aged (forties and older). In addition, 36 percent of the members were company employees (*kaisha-in*), 25 percent were self-employed (*jieigyō*), 22 percent were housewives, 9 percent were government workers (*kōmuin*), 6 percent were unemployed, and 2 percent were students. At that time also, 57 percent were male and 43 percent were female. In 1993, however, and here is where the greatest change took place, an NAK representative estimated that approximately 30 percent of the members were male and 70 percent were female.

For an initiation fee of ¥5000 ($45) and a yearly fee of ¥8000 ($73), a member receives *Songu Bukku* (Song Book), a monthly publication that features articles, interviews, news, and concert schedules, all related to enka, along with mini-singing lessons for specific enka songs. For additional fees, a member can also participate in singing lessons, workshops, regional karaoke taikai, and the yearly "*Guran Puri Taikai*" (Grand Prix Contest). NAK also sponsors social events, such as travel tour groups and parties, that may include professional enka singers.

NAK gives out its own annual awards, NAK Nihon Hayariuta Taishō. In 1992, those awards were for best song (including its singer, lyricist, composer, arranger, and director) and best newcomers (one male, one female), with a special award for career achievement. In addition, NAK compiles annual lists, based on member polls, of the "top 100" songs they most like to sing, songs they most like to listen to, and the singers they most enjoy. Enka songs and singers dominate all categories.

NAK's charter, which is printed in the pamphlet it supplies to prospective members, states the organization's four goals: 1) Members shall seek mutual friendship and interchange based upon respect through the appreciation (*kanshō*) and practice (*jissen*) of song; 2) Members shall endeavor to improve their individual, rich singing power (*kosei yutaka na kashō-ryoku*) with a deeper understanding of song; 3) Members shall work toward creating a society that is good to live in (*sumiyoi*), conducting their lives in good health and with abundant heart (*kokoro yutaka na*) while participating in the activities of the organization; 4) Members shall aim toward the creation of a popular song culture (*kayō bunka*) built upon adult sensibilities (NAK n.d.). Accompanying the charter are glossy color photographs of enthusiastic members—all smiling, clapping, and waving—not unlike those found in the promotional literature of religious sects.

The pamphlet also includes testimonials from various adherents to NAK. First it holds out the lure that spurs at least some karaoke enthusiasts: "one day, you too might become a star," and then it features three members who have become professional singers ("The birth of professional singers from NAK members!!"). Of these, the two females sing enka and the male sings "adult pops." In addition, the pamphlet quotes four amateur singers, who give further testimonials about NAK in somewhat cultic or religious terms. A sixty-two-year-old female company executive from Fukuoka prefecture claims, "I was born and changed through NAK" (*NAK de umare kawatta watashi*).[16] Other amateurs testify to NAK's life-enhancing abilities. A fourteen-year-old female middle school student from Osaka praises NAK, through whose training she has been able to win many karaoke taikai and make friends all over the country. A forty-two-year-old housewife from Ibaraki prefecture declares that, until she became a member of NAK and received training, her singing was like "coffee without cream" (*kurīpu o irenai kōhī*).¹⁷ A fifty-two-year-old Buddhist priest from Hokkaido admits that at first he felt embarrassed, even guilty, about his fascination with karaoke (presumably because of its incongruity with his life of priestly teaching), but since joining NAK and meeting other members, he has found karaoke to be life's "miracle remedy" (*jinsei no myōyaku*). Such validation by no less than a Buddhist priest helps sanctify karaoke in the eyes of prospective NAK members.

Through NAK, one can improve one's singing, win contests, and make friends, but one can also find the key to living. Through NAK, karaoke becomes an experience far beyond simply singing to prerecorded accompaniment: it becomes the way to a better social, aesthetic, and spiritual life. Indeed, what karaoke organizations such as NAK provide, at least for their more ardent members, is a patterned format for their enka fandom. If these enka fans enjoy the songs and sometimes sing to themselves or to small groups at parties, now, through karaoke, and in particular, through membership in a karaoke organization, their once formless pleasure becomes a structured regimen of regular singing, practicing, and doing.

Of course, not all enka lovers are necessarily karaoke lovers, much less members of karaoke organizations. Similarly, not all NAK members are enka fans, although the overlap here is much greater. For those who do fall into both categories, however, karaoke and NAK membership provide a social identity based firmly in enka and its imaginary. With karaoke (and NAK), they can "do" enka more legitimately. Their consumption of the genre becomes more active as they take to the stage to sing of emotions and "Japans" past, and as they practice enka every day at home, at a lesson, at a "circle" meeting, or at a karaoke bokkusu. Their singing has purpose, whether for the next lesson, the next contest, the next meeting, or the next performance. In this way, karaoke and karaoke organizations like NAK professionalize fandom. "Doing enka" becomes synonymous with embracing an organized, hierarchical arrangement of social roles, daily activities, and regular large-scale events. A song extends into a way of life through which an enka fan can live the imaginary.

CHAPTER SEVEN

Enka as Engendered Longing

Romance, Furusato, "Japan"

MALE:	*Furusato wa o-mae*	You are my *furusato*.
FEMALE:	*Furusato wa anata*	You are my *furusato*.

"Furusato" (Hometown) (*1990*)

Enka constructs a world of longing and suffering on a personal level that extends to the cultural and national levels. The two main arenas of suffering, romance and *furusato* (hometown), are defined along gender lines: brokenhearted romance for women (onna-gokoro/a woman's heart) and pining for furusato for men (part of otoko-michi/the path of a man). The separation between the two, however, is far from neat, as the lyrics from the song "Furusato" illustrate. Furusato is invoked within the context of romance for the power of its links to primacy, origins, and rootedness. One may therefore have a "'furusato' of emotions" or a lover who is one's "furusato." Moreover, there is considerable overlap between the gendering of the song and its focus (for example, men's songs of romance or women's songs of furusato). What ties the spheres of (women's) romance and (men's) furusato together is a sense of longing. Words such as *koishii* (long for, miss) and *akogare* (longing) focus the imaginary on yearning. A sense of longing infuses enka's gendered world, from the constructions of femaleness and maleness (whose kata allow for cross-gendering on stage), to the patterning of romance, to the invocation of furusato, and finally to this version of Japan's "Japan."

Romancing the Nation

The individual broken hearts of enka become collective broken hearts in the larger context of this "song of Japan" (*nihon no uta*). It matters little that others elsewhere sing songs like these, or that these songs have found a wide audience in other Asian countries. What matters is that in contemporary Japan, through deliberate processes of collective remembering and forgetting, aided by state institutions such as NHK, these songs have been infused with the aura of national culture. Here the suffering nation becomes the victim nation, and its stories transform that pain into moral, spiritual, and, ultimately, national virtue.

CONSTRUCTING FEMALENESS

In enka, "femaleness" follows the predictable lines of beauty, passivity, and longing. Female songwriters, as noted earlier, are few,[1] although significantly more women than men occupy the enka stage and concert hall. The genre molds female singers, songs, and subjectivities in its own male-dominant image. As a result, the discourse and performance of femaleness are determined by the men who control the genre rather than by the women who people it.

In enka, a woman is defined primarily by onna-gokoro (woman's heart): she is old-fashioned, out of step with modern times, and (traditionally) virtuous to the point of ridicule:

furui onna to warewareyō to	People may laugh at me, an old-fashioned woman,
hada wa dare ni mo yurusanai	But I will not surrender my body to anyone else [but you, who have died].

"Sake Kizuna" (Bonds of Sake) (1993)

Her heart also makes her foolishly stubborn in love.

onna-gokoro no oroka yue	It is all because of the foolishness of a woman's heart.

"Taki no Shiraito" [woman's stage name] (1988)

baka ne baka na onna ne	Foolish, huh? I was a foolish woman, wasn't I?
iji o hatteta watashi	I was foolishly stubborn.

"Yuki-guni" (Snow Country) (1986)

The inner life of her heart contrasts with her outer, physical beauty. Enka songs frequently remark on the transience of female beauty:

inochi o moyasu kisetsu wa mijikai	The season in which one's life burns brightly is short;
mashite onna no kirei na toki wa	Much shorter is the time when a woman is beautiful.

"Higurashi" (Cicada) (1993)

onna no sakari wa atto iu ma desu	A woman's prime is gone before you know it

"Hanamachi no Haha" (Flower Town [Geisha Quarters] Mother) (1973)

While her heart remains loyal, even foolishly so, her beauty (and thus her desirability) fades quickly.

A woman is, by definition, one who is socially embedded as daughter, lover, wife, mother. She is always part of a larger human unit. One of the most searing images, therefore, is that of *"onna hitori,"* a woman alone, socially adrift, untethered by the bonds of *ryōsai-kenbo* (good wife, wise mother), one of modern Japan's primary historicized female models. Of course, the woman is alone not by choice, and in no other way does she parade her failure more symbolically than by drinking alone. Like eating, drinking (especially alcohol) is supposed to be a social activity, whose etiquette requires that one pour another's drink or be served by another. Drinking alone, especially *tejaku-zake* (pouring oneself a drink of sake), thus takes on poignant significance as a lonely act. When the solitary drinker is a woman, its social transgressiveness increases:

inaka-zukuri no izakaya de	At this rustic-looking tavern
onna hitori no shinobi-ame	I [a woman] sit alone, drinking furtively.

"Ame Sakaba" (Rainy Night at a Bar) (1988)

onna hitori no sabishisa ni	I cling to the loneliness of a woman all by herself;
sugaru yo-ake no tejaku-zake	As dawn breaks, and I pour myself some sake.

"Tejaku-zake" (Pouring Myself Some Sake) (1992)

In these songs, woman is constructed as a victim of men's actions; the result is "the loneliness of a woman." Her position contrasts markedly with that portrayed in some American country and western songs, especially those written by women, which, through their anger and defiance, even threat of retaliation, proclaim an end to victimhood and mistreatment by men. The female enka songs I analyzed, however, express little anger or defiance and threaten no retaliation. Among these songs, the strongest expression of assertiveness appeared in "Sasori-za no Onna" (Scorpio Woman), a female song sung by a male singer (discussed in "Crossing Gender Lines" later in this chapter). The larger kata of "femaleness" is neatly summed up in the following lines:

moete koboreru onna no	I burn with desire and fall—
nasake . . .	the compassion of a woman . . .
nurete setsunai onna no	I am drenched with sadness—
namida . . .	the tears of a woman . . .
tsuite ikenai onna no kokoro	I cannot be with the one I love—
	the heart of a woman.

"Fuyu no Eki" (Winter Train Station) (1993)

"Compassion," "tears," "heart"—these define the enka woman, but they are themselves defined by the men who cast her as a victim of her own heart and the men she loves.

The kata of "femaleness" is also expressed in the musical patterning of enka. As noted earlier, composers of enka report that women's songs use a minor key more often than men's songs. Although I have not analyzed a large enough sample to be able to confirm this assertion, it is significant that composers themselves think in these terms, or at least say they do. Women's songs also tend to be slightly slower and less rhythmically driven than men's songs. A female singer is more likely to manipulate her voice to impart a sense of intimacy or pain, using techniques such as the whisper (PK-10), the sigh (PK-11), the groan (PK-12), and the sob (PK-13) (see Chapter 5). The female voice more readily exploits a break in the vocal register (PK-8), taking on a sobbing quality.

The intimacy conveyed through the female voice is matched by the intimacy expressed through bodily kata. In wearing the kimono, the female singer becomes emblematic of "traditional Japan." Although the kimono and its aesthetic restrict her outward movement and focus her attention inward, she might occasionally stretch out an arm in a gesture of longing. More than male singers, she "dances" throughout her performance, her movements small (sometimes barely perceptible beneath her kimono), graceful, curving, and artfully controlled—not action as much as aestheticized inaction.

Stereotypical stage effects reinforce this version of "femaleness." Foremost among these special effects is simulated fog, which is used most often during performances by female singers. The fog seeps onto the darkened stage, sometimes unrolling slowly like a carpet, sometimes swirling in a cloud around the feet of the spotlighted figure to create a dreamlike setting.

In televised performances, the camerawork, especially in shots of female singers, enhances this dreamlike quality. Although it is often static—a stationary camera captures the performer from the front—the camerawork sometimes aids in evoking a subjective world of fantasy. Female singers in particular are shot in extreme close-up and from the side rather than the front. One unusual camera angle is the pan from the rear to one side, taking in part of the shoulder, the nape of the neck, the tip of one ear, and the lower half of the face, as if the viewer were looking over the singer's shoulder from the intimate vantage point of a lover. Another unusual shot, one also more often used in photographing female singers, is the close-up of the singer looking off into the distance at an angle to the camera. What makes this so unusual is her position within the shot, gazing off beyond the edge of the frame—at what, we do not know. Her gaze finds no resolution.

A final noteworthy camera shot, one that I have seen used only with female singers in kimono, is the slow vertical pan from a tabi-clad foot to the top of a carefully coiffed head. This long pan, which subjects the objectified surface of the singer to a stereotypical "once-over," is electronically transmitted to thousands of television viewers. To a certain extent, the object of the gaze is the kimono, a wash of color and design: the eye follows the folds and the pattern of the fabric as the lens traverses the female body. The person encased within the kimono, however, is objectified by the camera's movement. Viewed in an angled close-up or as a full-length canvas, the singer subject to such scrutiny—and her pain—becomes an exquisite object of art.

Constructing Maleness

Enka songs about men, as noted earlier, speak of otoko-michi (the path of a man). The essence of being a man is committing oneself to a single path or dream and following it "to the end." In "Otoko-michi" (The Path of a Man), these lessons are passed down from father to son:

ichi-do kokoro ni kizanda	Once I etch a dream in my
yume wa	heart,

nani ga nan demo yari tōsu	I will pursue it, no matter what.
tsurai namida ya kuyashisa o	I will store my bitter tears and regrets
hara ni osamete niō-dachi	In my gut, standing firm with feet apart.
taete miseru ga	To endure and show one's face,
taete miseru ga otoko-michi	To endure and show one's face is the path of a man.
giri to ninjō no furi-wake nimotsu	"Within the heart of a man lies the double burden
se-ou otoko no mune no uchi	Of giri [duty] and ninjō [feelings]."
oyaji anta no kuchi-guse o	Father, I kept your favorite sayings
kokoro ni himete doko made mo	Concealed in my heart wherever I went.
yume o sakasu ga	The flowering of my dream,
yume o sakasu ga ore no michi	The flowering of my dream is this path of mine.

"Otoko-michi" (The Path of a Man) (1991)

Whereas women's faces and bodies display high emotion, those of men display stoicism. Even when men feel as deeply as women, songs like these imply that their feelings must be "stored" (in the words of the song), or kept inside, rather than exhibited. In fact, "storing" one's emotions is considered a sign of masculine strength, just as emotional display is considered a feminine art. While women's songs dwell on the private emotions of romance, men's songs tend to focus on more public emotions—the conflict between duty and human feelings (giri-ninjō) or longing for furusato.

In enka, a man stands alone, not, like a woman, in loneliness, but in spiritual strength, which helps him to endure:

yaru to kimetara otoko ja nai ka	I am a man, therefore I will do what I have set my mind to do.
hito ga waratte mo tada hito-suji ni	Even if people laugh, I will earnestly
ikiru zo jinsei o	Live my life!
moero moero moero	Let us burn, burn, burn!
(fuērmu furēmu furēmu)	(Flame, flame, flame)
honō no yō ni	Like a flame!
ai ai ai raiku enka . . .	I, I, I like enka! . . .
kaketa otoko no michi naraba	If this is the road of a man

	who wagered his life,
kui wa nai	Then I have no regrets.

"Honō" (Flame) (1992)

This song's premise lies in the poetics of "I am a man, therefore...." A man's spiritual strength and zeal come "naturally," as if they are a by-product of male hormones. The enka male antihero rises up committed to his path, even in the face of social censure. Passion, without regret, paves otoko-michi (here, *otoko no michi*, the "burning"). The song expresses this passion in part through repetition, including a phrase of English (ai ai ai raiku enka /I, I, I like enka), which is somewhat unusual for the genre.[2] Curiously, although enka is directly implicated, the actual connection between song and passion is not made clear.

Not all constructions of "maleness" in enka display this public virility. As several song lyrics attest, "to be strong is not all there is to being a man" (e.g., "Honō" [Flame], 1992; "Otoko no Jōwa" [A Man's Love Story], 1989; "Senshū Harukikō," [old name for Osaka Harbor], 1992). In love, a man's heart weeps just as a woman's does.

sake ga furaseta otoko no	The sake makes my tears flow—
namida	the tears of a man.

"Suika" (Drunken Song) (1990)

This show of heart, of private vulnerability, infuses the construction of "maleness" with greater complexity. A man is one who may be outwardly strong but inwardly vulnerable to love and heartbreak.

A man learns the lessons of attachment at his mother's knee, but he also learns them through homosocial bonds—father to son, brother to brother, buddy to buddy. Far more often than women's songs, men's songs express deep attachments between persons of the same sex. Just as the song "Otoko-michi" (The Path of a Man) tells of the lessons of life learned from a father, the following song tells of blood-based affective ties between brothers and between father and son:

kyōdai-bune wa oyaji no katami	This ship of brothers is the pride of our father.
kata wa furui ga shike ni wa tsuyoi ...	It may be old, but in a storm, it is strong ...
keredomo oki no ryōba ni tsukeba	When we arrive at the fishing grounds of the open seas,

yake ni ki no au kyōdai-	We become brother gulls who
kamome	pull together fiercely.
chikara awasete yo ami o	We join forces and hoist our
maki-ageru....	nets....
yo oyaji	It is hot, this blood of ours,
yuzuri da ze	passed down from our father.

"Kyōdai-bune" (Ship of Brothers) (1982)

A father passes down to his sons not only a boat but a way of life based on brotherly interdependence and passion. This way of life allows father and sons to withstand the natural elements and to harness them to make a living.

Another kind of homosociality exists between friends:

...naniwa-machi	... In this town of Naniwa [Osaka],
hoshi no kazu hodo aru sono	Where there are as many people
naka no	as there are stars,
tatta futari ga shiri-atte	The two of us became friends,
otoko-dōshi no sake o kumu	And now drink together as buddies.[3]

"Otoko-bore" (Admiration Between Men) (1992)

Men "bare their souls" to each other through drink; many men's songs address the general public or other men. Most women's songs, in contrast, are almost soliloquies addressed to oneself or to an absent lover.

Constructions of "maleness" emphasizing positive action, strength, and inner drive are given distinctive musical expression. The compositional musical kata of maleness (see Chapter 5) are reputed to make more frequent use of major keys and faster tempos, and to demonstrate a greater sense of rhythmic drive. Men's performative kata include such vocal techniques as the guttural rasp (PK-14), the grunt (PK-15), and the nonsemantic shout. These sometimes explosive utterances convey an impression of energy released, not controlled.

Physically, male singers hold a different position on the "slide-rule" of performer-audience interaction (see Chapter 4) than female singers. They are less aestheticized, less theatrical, less performative. Some simply stand on stage facing the audience and sing (see Chapter 5). Others move rhythmically to the music, although no more so than crooners in the United States and elsewhere, their movements conveying energy but not necessarily grace.

Although men feel and cry, most of the drama, tension, and tear-filled emotion rests with women.

Crossing Gender Lines

The kata of gender provides a language that makes crossing the lines of gender on the enka stage not only possible but quite reasonable. If "femaleness" and "maleness" are constructs built upon kata, then theoretically, anyone can perform them. "Crossing" in enka—whether this refers to a female singing a man's song or to a male fully costumed as a woman—shows kata as sheer performance, unburdened by the biological housing of the male or female body.[4] And far from being some kind of fringe or avant-garde stage presentation, such crossing is a part of national culture.[5]

The simplest form of crossing is through song. Men's songs and women's songs are differentiated by language and by narrative. In enka, male and female singers may sing both types with lyrics unchanged. The song is itself a kind of kata that is separate from the singer. It is important to note, however, that the question of who sings which song is not completely open to chance. In other words, it is not all a matter of kata. If it were, then half of men's songs would be sung by females, and half by males. Instead, the majority of men's songs are sung by male singers. But it is also true that a Japanese audience does not consider it unusual for a female singer to sing a man's song or for a male singer to sing a woman's song.

"Funa-uta" (Sailor's Song), for example, is a man's song made famous by Yashiro Aki, a female singer known for performing in a full, floor-length evening gown and a sparkling tiara.

o-sake wa nurume no kan ga ii	I prefer my sake warmed up.
sakana wa abutta ika de ii	I prefer grilled squid for a chaser.
onna wa mukuchi na hito ga ii	I prefer women who don't talk too much.
akari wa bon-yari tomorya ii	I prefer lights that are dim.
shimi-jimi nomeba shimi-jimi to	If I drink to the core, then
omoide dake ga yukisugiru	Only those memories from the core will come flooding back.
namida ga porori to koboretara	When my tears well up and spill over,
utai-dasu no sa funa-uta o	I begin to sing the sailor's song.

oki no kamome ni fuka-zake sasete yo	Let the seagulls get drunk so that
itoshi ano ko to yo asane suru dancho ne	I can sleep late in the morning with my sweet maiden.

"Funa-uta" (Sailor's Song) (1979)

During her performance, Yashiro gives no hint in her dress, make-up, gestures, or vocal intonation that this is a man's song. She sings it as she would any love song, in a straightforward manner.

Male singers also sing women's songs, lyrics unchanged, and for some, this kind of crossing has become the basis of a singing career. Mori Shin'ichi (see Chapter 6), for example, is known as "a woman's man" because he sings both women's songs (i.e., crossed) and songs about mother (i.e., uncrossed). When he performs, he usually wears a tuxedo, giving no physical hint of the crossed nature of some of his performances. His fans, primarily female, say that he understands women's feelings especially well, although it is unclear whether this empathy is innate or whether he learned it from the songs.

A few female enka singers extend "crossing" beyond song to gesture and singing style. A case in point is Sakamoto Fuyumi (see Chapter 3), whose manager has deliberately contrived a cross-gendered image for her. The following is an excerpt from her debut man's song:[6]

guchi wa iu-mai genkai sodachi	I am not one to complain; I was raised on the rough seas of Genkai.
otoko inochi o nasake ni kakete	I put all my manly passion into
tataku taiko no abare-uchi	The wild beating of the drum.
sake to kenka wa ato e wa hikanu	No one can match me when it comes to drinking sake or fighting.

"Abare-daiko" (Wild Drums) (1987)

Sakamoto's performance is partially mimetic. She adopts some men's kata, using drum-beating gestures, clenched fists, and extra-musical grunts. Yet in her hair, clothing (*furisode*, the long-sleeved kimono of an unmarried girl), make-up, and gestural grace she retains women's kata. Her expressions of masculinity are highly contained and stylized, even feminized. Sakamoto always appears *onnarashii* (feminine), even when her femininity encompasses these quasi-men's kata. In fact, her use of men's kata eroticizes her image, placing her in "anodyne modes" of "manly passion" (Senelick 1993: 81).

A performer whose crossing goes beyond song and gesture to include costuming and make-up is Mikawa Ken'ichi (b. 1946), a male enka singer who, after his debut in 1965, successfully boosted his career by gradually adopting more feminine clothes, make-up, and mannerisms, and singing women's songs. He designs many of the outfits he wears; in 1994, a well-known Tokyo department store held an exhibition of his costumes.

Mikawa's crossing is partially mimetic but still within well-defined limits. He never wears a dress or a skirt, yet any viewer would interpret his clothes as feminine. He favors beaded pant suits, tunics with loose pants, or glittery hip-length jackets and pants in bright (female coded) colors; on one televised variety show he wore ensembles of emerald green, canary yellow, and cerulean blue, one after the other. He may accessorize his outfits with a turban, a long scarf, or a feather boa. On his feet, however, he wears low pumps rather than high heels, and even these are discreetly hidden by the hem of his pants. His hair is styled in an ear-length unisex bob that sweeps across his forehead, and his make-up is modest. He also favors rings and gold chains but never wears earrings.

The songs he sings, such as "Sasori-za no Onna" (Scorpio Woman), his signature song, are women's songs:

iie watashi wa sasori-za no onna	Well, I am a Scorpio woman.
oki-no-sumu made warau ga ii wa	You may laugh all you like.
anata wa asobi no tsumori demo	Even if you only intend to love me in jest,
jigoku no hate made tsuite yuku	I will follow you to the ends of hell.
omoi kondara inochi- inochi-	If I have fallen head over heels in love,
inochi-gake yo	Then it's for life.
sō yo watashi wa sasori-za no onna	Yes, I am a Scorpio woman
sasori no hoshi wa ichizu na hoshi yo	And a person born under the Scorpio constellation loves with all her heart.

"Sasori-za no Onna" (Scorpio Woman) (1972)

When Mikawa, wearing his characteristic clothing, hair style, and make-up, and swaying to the music in a female-kata gesture, sings these words in his low, nasal, obviously masculine voice, the effect is nothing short of striking.

Unlike Sakamoto's crossing, which eroticizes, Mikawa's serves as a neutering device that makes him a safe haven for the middle-aged housewives who are his primary fans. An entertainer like Mikawa can create a cross-gendered spectacle unlinked to any particular sexual orientation. Various Japanese with whom I spoke emphatically denied that Mikawa is homosexual; in fact, they considered him asexual. His fans like him, according to a fan club spokesperson, because he sings women's songs and understands women's feelings. His crossing allows him access to the emotions of these female fans while posing no (hetero)sexual threat.[7]

One of the most fascinating examples of crossing within the tangential reaches of the enka world is Umezawa Tomio, nicknamed "Shitamachi no Tamasaburō" (Downtown's Tamasaburō) after the well-known kabuki *onnagata* (male performer of female roles), Tamasaburō.[8] Umezawa performs as a member of Umezawa Takeo Gekidan, a family-based itinerant troupe, in a vaudeville-like form of entertainment called taishū engeki (theater of the masses), about which Marilyn Ivy has written extensively (1995: 192–239). As she points out, this form of theater represents "an older, vanishing aesthetic that is rooted in a conception of the *taishū* [the masses] as down-home, lower-middle-class, and raised on the pre-war ethics and aesthetics of samurai drama" (1995: 209).

A typical performance by this troupe is much like the enka performance I describe in the Prologue. It includes 1) period drama; 2) a song show, during which Umezawa appears as the troupe's crooner; and 3) a dance revue of quasi-classical dance, during which Umezawa appears as the troupe's onnagata. A commercial video of Umezawa's performances, *Mei Bamen Shū* (Collection of Famous Scenes), highlights his artistry. Dressed and made up as a woman, he is sultry and erotic, his eyelids half-lowered, his lips half-parted. His hair (a wig), strands of which trail down the sides of his face, is on the verge of disarray. His kimono is open at the neck and down the back in an exaggerated fashion. Within a kimono aesthetic that emphasizes the nape of a woman's neck as visually erotic, Umezawa Tomio not only exposes the nape of his neck, he allows his kimono to plunge almost halfway down his back. Several still shots in the publicity brochure that accompanies his

Taishū engeki Performer Walking Near Congratulatory Displays

performance show him holding a scarf or a sleeve in his teeth, a gesture not uncommon in the premodern period but one which today, in combination with his make-up, hair, dress, and demeanor, suggests a smoldering sexuality. His appearance is one of complete and seductive mimesis.

It is interesting to note that the troupe includes female members who could perform the women's parts. Umezawa, however, does not play the part of a woman; he is an onnagata, a representation of womanhood constructed by men and for men.[9] The erotic, premodern onnagata and the suave modern male crooner are contained within one person and within successive acts of the same performance. Umezawa crosses temporal and gender boundaries with sensual ease, and in so doing, becomes one of the most potent examples of gender as kata.

In the historically linked context of the taishū engeki stage, crossing (male to female) occurs more completely because of the frank performance of gender. Likewise, in period dramas, female enka singers may appear as swashbuckling swordsmen (female to male crossing). In modern enka stage contexts, however, crossing has its limits. In general, male singers do not adopt women's clothes or movements, although they may sing women's songs. The few who do, such as Mikawa Ken'ichi, depoliticize their transgressive actions through self-deprecating humor and careful attention to the boundaries placed upon crossing. Put simply, one is freer to cross and to do so more completely in a kimono (coded as Japanese and historic) than in an evening gown or tuxedo (coded as Western and "modern"). This points not only to the interrelationship of the past and the present in Japan, but also to the complexity of the resulting gender system.

What are the effects of these crossed performances? How do notions of "femaleness" and "maleness" iterate targets of the cultural imaginary? When a female sings a man's song, her performance is considered chic, *furesshu* (fresh), even *sekushii* (sexy), as having a sense of *iki* (stylishness), an evaluation that for the most part addresses only the concerns of male desire (cf. Mulvey 1989). When a male sings a woman's song, however, his performance is considered sensitive and empathetic, and while these qualities may evoke female desire, they also convey significant cultural values that embed him tightly within the social order. In effect, what these crossed performances demonstrate is that the cultural imagination places women at men's (sexual) service, but men at society's service. The persistence of these performances on the enka stage is thus a running commentary on constructions of femaleness and maleness, and on the interactions of women and men in heteronormative romance.

THE KATA OF ROMANCE

Women and men connect, as sexual beings, through the structures of hetero-normative romance, which determine the circumstances—the ways, reasons, and objects—of desire. In enka, the kata of romance is framed as a negotiation between desire and duty, between the individual and the group, and between the heart and the nation.

In enka, a distinctive aspect of romance is its brevity. At the extreme, romance may be as fleeting as a one-night stand or *"wan naito rabu"* (one-night love), as the song "Ma-yonaka no Shawā" (Shower in the Middle of the Night) puts it:

ma-yonaka ni atsui shawā o abite	In the middle of the night, I took a hot shower.
natsu ga kureta wan naito rabu	The "one-night love" which summer bestowed upon me

shizuku ni shite mita kedo	Is what I tried to wash away with each drop of water,
sore wa munashii doryoku mitai	But it seems that my efforts were in vain.
kagami no naka de aitai kokoro ga tokimeku	In the mirror, my heart, which wants to be with you, throbs.

"Ma-yonaka no Shawā" (Shower in the Middle of the Night) (1990)

And again,

shinu made kono koi moyashite itai	I want this love to burn until death,
hito-yo no nasake ni mi o makase	This one-night love to which I surrender.

"Kizuna-gawa" (River of Bonds) (1992)

This "one night" pattern informs an extremely poignant view of romance as the stuff of dreams, fantasy, and illusion. This is not romance lived but romance imagined. The prime imaginer is the woman, who fabricates romance out of passion and contrives commitment out of capricious fancy. For her, "one night" initiates an eternity of loyalty and longing. She anchors her love in a fleeting moment of happiness and proves its value through her subsequent devotion and desire.

In clichéd metaphors of fleetingness, enka songs express the evanescence of happiness:

shiawase mijikai ichinen sō	Happiness is brief for an annual plant.
hōsenka hōsenka	Touch-me-not flower, touch-me-not flower!

"Hōsenka" (Touch-me-not Flowers) (1981)

hanabi mitai na hito-yo demo	Even if our one last night is fleeting like fireworks, ...
koi wa hakanai koi wa hakanai niwaka-ame	Love is fleeting, love is fleeting, Like a sudden rain shower.

"Niwaka-ame" (Sudden Rain Shower) (1991)

Here again, evanescence is not merely a fact of life but a criterion of aesthetic value. The beauty of a flower (like the beauty of a woman) is that much more precious because it is perishable. So, too, romance is that much more cherished because it is transitory.

In these songs, men's and women's roles are dichotomous by nature:

otoko ni wa hito-toki de sugiteku arashi	For a man, love is a mere passing storm;
onna tadayou kami no fune	But for a woman, love drifts on in a paper boat.

"Kami no Fune" (Paper Boat) (1991)

otoko no koi wa hito-yo no nasake	A man's love is the tenderness of a single night.
onna no koi wa shinu hi made	But a woman's love lasts until the day of death.

"Nakase Ame" (Rain Which Makes One Cry) (1991)

A woman's love gains cultural value through its single-mindedness and its loyalty. At the same time, it makes her an object of ridicule, as in "Sake Kizuna" (Bonds of Sake), "Taki no Shiraito" (woman's stage name), and "Yukiguni" (Snow Country) quoted earlier: people laugh at the "old-fashioned woman," at the "fool." Ironically, a man also possesses single-mindedness and loyalty, but for different ends and more public purposes, and with no hint of ridicule. In these songs of romance, both women and men are seen as noble, but women's nobility is trivialized by its romantic focus.

Another important aspect of romance in enka is its reliance upon fate.

umareru mae kara musubarete ita	We were connected even before we were born—
sonna ki ga suru beni no ito	This is the red thread of fate that I feel.
dakara shinu made futari wa issho	Therefore, we will be together until death.

"Inochi Kurenai" (Crimson Life of Passion) (1986)

Fate, viewed so often in these songs as a river, becomes an immutable force moving along a predetermined course. On this river of fate, women and men can do no better than to accept its course, which guides life and love, as their own and try to stay afloat. Fate determines everything about romance: who loves, for how long, under what circumstances, and with what result.

The ways in which men and women love are also patterned. Men love actively, even passionately, but leave abruptly. Women, on the other hand, love passively, sometimes pleadingly, as in the following woman's song:

suteru koto mo kamawanai	I don't care if I throw my life away,
dakara onegai soba ni oite ne	Just please let me be here by your side.

"Nagare ni Mi o Makase" (Surrender to the Flow of Time) (1986)

Women love by giving all they have:

kono inochi hoshii nara	If you want my life,
itsu demo shinde misemasu wa	I would die in a moment and present it to you.

"Kaze no Bon Koi Uta" (Love Song of Owara *Bon* Festival) (1989)

kokoro kokoro kokoro kokoro	Heart, heart, heart, heart!
kokoro agemasu onna no kokoro	I give you my heart, this heart of a woman.
hoka ni nan ni mo nai ageru mono nante	I have nothing else To give.

"Onna no Defune" (Woman of the Sailing Ship) (1983)

The tone of these songs is one of unabashed begging and pleading—in some cases even groveling—yet women's offers of their lives and love to men go unheeded. A woman clings and waits:

mi-sutenai de to sugatte mo	Even if I cling to you, begging you not to forsake me,
yurete omokage	Your flickering visage
tō-zakaru tō-zakaru	Grows distant, grows distant.

"Nakase Ame" (Rain Which Makes One Cry) (1991)

watashi itsu made machimasu to	Tell the ship [with my lover aboard] in one brief moment
fune ni tsutaeru tsuka no ma o	That I will wait forever.

"Namida no San-bashi" (Wharf of Tears) (1987)

Men leave without warning or explanation:

doko e iku to mo iwanai de	Without saying where he was going
yo-ake ano hito fune no ue ...	He left aboard the ship at dawn....

nani mo oshiezu iku nante	He left without telling me anything.
ikanai de ikanai de	Please, do not go, do not go,
ikianai de	Do not go!

"Namida no San-bashi" (Wharf of Tears) (1987)

On the river of fate, men appear and disappear, leaving women the victims.

The one-sidedness of this version of romance is unremitting. Inasmuch as a woman may be defined by her loyalty in love, a man may be defined by his disloyalty, even alongside his loyalty in public affairs. According to this convention, a man is one who leaves the woman who loves him, while upholding the moral fabric of the community and the state.

Women (and men) love because they were so destined; but just as their love is destined, so too is their heartbreak. The following example shows a kata of parting that is situated in the past:

namida namida namida namida	Tears, tears, tears, tears!
namida karete mo kareru na koi yo	Even if my tears run dry, it won't mean that my love has withered.
fune ni watashi wa noru	I board the ship, while
anata san-bashi de	You remain on the pier.
shiroi tēpu o hiku	The white streamers unfurl—
o-wakare hatoba	The pier of parting.
sayonara sayonara onna no defune	Goodbye, goodbye! I am a woman of the sailing ship.

"Onna no Defune" (Woman of the Sailing Ship) (1983)

The ship recedes slowly in the distance, a gradual, drawn-out process and one that gives this kind of parting a particular poignancy. Moreover, the "white streamers" thrown by the person on the ship to the person left behind on the pier become a last physical bond uniting the two. As the ship departs, the streamer unfurls until finally, it can connect the two no longer. The result, symbolized by the streamer, is heartbreak.

For a woman, heartbreak rapidly transforms itself to *miren* (lingering affection), but I have heard of only a few instances in which miren was used in reference to men. This kind of structural poignancy seems to be the purview of women, as passive in heartbreak as they are in loving:

onna-gokoro no miren deshō	Is this the lingering affection of a woman's heart?

"Kita no Yado kara" (From an Inn in the North Country) (1975)

aa miren tsunaide	Ah, but I [a woman] cannot help this lingering affection.

"Ame Yo-zake" (Sake on a Rainy Night) (1988)

Lingering affection, considered foolish yet normalized as a part of "femaleness," gives the woman a certain moral currency. She exemplifies loyalty, beauty, and passivity. Within an aesthetic built on pathos and evanescence, her love, in miren, becomes exquisite and touching.

The combination, however, is also volatile. In a tumult of emotion, she may love and hate at the same time:

itoshiku natte wa nikuku naru	Loving you can also mean hating you.

"Kizuna-gawa" (River of Bonds) (1992)

ai suru kimochi to onaji dake	My feelings of love are matched by
midarete saite mo hana wa hana	My growing feelings of hate.

"Midare-bana" (Strewn Flowers) (1988)

anata urande koishigaru	[My lips] Will not forgive you, yet long for you.

"Koi-bune" (Boat of Love) (1990)

hada ga samishii hada ga samishii	My body is so lonely, my body is so lonely.

"Koi Banka" (Love's Elegy) (1991)

In many enka songs, the failure of romance is culturally structured but individually wrought. In others, however, the failure is culturally structured and socially wrought. What keeps men and women apart is society itself:

suki de soenai hito no yo o	I cry with bitterness toward a world that keeps me apart from the one I love.

"Kanashii Sake" (Sorrowful Sake) (1966)

Whatever the specific reasons for societal censure—barriers of social class, family feud, morals—they themselves are less important than the fact that they are unchangeable and insurmountable.

These romantic relationships must be conducted in secret, hidden from "the eyes of the world" and the glaring social spotlight of gossip.

hito-me shinonde fune o kogu	Hiding from the eyes of the world, we will ply our boat....
yukue mo shirenu saza-nami no	Without knowing our destination, we find the ripples of
uwasa ga tsurai ko-no-ha-bune ...	Gossip harsh on our boat of leaves.

Kinokawa" (Kinokawa River [Wakayama Prefecture]) (1991)[10]

Through gossip, the "eyes of the world" become effective watchdogs against infractions of the moral and ethical code.

Romance in these songs goes against the grain of the social order. Individual desire is at odds with the family, the village, and, potentially, the nation. Lovers become violators of the moral code. And yet the stages of romance—meeting by chance, loving, parting, and longing—in effect reaffirm the values that hold the nation together: acceptance of fate, emotional strength, endurance of hardship, and perseverance. Those who go against the grain, in an ironic turnabout, become upholders of the nation's values.

These melodramatic patterns of romance may not be literal reflections of everyday lives, but they are grounded in what is construed as a common heart, one that can empathize with them to the point of tears. The ultimate failure of romance and the heart-wrenching longing portrayed in enka songs become metaphors (if exaggerated) for the everyday processes and practices of ordinary people. Fans of enka assert the contiguity between the highly saturated lives of the songs' characters and their own relatively ordinary lives. I would contend that the contiguity rests in shared tears—there public, here private. These melodramas also suggest larger cultural lessons. Men and women fall in love stereotypically, defining themselves through action (or inaction). The active man who loves and leaves holds controlling power. The passive woman who loves and longs grovels in powerlessness, her life bound up in tension, emotion, and internal drama. Men and women both play victim to fate and society, the larger forces that control them.

What does the enka version of romance give women? In important ways, it subverts the nineteenth-century "good wife, wise mother" paradigm upon which the modern Japanese nation was built, replacing it with a "mistress, bar hostess" paradigm of female antiheroes at the margins of society. And if its cast of characters is subversive, so also is its glorification of their actions—engaging in illicit love affairs, fleeing from social scorn, hiding from the eyes of the world—which contradict the culture's idealization of the family, the village, and the nation. At the same time, the songs endorse the moral substance underlying the traditional paradigm: sincerity, loyalty, and devotion.

Failure is intrinsic to the enka version of romance. In their unfulfilled longing, enka songs create a bond of suffering between singer and audience, and between listener and listener, a pact sealed in tears that draws the nation closer together. Emotional bonds born of romance are sustained by its failure. By negotiating between desire and duty, the individual and the group, romance constructs nationhood. It is a nationhood in affirmation of what is considered "right" about "traditional" Japan: warmth of human feeling, loyalty to commitment, duty. It is also a nationhood that negates what is considered "wrong" about modern Japan: urban anonymity, electronic dehumanization, a waning sense of personal loyalty. Ultimately, it is a nationhood built on the glorification of suffering—in romance, but also in the workplace, on the factory line, in the home. In romance, as in contemporary Japan, one accepts the flow of fate and suffers valiantly and passively, one's private tears falling unchecked.

Longing for Furusato

Tears of longing also flow for furusato (hometown). In enka's imaginary, furusato creates what is perceived to be a particularly (although not exclusively) male arena of longing.

"Virtual" Furusato

The close link between enka and furusato is epitomized in such television broadcasts as Terebi Tokyo's weekly daytime song show *Enka no Furusato* (The Hometown of Enka), whose final program aired in March 1993. Each program featured a "rural" region of Japan and brought representatives of the region together with several enka singers and the two regular (male and female) hosts. The regional representatives usually included a member of the local tourist board, who displayed the *meibutsu* (well-known products of the area) and offered regional food for tasting. At the end of the show, the hosts produced a map of the area and explained how to get there from Tokyo. Through shows like these, enka, furusato, and tourism have become discursively linked.

Enka no Furusato's opening sequence deserves closer scrutiny because it introduces some of the iconography of furusato (cf. Daniels and Cosgrove 1988).[11] The program title, superimposed on a background shot of a castle, links the present not merely to a premodern past, when those inhabiting such castles held power, but to a seventeenth- and eighteenth-century past, when regional castle towns (*jōka machi*) dominated the country economically and politically. The next shot, a blur of green, gradually comes into focus as a close-up of maple leaves. Green—a signifier of nature, freshness, and youth—is one of the most common visual evocations of furusato. The final shot, a train crossing a bridge over a ravine and heading into a tunnel, is, on closer inspection, not an ordinary electric train but an old-fashioned steam-powered locomotive with open-air cars transporting tourists deep into the mountainous countryside.[12]

Although each week's program purported to showcase a specific area of Japan, discussion was not restricted to that area. The enka singers sang songs with no relationship to the featured region, and when they talked about their own furusato, which might or might not be the featured region, what they said could also apply to many others. The result was a generalized discussion of furusato tied together through enka.

Comments about furusato tended to focus on several themes: 1) it is peaceful and quiet; 2) it has many beautiful natural features; 3) it is a place where one can hear, see, and smell nature (e.g., the sound of cicadas, the color green, the fragrance of flowers); 4) the food is especially good (and there are often specific references to the freshness of the harvest); 5) there are *onsen* (hot springs); 6) there are matsuri (festivals); 7) there are rice paddies, evocative of Japan's agrarian, rice-based past; 8) one's childhood there was blissful; 9) one's parents are there, especially one's mother.

The version of furusato portrayed here, however, is sanitized: there is no talk of the long hours of labor, the poverty, the lack of modern amenities, the depopulation, or the gossip prevalent in small towns. This furusato is sensualized: program guests are asked to taste the products of the region, and at least one invariably comments on smell, whether in reference to the food they are sampling or a new perfume made from regional flowers, or they recall the pleasure of bathing in the hot waters at the onsen, with its particular smells and sensations. This furusato is commodified: one can buy a taste of it or a piece of it as a souvenir. Finally, this furusato is exoticized: it is "hometown" seen from afar, a Tokyo resident's nostalgic tourist destination. Nobody claims they want to live there; they only want to visit.

Even those television shows that do not overtly attempt to establish this kind of link between enka and furusato do in fact assume such a link. The major enka television program of the 1990s was Terebi Tokyo's primetime weekly show *Enka no Hanamichi* ("Flower Way"/Stage Passage of Enka; see Chapter 4). In a special interview marking the fifteenth anniversary of the show, producer Hashiyama Atsushi explained its purpose: "I want to create a furusato of emotions. Everyone probably has a furusato, a place to which he or she wants to return. Probably people who have left their rural hometown, as well as those who have no such rural hometown, have a nostalgic desire to return. However, in reality, there are few people who have the luxury of actually visiting these places. Therefore, the purpose of this program is to give the sense of a temporary return through music and images" (Anonymous 1993d: 14).

Hashiyama's explanation suggests that furusato is no longer a place: it has become a concept, an abstraction, a kind of "atmosphere" (cf. Field 1989). And the more abstract the concept, the more effective the metonymic shorthand. Here, the music and visual images that effect this return to furusato are those of enka, sung in a dimly lit country inn or a forlorn bar on a wharf.[13] For many in the listening and viewing audience whose own life experience does not necessarily include such places, such referents become symbolically evocative. These homelands are theatricalized settings for the emotions defining this version of the nation.

The introductory segment of a January 1993 broadcast of *Enka no Hanamichi* drew on these images of the enka imaginary: "I have nothing but unforgettable memories of that trip to the snowy north country. I think over and over of that person, the awakening of love [*koi-gokoro*] in me. When I look at the sky that flows onward to the north, it touches my heart [*mi ni shimu*]. These are songs of the heart [*kokoro uta*]." These images—snowy north country, memory of past love, and most important, songs of the heart—define enka. The heart is the link between enka's two main themes, failed romance and a yearning for home. Furusato (homeland) becomes the place where the heart is.

Performing Furusato

In the following song, a regional matsuri (festival) that supplies the rhetoric for the local also extends to the national:

(*1.*) *otoko wa matsuri o sōsa*	Men bearing the festival palanquin
katsuide ikite kita	On their shoulders were living life to the fullest.
yama no kami umi no kami	God of the mountains, god of the seas,
kotoshi mo hontō ni arigatō	We truly thank you for this past year.
shiroi fundoshi hiki-shimeta	The snow swirls atop the young men
hadaka wakashu ni yuki ga mau	In white loincloth[s].
matsuri da matsuri da	Festival! Festival!
matsuri da	Festival!
hōnen matsuri	It's a festival for the year of abundance.
tsuchi no nioi no shimi-konda	These young men, who have become permeated with the smell of the earth—
segare sono te ga takaramono	Their hands, which till the soil, are treasures.
(*2.*) *otoko wa matsuri de sōsa*	At the festival men
otoko o migakunda	Honed themselves as men.
yama no kami umi no kami	God of the mountains, god of the seas,
inochi o hontō ni arigatō	We truly thank you for life.
(*3.*) *moero yo namida to ase*	Burn! The life of a man is
koso otoko no roman	one of sweat and tears.
ore mo don-to mata ikite yaru	I am living to the fullest.
kore ga nippon no matsuri da yo	This is a festival of Japan!

"Matsuri" (Festival) (1984)

Although there is in fact no one festival that might be called a "festival of Japan," here the particular is generalized; a local festival becomes a generic festival representing a version of nationhood (Ivy 1995: 12–13).

This song was performed in 1993 by the veteran male singer Kitajima Saburō (see Prologue) as the finale of NHK's 44th annual Kōhaku Uta Gassen (Red and White Song Contest), whose theme was "*kawaranu Nippon*" (unchanging Japan). Through song, particularly through enka, the program presented the nation to itself as unchanging and stubbornly refusing to be changed. Kitajima's performance included a panoply of the symbols of furusato *cum* Japan—cherry blossoms, festival, fans, rice, traditional costume, and enka—amid the public virility of this version of nationhood.

Musically as well, the "exoticism" of enka's vocal technique thrusts it into the enclaves of the furusato imaginary. I use the word *exoticism* to highlight the fact that many of enka's performative kata are not common in the world of popular music. They find precedent instead in Japanese narrative genres, such as *gidayū-bushi* (narrative song in *bunraku* puppet theater) and *naniwa-bushi* (narrative song originally from Osaka). Moreover, the very aesthetic of the genre—that what is important is not a "beautiful voice" but the ability to tell a story effectively or inspire tears—links it to premodern vocal genres.

The intertwining of distant places and times in enka is further confirmed by the language enka singers speak, the image they cultivate, and the clothes they wear. As Godai Natsuko, one of the top "enka bijin" (enka beauties), proclaimed during a Honolulu news conference in July 1994, "I am a real Edokko [Tokyoite of the premodern period, when the city was called Edo] and can only speak Japanese." She invokes not only shitamachi (downtown)/"furusato Tokyo," but also uncosmopolitan "furusato Japan," which projects Tokyo back to Edo, a sophisticated urban culture of nineteenth-century Japan little touched by Western influence.

Female singers invoke the past by wearing kimono, while their male counterparts wear Western suits. Both male and female singers further enhance an image of rootedness in the past by appearing in nonsinging dramatic roles in televised *jidai-geki* (period dramas) most often set in the Tokugawa Era (1600–1867), or in month-long runs of period plays performed in combination with concerts (see Prologue). The past is not remote in time; it is compartmentalized within daily life.

As an "internal exotic," furusato is an important element in enka song texts. Many songs are set outside big cities, often, as their titles suggest—

"Kita-guni no Haru" (Spring in the North Country), "Kita no Daichi" (The Land of the North), and "Kita no Yado Kara" (From an Inn in the North Country), for example—in the wintry countryside of northern Japan. The north becomes a place of "otherness" not only because it is remote but because it involves inherent physical hardship. And as the composer Yoshioka Osamu has discovered, the more remote, the better. One of his most famous songs, "Settchūka," was originally set in Niigata (a prefecture in the northwest of Honshu). Subsequently, however, especially in view of the high-speed trains that linked the area to Tokyo, he decided that Niigata had become too familiar in the public mind and substituted the Echizen *misaki* (cape) in the more remote Fukui prefecture. The song became one of his biggest hits (Nippon Hōsō Kyōkai 1992).[14]

Several songs, such as the duet quoted at the beginning of this chapter, link furusato and romance. "You are my furusato," an image that draws on the emotional ties of kinship and place, becomes the ultimate statement of intimacy. Furusato conjures up family members who live in the hometown but also the lover long ago left behind. The unbridgeable distance between "here" and "there" echoes the heartbreaking sadness of lost love:

umi no tori sae tsubasa o yosete	Even sea birds spread their wings,
haruka kaikyō koete yuku	And cross the broad channel.
shima wa miete mo watarenai	I can see the island, but I cannot cross over to it.
kokoro hiki-saku mujō no umi yo	It tears at my heart—the cruel sea....
aitai yo aitai yo	I long to see you, I long to see you.
umi no mukō ni furusato ga aru	My furusato is there across the sea.
aitai yo aitai yo	I long to be with you, I long to be with you.
shima wa miete mo watarenai	I can see the island, but I cannot cross over to it.
umi no nikurashisa	The sea's heartlessness.

"Mujō no Umi" (Cruel Sea) (1992)

These songs place furusato, like romance, on the far side of a "cruel," "heartless" distance: it is visible but unreachable, and the fact that one can see the object of one's desire (even if only in the mind's eye) increases the frustration. The cultural logic of enka's poetics maintains a constant state of longing. The physical remoteness of furusato is one reason for its desirability: a common refrain is *"Kaeritai kaerenai"* (I want to go home, but I cannot). In fact, the entire discourse of longing, for furusato as for romance, hinges upon the juxtaposition of desire (*-tai*) and failure (*-enai*). Here is Susan Stewart's (1993) "desire for desire" reiterated as unquenchable longing (see Chapter 1).

MOTHER AND FURUSATO

Ties of kinship connect furusato to family, but more specifically, to mother, one's "biological furusato." The figure of mother herself rarely appears in enka songs; she surfaces instead as "mother remembered," especially by sons. The construction of femaleness represented in "mother" is different from that found in romance: these women are not fragile and passive, not victims, but stalwart and active, the practical and emotional backbone of the family. These are "country" women who recuperate a different kind of space within the patriarchy as active shapers of their surroundings.

Memories of mother are primal and sensory. Several enka songs speak nostalgically of mother's breast, of listening to her lullabies and sleeping in her arms:

haha no yasashii te-makura de	Lying on my mother's gentle arm like a pillow,
nemuri-tsuku made komori-uta	I listened to her lullabies until I fell asleep.
yume de yume de mezameta toki wa	I dreamt and dreamt, and upon awakening,
itsumo sagashita haha no mune	I always searched for my mother's breast.

"Haha-goyomi" (Calendar of Memories of Mother) (1988)

ima mo chichi-kusaku hito-suji ni shita	Even now, I earnestly long for the smell of my mother's milk.
haha no omokage namida ga koishii . . .	I yearn to see her face, her tears. . . .
tōku e moshi mo kaereru naraba	If I could only return to that distant time and place.

"Haha-kage" (The Figure of Mother) (1992)

The sensuality with which mother and child coexist, sleeping together and bathing together, becomes a model of national knowing, a cultural ideal of sociality based in infancy and early childhood.

Enka songs also portray the child grown older and able to appreciate mother's wisdom:

o-fukuro-san yo o-fukuro-san	Mother dear, mother dear,
sora o miagerya sora ni aru	I look up to the sky and find memories of you.
ame no furu hi wa kasa ni nari	On rainy days, you are my umbrella;
o-mae mo itsu-ka wa yo no naka no kasa ni nareyo to oshiete kureta	You taught me to become an umbrella For others in this world.
anata no anata no shinjitsu wasure wa shinai	I will never forget The truth of your words.

"O-fukuro-san" (Mother Dear) (1971)

When Mori Shin'ichi sings this song (see Chapter 6), it brings tears to the eyes of his audience, which consists mainly of mothers in their fifties and sixties. "Mother remembered" is furusato, the site of natal origins, the moral standard bearer and spiritual teacher.

Mother is also the bearer of national tradition, the keeper of the household in which Japanese citizens are molded. In the following song, a humble soup served at breakfast, lunch, or dinner, becomes the focus of Japaneseness:

(Serifu) shibareru nē	It's freezing, isn't it?
fuyu wa samui kara miso shiru ga umai n da yo ne	Winter is so cold, making miso soup delicious.
umai miso shiru attakai miso shiru	Delicious miso soup, hot miso soup,
kore ga o-fukuro no aji na n da nē . . .	This is the flavor of my mother, isn't it? . . .
(1.) itsu-ka otona ni natta toki	Why is it that when people become adults,
naze-ka eraso na kao suru ka . . .	they put on fancy airs like big shots . . .
atsui miso shiru nomu tabi	But when they drink hot miso

ni	soup,
omoi-dasu no sa o-fukuro o	they think of their mother
wasurecha naranē otoko iki...	and cannot forget her—such is the male spirit...
(*Serifu*) *neru no wa futon*	We should sleep on futon [mattress],
shitagi wa fundoshi	and our underwear should be *fundoshi* [loincloth],
gohan no koto o raisu da nante	And don't call *gohan* [rice]
iu n ja nai yo	"ra-i-su"!
sore ni shite mo chikagoro no	Yes, people these days forget
hito wa nani-ka wasureteru ne	the important things in life.
kore de mo nihonjin nan da	Can we still call them
beka nē	Japanese?
(2.) *nipponjin nara*	If people are Japanese, they
wasurecha komaru	shouldn't forget
furusato to miso shiru o...	their furusato and their miso soup...
(*Serifu*) *furusato o dete kara*	It's been sixteen years now since I
jū-roku-nen	left my furusato,
itsumo o-fukuro-san no futokoro o	and I always see my mother's
yume mite orimashita	breast in my dreams.
omoi-dasu tabi ni kono mune	When I recall thus, my heart
ga kyū' to itaku naru n desu.	aches terribly.
omowazu namida ga dete kuru n da nā...	Without realizing it, I find tears welling up in my eyes...
o-fukuro-san no misoshiru ga	I want to taste my mother's
kuitai nā	miso soup again.
kā-cha-a-n	Mama!!

"Miso Shiru no Uta" (Song of Miso Soup) (1980)

Mother—the maker of soup, the keeper of a house in which people still sleep on futon, wise in her moral teachings, hard working, uncomplaining—becomes the repository of the homeland and, by extension, of all things Japanese.

This mother-child or, more specifically, this mother-son relationship, establishes a pattern of interaction that extends to heterosexual romance. In many enka songs, one of the ways in which a woman expresses her love for a man is by tending and nurturing him as a mother would. Parts of the following song could as easily be spoken by a mother to her son as by a woman to her lover:

anata kawari wa nai desu ka	How are you, my dear?
hi-goto samusa ga tsunorimasu	Day by day the cold weather gets worse.
kite wa moraenu sētā o	Although I will never see you wear it,
samusa koraete andemasu	I knit this sweater for you, enduring the cold.
onna-gokoro no miren deshō	Is this the lingering affection of a woman's heart?
anata koishii kita no yado	I long for you from the inn in the north country.

"Kita no Yado kara" (From an Inn in the North Country) (1975)

Both relationships (mother-child, lover-lover) share a similar core of amae (dependency). As child to mother, so lover to lover: the child/lover seeks and accepts dependency, but that acceptance is contingent upon the presumed indulgence of the mother/lover. When romantic relationships are patterned after familial ones, men are placed in the position of children and women in the position of mothers, an arrangement that would seem to contradict the pervasive pattern of male domination in Japanese society. But just as there are active and passive dependencies, there are also different kinds of power. The dependent child wields power in his very helplessness because things are done for him, while the indulgent mother holds power by doing those things. As Dennis Wrong points out, the child retains "power over," while the mother retains "power to" (1995: xv). If one rethinks the child-mother relationship in terms of a master-servant relationship, the master/child/man and servant/mother/woman dynamic of lovers is more obvious. Mother-as-servant becomes the woman who empathetically anticipates the needs of others.

Within Japan's nation-as-family (*kazoku kokka*) ideology, mother becomes the source of national as well as personal identity. In reifying the most physically intimate of relationships, that of mother and child, enka songs establish a sensual link between all Japanese citizens (particularly men) as children of mothers. As the primary caregiver in the Japanese family, mother is the primary socializer, the primary nationalizer. Through her, whether from the foods she cooks or from her example of humility, diligence, and suffering, a child learns what it means to be Japanese. In evoking mother, enka songs establish a biological definition of national identity that is powerful and irrevocable. Just as an adult, especially a man, will always be the child of a mother, so, theoretically, Japanese will always be Japanese. National identity, particularly masculine identity, courses in the blood. Through mother, these enka songs also create an emotional definition of national identity, which gives that identity a different, but no less important, kind of potency. Just as a man will always love and yearn for his mother, so, theoretically, will Japanese always love and yearn to be Japanese. Enka thus roots national identity in the heart.

The relationship between child and mother, however—and between Japanese and their identity as Japanese—becomes ambiguous. The child, separated from his mother, forever seeks her. In the same way, according to the logic of enka, Japanese separated from their furusato now seek to reclaim the sources of their own Japaneseness. This internal monologue of song seems to be saying, "We long for our past Japanese selves." Nostalgia, expressed in enka, becomes a means through which this imaginary of furusato takes hold, keeping desire in place.

"Japan"

The nostalgia expressed in enka occupies a particular niche in the social practice of contemporary Japan. One may "do" enka—buying tapes, requesting particular songs, tuning in to radio and television programs, listening to and watching performances, attending concerts, joining fan clubs, singing at karaoke—and in the doing, participate in this one form of commercially based national culture. This is not to say that enka's adherents accept all its ideological aspects or even agree on its meaning. "Doing" merely serves to keep enka afloat in whatever guise and with whatever meaning individual doers seek and find for themselves.

Yet this is a "Japan" circumscribed by its borders, whose local hometowns have become nationalized as Homeland. Enka, a commercial cultural product, brings the traditional hearth of furusato to the center of cultural nationalism, drawing the nation around it through the fluids of intimacy—mother's milk, tears of longing, the sweat of exertion. With the faces of the homeland on television, with the sounds of furusato overheard, enka makes visible and audible the nation as imaginary. Japan becomes "Japan," and its peripheries, its center.

This "Japan" serves different masters, not all of whom may be found in government ministries or business conglomerates. But it is this very multiplicity that gives it force. Some aspects of this imaginary would certainly be approved by the government, while others, which glorify antiheroes as repositories of past ways and values, are subversive of the social order. Nor is this solely big business dominated by male producers at the expense of unwitting female consumers and aspiring singers. As formulaic as much of enka is, there is no guarantee of success for either singers or songs. Male and female consumers select products and use them for purposes beyond the control of producers. What they select affirms their participation as consumers of this "Japan," as official citizens of this national culture.

The enka imaginary constitutes a "Japan" uncertain about its relationship to the outside world and to its own past. But instead of confronting these uncertainties, the imaginary withdraws into an insular notion of a common heart. The tales it tells—of emotional pain, of failed romance, of longing for furusato, of nostalgia for a past just out of reach, of suffering as moral virtue—provoke tears of empathy and recognition. In these tears lie the critical links of the self to the imaginary, of the home to the nation, and ultimately, of Japan to "Japan."

Epilogue

The final applause for Kitajima Saburō dies down, the house lights go up, and I begin to gather my things together. As I shuffle out of the Shinjuku Koma Gekijō theater with the rest of the audience, I overhear random comments: "Oh, that was good, wasn't it!" "Sabu-chan must be tired" "That was really something!" In general, however, the crowd is quiet, as if savoring a satisfying meal. Their relative silence resounds as a kind of contented communal clucking.

For contemporary audiences, enka has become the emblem of a constructed past, one in which men followed a life-long path and women followed their hearts. In this past, men became noble through single-mindedness and sheer effort. They were not concerned about fulfilling production quotas or enduring a long daily commute to a high-rise office building (the dangers of *karōshi*, death through overwork, had not yet replaced the threat of the sword). These were men of duty and honor, of life-or-death commitment. In this past, too, women loved one only, and enduringly, until death and even beyond. Their work took them to fields and teahouses, not offices.

According to this version of the past, men and women lived in close connection with the land and the seasons, surviving through hard physical labor at sea and in the rice fields. Women tended their children much as their own wise mothers had tended them. Other, less fortunate women yearned in lingering affection. In the nostalgic haze of song, romance, even failed romance, is noble.

Enka fans embrace this version of the past wholeheartedly, savoring the opportunity to cry alone and together over the inevitability of life's sorrows—over lovers who must part, children whose parents die, wanderers who never return home. Their tears are proof of their empathetic hearts, which reach out to the intimacy and sincerity they see portrayed on stage. In crying, they create and reaffirm their connections with one another and their own sense of a common past.

As connoisseurs of the familiar, audience members like those who attended Sabu-chan's performance cherish the opportunity to hear the same song one more time. And even when the titles change, the themes and the words—*giri-ninjō* (duty, loyalty), *yume* (dream), *kokoro* (heart/soul), *namida* (tears), *sake*, *furusato* (hometown)—do not. Neither do the sounds, the rhythms, the guitar riffs, or the melodic phrases. These songs could have been written years ago or only yesterday. By invoking and reaffirming past experience, they offer soothing comfort, encouraging listeners to forget the everyday world beyond the theater doors.

In reinhabiting the nostalgia of a constructed past, audiences also savor other aspects of the enka imaginary. They enjoy the latest technology, from laser beams to hydraulic stages to swirling lights, with appreciative gasps and eager applause. They savor the sheer theatricality of the performance. When Sabu-chan, ever the showman, performs, he wears one expensive, glittery suit after another and surrounds himself with a bevy of dancers whose colorful movements form a counterpoint to his stillness. Most important, he makes each song into a personal, small-scale melodrama, drawing on a variety of vocal techniques, shadings, and textures to weave a seductive net of storytelling.

Also appealing is his sincerity. Sabu-chan, the country boy, never lets his audience forget that he is the "real" thing. In spite of the tuxedos and the glitter, his look remains rough and unrefined. He sings each song with such complete conviction that he becomes the song's character, a likely complement to his image. Between songs, with equal sincerity and ease, he is Kitajima Saburō, the bumpkin from Hokkaido, who chats in a provincial accent and jokes self-deprecatingly. He makes the audience feel as if they are enjoying a drink with him at the local bar.

The audience also responds to the songs, which speak of the ephemeral, of fleeting love, the brief bloom of a flower, the sudden burst of fireworks that slowly fades in the dark sky. Life flows on like a river, and nothing remains the same for long. There is a certain poignant beauty in this aesthetic of ephemerality, this evanescence, this striving to capture the elusive, but there is also a parallel irony. The rapid change, the very ephemerality of contemporary Japan is often bewildering, especially in the eyes of older Japanese men and women, who have lived through prewar, wartime, and postwar difficulties and disappointments. It is this bewilderment, in part, that drives audiences to enka performances. Here, change is managed through nostalgia. In these songs, they can savor longing itself—of men and women for each other, for their furusato, for their mothers. They can long for a time and place in which they might revel in deliberate helplessness and wield the subtle power of passivity and powerlessness. They can pine for a Japanese self that can only be retrieved in the floating world of the spectacle, the stage, the memory, the dream. The longing itself becomes virtuous. It is not that the young do not, or cannot, feel this longing, but that older adults, with their accumulation of life experience, possess knowledge that gives them a certain authority. Longing validates their lives.

The kata of nostalgia and yearning in enka invokes not only the object of desire but also the inevitable obstacles to desire, including group norms, family obligations, and society itself. Outside the theater, these obstacles form the social order. Within the confines of the theater, that social order is always problematized as a constraining force against which an individual must struggle in a classic giri-ninjō (duty vs. human feelings) confrontation. Yet the struggle finds no resolution. All enka can offer listeners is an emotional contract that promises frustration, sorrow, and resignation. In these songs, a mature adult is one who longs without expecting fulfillment, and it is longing that defines this poignant view of citizenship.

Like a bag that assumes the shape of its contents, the audience is filled, and the filling helps to define them. They attend enka performances as active participants, watching and listening but also laughing and crying. They choose (and pay) to come to the theater. Once there, they cheer those aspects of the performance they like and ignore those they do not. They also speak with their wallets by buying Sabu-chan songs and souvenirs to prolong the experience. They join fan clubs, which bring them into closer contact with this tsukutta-mono (made thing), this industry commodity called "Kitajima Saburō." By joining his fan club, they gain (and pay for) the right to in-group status, officially becoming his supporters. At home and at karaoke, they sing his songs, adopting his vocal mannerisms, forming their lips around his words, celebrating Sabu-chan. In the theater, they reach out to him and very much feel that he reaches out to them. He touches their hearts with his words, and they meet him more than halfway, touching his words with their hearts.

Enka's patterned expression relies on familiar scenarios and stereotypical words sung in well-rehearsed ways by singers who move through set poses. By definition, its predictable clichés operate within an aesthetic of replication. And yet somehow it continues to move human hearts. Through its sheer emotional force, the poignancy of its expression fine-tuned within limited means, it succeeds in shattering the artifice of its own art. It moves audiences through the "expressiveness of the back."

Popular discourse on enka, this expression of the "heart/soul of Japanese" (nihonjin no kokoro), ascribes to it a nationalistic ideology. An affinity for enka is said to run in the (Japanese) blood; those who dislike it have allowed themselves to be seduced away from their own innate Japaneseness. In contemporary Japan, as the number of its devotees declines, enka has remained that internal place (or one of those places) where "Japaneseness" still exists. Thus surveyed and mapped, enka has become the nation's emotional "preserve." This version of the "heart/soul of Japanese" finds affirmation in the posters of enka singers on display at every post office and in the enka songs played one after another during NHK's Kōhaku Uta Gassen. But it glosses over the very real tensions that accompany these claims.

The contested space of enka epitomizes the sociopolitical conflicts of contemporary Japan: state and commercial institutions with a vested interest in keeping this expression of national music afloat intervene directly, even as enka's persistence confounds its declining numbers. What may appear to be systematic and orderly is in fact a disorderly human zigzag of guesswork, conflict, and accommodation. The commercial production of emotional nostalgia leaves little room for true messiness, so the industry relies on formulas to eliminate guesswork. Yet—and this is a big yet—somewhere amid the stereotypes and the sameness, the human element persists. Hit making may be formulaic, but popular success can never be guaranteed. A raspy, unconventional voice may have appeal as a sign of adversity overcome. A mole near a perfectly painted mouth can be as important as the years spent practicing a sung sob. What is promoted under the "song of Japan" (nihon no uta) banner finds its life force in the messiness of unwiped tears.

In the end, the "Japan" of enka remains elusive. As in *Rashōmon*, it changes as the the point of view changes.[1] For many at the Shinjuku Koma

Gekijō, enka's "Japan" is their "Japan," and they possess it bodily. Sabu-chan, whatever his actual hometown, is their own "hometown boy." The emotions he expresses seem reassuringly familiar. Audience members have heard these songs many times, but when he sings them they feel these emotions all over again. As they listen to singers from Korea and Taiwan sing "their" "song of Japan" and hear rumors that one or more top enka stars is of Korean ancestry (despite a Japanese name) or that another comes from a *burakumin* (outcaste) background, the smooth surface of this nostalgic "Japan" begins to show tiny cracks. These theater-goers know that when they file out of the theater, they leave this intimate spectacle for a world filled with cracks large and small, one in which they sometimes feel dispossessed.

And yet enka also belongs to that contemporary world, where it has become isolated and elevated, where the folk, the yakuza, and the laboring masses become national antiheroes. Contemporary Japan's discursive tropes—homogeneity, uniqueness, island country, island people—have been embraced as true myths; enka, as the "song of Japan," is yet another. This "Japan" belongs to its antiheroes as well as to its hero-makers.

The crowd thins out as it moves through the lobby and into the street. The rain continues, and some remove their umbrellas from the plastic casings handed out earlier at the theater entrance. Each of us gradually becomes reabsorbed into the outside world, the garishness of Shinjuku's Kabuki-chō now muted by the gray dampness. We head for the train station in haphazard procession, some in clusters of two or three, others, like me, by themselves. We wait at the corner for the light to turn green and then cross en masse to the tune "Comin' thro' the Rye."[2] It feels like a march, and I am still part of it. Once across the street, however, we disperse, absorbed by the constantly moving crowds. Soon, among the people around me, I no longer recognize anyone who sat with me only ten minutes ago, applauding Kitajima Saburō at the Koma Gekijō. The moment has passed. I check my wallet to see if my souvenir Sabu-chan telephone card is still there, and of course it is. The Yamanote-sen train arrives on schedule at 4:31 P.M. I am near the back of the crowd and step into the train only seconds before it leaves. The doors close firmly behind me.

Appendix A: Major Record Companies That Produce and Market Enka

This list is derived from *Orikon Nenkan 1992 Nenban* (1992 Oricon Yearbook) and *Orikon Nenkan 1993 Nenban* (1993 Oricon Yearbook). The names of companies and their major singers appear in the order given in these sources. The date indicates the year in which the record company was established; the amount of capital is that reported for 1992, the central year of my fieldwork (to avoid long numbers I have used the Japanese numbering system: *oku* = one hundred million; *man* = ten thousand; *sen* = one thousand). The year in parentheses following a singer's name indicates when the singer joined that particular company.

Nippon Columbia	1911	¥67 oku 8,300 man	Ōkawa Eisaku Kanmuri Jirō Hosokawa Takashi Ishikawa Sayuri (1992) Kaneda Tatsue Shimakura Chiyoko Matsubara Nobue "Marcia" (Marushia) Miyako Harumi Yashiro Aki
Victor Ongaku Sangyō [Music Industries]	1928 (1972)	¥10 oku	Mori Shin'ichi Misawa Akemi Nagayama Yoko

King Records	1952	¥8 oku	Ōtsuki Miyako Harada Yūri Shimazu Etsuko
Teichiku Records	1935	¥1 oku 2,355 man 2 sen	Sugi Ryūtarō Tendō Yoshimi
Polydor	1954	¥4 oku 8,000 man	Kōzai Kaori (1993)
Apollon	1956	¥1 oku 5,000 man	Nagahō Yuki
Toshiba-EMI	1961	¥16 oku 67,000 man	Koda Shin Murata Hideo Yamakawa Yutaka Kei Unsuku Sakamoto Fuyumi Nakamura Mitsuko
Nippon Crown Records	1964	¥2 oku 5,000 man	Kitajima Saburō Suizenji Kyōko Segawa Eiko Toba Ichirō Mikawa Ken'ichi
Tokuma Japan Communications	1966	¥2 oku 7,000 man	Itsuki Hiroshi Sen Masao Moriwaka Satoko Yoshi Ikuzō
Pony Canyon	1967	¥2 oku	Maekawa Kiyoshi Yamamoto Jōji Ishikawa Sayuri (1993)
Sony Music Entertainment	1968	¥496 oku 6,000 man	Godai Natsuko Nagai Miyuki Fuji Ayako

Warner Music Japan, Inc.	1970	¥1 oku	Kōzai Kaori (1992) Kobayashi Sachiko Chō Yonpiru
Polystar	1980	¥9,000 man	Takayama Gen Horiuchi Takao
Vap Records	1981	¥5 oku	Kim Yonja
Taurus Records	1981	¥1 oku 2,000 man	Teresa Ten Makimura Mieko
Century Records	1982	¥5,300 man	Cool Five
BMG Victor	1987	¥4 oku 5,000 man	Kadokawa Hiroshi Nishikata Hiroyuki
Newcreek Records (subsid. of Tokuma Japan Corp.)	1981	¥1 oku 2,000 man	Itsuki Hiroshi

Appendix B: Regular Mass Media Enka Programs in the Tokyo Area, 1992

Radio

The following list of Kantō radio stations that broadcast prerecorded enka is derived from a request list published in a 1992 fan club newsletter. Other general popular music programs, however, also included enka.

Bunka Hōsō
    Fuji Card Zenkoku Kayō Best Ten   Sat.   3:10–4:00 P.M.
    Honki de Don Don   Mon.–Fri.   11:00 A.M.–1:00 P.M.
    Hashire/Kayōkyoku Oyōbi no Kei   Mon.–Sun.   3:00–5:00 A.M.

Nippon Hōsō
    Kayō Den Request   Mon.–Thurs.   6:30–8:00 P.M.
    Moyamoya Kayō Center   Sat.   4:35–5:00 P.M.
    Kayō Parade Nippon   Mon.–Fri.   1:00–4:00 P.M.

Rajio Nippon
    Yugata no Wide Show Enka Da Yo   Mon.–Fri.   4:05–5:33 P.M.
    Nihon Rettō; Enka de Omakase   Fri.   1:00–3:00 A.M.

TBS Rajio
    Kayō Best Ten   Sun.   8:05–9:00 A.M.
    Sore Yuke ... Genki Maru   Mon.–Fri.   1:00–3:55 P.M.
    Utau Headlight   Mon.–Fri.   3:00–5:00 A.M.

Appendix B

Television

This list of Kantō television programs broadcasting enka is derived from the 1992 *TV Gaido* (TV Guide), a weekly magazine of program listings and brief articles. It does not include various karaoke shows, such as *Nodo Jiman* (literally, "pride in one's voice"), an amateur song contest on NHK (Sun. 12:15–1:00 P.M.), or "Onna Nodo Jiman," the women's amateur song contest segment of the program *Rukku* (Look) on Nihon Terebi (Wed. 8:30–10:00 A.M.), most of which feature enka, although not exclusively.

NHK
    NHK Hitto Sutēji   Tues.   8:00–8:45 P.M.

Terebi Asahi
    Enka TV   Sat.   5:00–5:30 A.M.

Terebi Tokyo
    Enka no Furusato   Tues.   5:30–6:00 A.M.
    Enka no Hanamichi   Sun.   10:00–10:30 P.M.

Appendix C: Listing of Songs in the Corpus

The following 115 songs formed the corpus of my textual analysis (see Chapter 5). The list includes the title of the song and an English translation; the category: man's (m), woman's (w), duet (d), ambiguous solo song (m/w); the name of the singer who made the song popular (and, where applicable, the name of a second singer who made it equally or more popular in a rerelease); the name of the recording company; and the year of release and/or copyright. Those songs analyzed musically in the text are marked with an asterisk.

Abare-daiko (Wild Drums), m
    Sakamoto Fuyumi, Toshiba-EMI 1987

Airenka (Song of Pity), w
    Kim Yonja, VAP 1992

Amagi-goe (Amagi Pass), w
    Ishikawa Sayuri, Nippon Columbia 1986

Ame Sakaba (Rainy Night at a Bar), w
    Kōzai Kaori, Warner Pioneer 1988

Ame Yo-zake (*Sake* on a Rainy Night), w
    Fuji Ayako, Sony Records 1988

**Bōkyō Jonkara* (Song of Homesickness), m
    Hosokawa Takashi, Nippon Columbia 1985

Funa-uta (Sailor's Song), m
   Yashiro Aki, Nippon Columbia 1979

Furusato (Hometown), m
   Itsuki Hiroshi, Newcreek Records 1973

Furusato (Hometown), d
   Yamakawa Yutaka & Kei Unsuku, Toshiba-EMI 1990

Fuyu-Geshō (Winter Make-up), w
   Kobayashi Sachiko, Warner Music Japan 1991

Fuyu no Eki (Winter Train Station), w
   Ōtsuki Miyako, King Records 1993

Ganpeki no Haha (Mother at the Wharf), w
   Kikuchi Akiko, Teichiku Records 1954
   Futaba Yuriko, King Records 1971?

Ginza no Koi no Monogatari (Ginza Love Story), d
   Ishihara Yūjiro & Makimura Junko, Teichiku Records 1966

Haguresō (Drifter), w
   Kōzai Kaori, Polydor 1991

Haha-gokoro (Mother's Heart), w
   Mikasa Natsuko, 1986

Haha-goyomi (Calendar of Memories of Mother), w
   Harada Yūri, King Records 1988

Haha-kage (The Figure of Mother), m
   Chō Yonpiru, Warner 1992

Hana Banka (Flower Elegy), w
   Kōzai Kaori, Polydor 1992

Hanamachi no Haha (Flower Town [Geisha Quarters] Mother), w
   Kaneda Tatsue, Nippon Columbia 1973

Hatoba Shigure (Late Autumn Passing Showers on the Pier), w
   Ishikawa Sayuri, Nippon Columbia 1985

Higurashi (Cicada), w
  Nagayama Yōko, Victor 1993

Hi no Kuni no Onna (A Woman of Volcanic Land), w
  Sakamoto Fuyumi, Toshiba-EMI 1991

Honō (Flame), m
  Kanmuri Jirō, Nippon Columbia 1992

Hōsenka (Touch-Me-Not Flowers), w
  Shimakura Chiyoko, Nippon Columbia 1981

Hotaru (Firefly), w
  Matsubara Nobue, Nippon Columbia 1990

*Inochi Kurenai (Crimson Life of Passion), w
  Segawa Eiko, Nippon Crown Records 1986

Iwai-zake (Congratulatory Sake), m
  Sakamoto Fuyumi, Toshiba-EMI 1988

Izakaya (A Bar), d
  Itsuki Hiroshi & Kinomi Nana, Newcreek Records 1982

Izakaya "Fujino" ("Fujino" Bar), w
  Segawa Eiko, Nippon Crown Records 1991

Jinsei Iroiro (Various Lives), w
  Shimakura Chiyoko, Nippon Columbia 1987

Jinsei Tsuzura-zaka (The Winding Slope of Life), w
  Segawa Eiko, Nippon Crown Records 1991

Kaerō Ka Na (Shall I Go Home), m
  Kitajima Saburō, Nippon Crown Records 1965

Kaji (Rudder), m
  Kitajima Saburō, Nippon Crown Records 1992

Kami no Fune (Paper Boat), w
  Shimazu Etsuko, King Records 1991

*Kanashii Sake (Sorrowful Sake), w
  Misora Hibari, Nippon Columbia 1966

Kawa no Nagare no Yō ni (Like a River's Flow), w
    Misora Hibari, Nippon Columbia 1988

Kaze no Bon Koi Uta (Love Song of Owara *Bon* Festival), w
    Ishikawa Sayuri, Nippon Columbia 1989

Kinokawa (Kinokawa River [Wakayama prefecture]), m/w
    Nishikata Hiroyuki, BMG Victor, Inc. 1991

**Kita-guni no Haru* (Spring in the North Country), m
    Sen Masao, Tokuma Japan 1977

*Kita no Daichi (The Land of the North), m
    Kitajima Saburō, Nippon Crown Records 1991

**Kita no Yado kara* (From an Inn in the North Country), w
    Miyako Harumi, Nippon Columbia 1975

Kizuna-gawa (River of Bonds), m
    Ōkawa Eisaku, Nippon Columbia 1992

Koi Banka (Love's Elegy), w
    Godai Natsuko, Sony Records 1991

Koi-botaru (Firefly of Love), w
    Kobayashi Sachiko, Warner Music Japan, Inc. 1992

*Koi-bune (Boat of Love), w
    Kōzai Kaori, Warner Pioneer 1990

Koi Momiji (Autumn Leaves of Love), w
    Kōzai Kaori, Polydor 1992

Koi Uta Tsuzuri (Love Song Spelling), w
    Horiuchi Takao, Polystar 1989

Kokoro Kōrasete (Freeze Our Hearts), w
    Takayama Gen, Polystar 1993

*Kokoro-zake (Sake of the Heart), w
    Fuji Ayako, Sony Records 1991

*Kyōdai-bune (Ship of Brothers), m
    Toba Ichirō, Nippon Crown Records 1982

Mabuta no Haha (Mother of My Memory), m
  Nakamura Mitsuko, Toshiba-EMI 1991

Matsuri (Festival), m
  Kitajima Saburō, Nippon Crown Records 1984

Ma-yonaka no Shawā (Shower in the Middle of the Night), w
  Kei Unsuku, Toshiba-EMI 1990

Meoto-zaka (A Couple's Struggles), w
  Miyako Harumi, Nippon Columbia 1984

Michinoku Yuki Akari (The Gleam of Snow in the Northern Hinterlands), w
  Harada Yūri, King Records 1992

Michi-zure (Traveling Companions), m
  Watari Tetsuya, Polydor 1978

Midare-bana (Strewn Flowers), w
  Ōtsuki Miyako, King Records 1988

*Midare-gami (Hair in Disarray), w
  Misora Hibari, Nippon Columbia 1987

Minato Machi Burūsu (Harbor Town Blues), w
  Mori Shin'ichi, Victor 1980

Minato Uta (Harbor Song), w
  Ishikawa Sayuri, Nippon Columbia 1991

Miso Shiru no Uta (Song of Miso Soup), m
  Sen Masao, Tokuma Japan 1980

Mizu-nashi-gawa (Dried-up River), w
  Godai Natsuko, Sony Records 1989

Mugon-zaka (Silent Slope), w
  Kōzai Kaori, Polydor 1993

*Mujō no Umi (Cruel Sea), w
  Matsubara Nobue, Nippon Columbia 1992

*Nakase Ame (Rain Which Makes One Cry), w
  Mori Shin'ichi, Victor 1991

Namida no Renraku-sen (Ferryboat of Tears), w
   Miyako Harumi, Nippon Columbia 1965

Namida no San-bashi (Wharf of Tears), w
   Matsubara Nobue, Nippon Columbia 1987

Niwaka-ame (Sudden Rain Shower), w
   Nagahō Yūki, Apollon 1991

Noto wa Irankai ne (Don't You Want to Come to Noto?), m
   Sakamoto Fuyumi, Toshiba-EMI 1990

Nukumori (Warmth), m
   Kanmuri Jirō, Nippon Columbia 1992

*O-fukuro-san (Mother Dear), m
   Mori Shin'ichi, Victor 1971

Omoide no Yado (Inn of Memories), w
   Harada Yūri, King Records 1992

Omoide-zake (Sake of Memories), w
   Kobayashi Sachiko, Warner Music Japan 1979

*Onna no Defune (Woman of the Sailing Ship), w
   Matsubara Nobue, Nippon Columbia 1983

Onna no Kawa (Woman's River), w
   Moriwaka Satoko, Tokuma Japan 1992

Ōsaka Jōwa (Osaka Love Story), w
   Nakamura Mitsuko, Toshiba-EMI 1990

*Ōsaka Shigure (Late Autumn Rain in Osaka), w
   Miyako Harumi, Nippon Columbia 1980

Ōsaka Suzume (Osaka Sparrow), w
   Nagai Miyuki, Sony Records 1992

Oshidori (Mandarin Ducks/Love Birds), m
   Itsuki Hiroshi, Tokuma Japan 1991

Otoko-bore (Admiration Between Men), m
   Sakamoto Fuyumi, Toshiba-EMI 1992

Otoko-michi (The Path of a Man), m
    Nakamura Mitsuko, Toshiba-EMI 1991

Otoko no Jōwa (A Man's Love Story), m
    Sakamoto Fuyumi, Toshiba-EMI 1989

Ringo Oiwake (Apple Folk Song/Packhorse Driver's Song), w
    Misora Hibari, Nippon Columbia 1952

*Sadame-gawa (River of Fate), w
    Chiaki Naomi, Nippon Columbia 1975
    Hosokawa Takashi, Nippon Columbia 1986

Sado no Koi Uta (Love Song of Sado Island), m/w
    Hosokawa Takashi, Nippon Columbia 1991

Sakaba (A Bar), m
    Kanmuri Jirō, Nippon Columbia 1990

Sakaba Hitori (Alone at a Bar), w
    Nakamura Mitsuko, Toshiba-EMI 1992

*Sake Kizuna (Bonds of Sake), w
    Tendō Yoshimi, Teichiku 1993

*Sake Yo (Sake!), m
    Yoshi Ikuzō, Tokuma Japan 1988

Sasame-yuki (Light Snowfall), w
    Itsuki Hiroshi, Newcreek Records 1983

Sasori-za no Onna (Scorpio Woman), w
    Mikawa Ken'ichi, Nippon Crown Records 1972

*Sazanka no Yado (The Inn of Sasanqua Flowers), m
    Ōkawa Eisaku, Nippon Columbia 1982

Senshū Harukikō [old name for Osaka Harbor], m
    Toba Ichirō, Nippon Crown Records 1992

*Settchūka (Flowers in the Snow), w
    Godai Natsuko, Sony Records 1992

Shiawase-zake (Sake of Happiness), m
    Nakamura Mitsuko, Toshiba-EMI 1990

Shigure-gawa (Wintry River), m
    Yamakawa Yutaka, Toshiba-EMI 1990

Shinobu Ame (Enduring Rain), w
    Godai Natsuko, Sony Records 1990

Shiroi Kaikyō (White Straits), w
    Ōtsuki Miyako, King Records 1992

Shūchaku Eki (Last Train Station), m
    Itsuki Hiroshi, Tokuma Japan 1992

Suika (Drunken Song), m
    Yoshi Ikuzō, Tokuma Japan 1990

Suzume no Namida (Tears of a Sparrow), w
    Kei Unsuku, Toshiba-EMI 1987

Taki no Shiraito [woman's stage name], w
    Ishikawa Sayuri, Nippon Columbia 1988

Tejaku-zake (Pouring Myself Some Sake), w
    Kōda Shin, Toshiba-EMI 1992

Tō-hanabi (Far-off Fireworks), w
    Nishikata Hiroyuki, BMG Victor 1989

Tokai no Tenshi-tachi (Angels of the City), d
    Horiuchi Takao & Kei Unsuku, Toshiba-EMI, Polystar 1992

Toki no Nagare ni Mi o Makase (Surrender to the Flow of Time), w
    Teresa Ten, Taurus Records 1986

Tokyo da yo Okka-san (This Is Tokyo, Mother Dear), w
    Shimakura Chiyoko, Nippon Columbia 1957

**Tsugaru Kaikyō Fuyu-geshiki* (Winter Scape of the Tsugaru Straits), w
    Ishikawa Sayuri, Nippon Columbia 1977

Utakata (Bubbles/A Moment), w
    Ishikawa Sayuri, Nippon Columbia 1990

**Yagiri no Watashi* (Yagiri Crossing), w
    Chiaki Naomi, Nippon Columbia 1976
    Hosokawa Takashi, Nippon Columbia 1983

Yanagase Burūsu (Blues of Yanagase [Fukuoka]), w
    Mikawa Ken'ichi, Nippon Crown Records 1966

Yoi-gokoro (Drunken Heart), w
    Tendō Yoshimi, Teichiku 1992

Yo-zakura (Evening Cherry Blossoms), m
    Yamakawa Yutaka, Toshiba-EMI 1992

Yuki-guni (Snow Country), w
    Yoshi Ikuzō, Tokuma Japan 1986

Yume Ichi-byō (One-Second Dream), w
    Maekawa Kiyoshi, Pony Canyon 1992

Reference Matter

Notes

Prologue

1. In giving Japanese names, I follow the standard Japanese practice of surname first, then personal name. When I give someone's age, it is at the time of the events described. In addition, all translations in the text are my own.

2. These figures are based on an exchange rate of ¥110 to U.S. $1, the average rate during most of my stay in Japan, from 1991 to 1993. Dollar figures are rounded to the nearest dollar.

3. The Diet approves the budget and the administration of NHK and appoints its steering committee.

4. Yoshino cites a near-carbon-copy explanation given by Shōichi Watanabe, who wrote in a 1974 publication, *Nihongo no Kokoro* (The soul of the Japanese language), that many non-Japanese may read, write, and speak Japanese fluently, but only those who are ethnically/racially Japanese can compose or fully appreciate good *waka* (31-syllable Japanese poetry) (1998: 21–22).

5. Ten's tragic death in 1995 was greatly mourned in Japan. Tributes to her after her death attend to some of the issues of enka's foreign Asian singers. One article called Ten the "Singing Princess of Asia," who "captivated many Japanese fans as a foreigner who sang about the Japanese soul" (Anonymous 1995: 13).

6. My information has been gathered from the following sources: 1) background readings; 2) interviews with fans, producers, composers, lyricists, and singers; 3) participant-observation as a student of enka with three teachers, Mr. Noda Hisashi and Mr. Ueno Naoki in Japan and Mr. Harry Urata in Hawai'i, totaling over two years; as a singer at karaoke gatherings, recitals, public performances, and a contest; and as a member of two different enka fan clubs (Mori Shin'ichi, Yashiro Aki);

4) attendance at 38 live professional enka performances during the primary fieldwork period, as well as at several others in Japan and Hawai'i; 5) analysis of the enka fan magazine *Enka Jānaru* from March 1989 to March 1999 and of other selected magazines, such as *Karaoke Taishō* and *Karaoke Fan*; and 6) analysis of over 200 hours of televised enka performances.

7. Local teachers include Japanese nationals, *kibei-nisei* (Japanese-Americans born outside Japan but raised in Japan, who have returned as adults to live in their place of birth), and other Japanese-Americans. Some, but not all, have had training in singing in Japan.

Chapter 1: The Cultural Logic of Enka's Imaginary

1. Nativism and nostalgia are not the sole purview of Japan's modern period. Earlier nativistic movements include the eighteenth-century *kokugaku* (national learning) movement, which Nosco has analyzed as having clear seventeenth-century antecedents (1990).

2. These dichotomizations persist in spite of constant blurring, as in *tarakko* (cod roe) spaghetti and rice burgers. The point is not so much that different cultural strands are kept distinct and separate in practice (in some instances they are; in others they are not), but that distinctiveness and separateness are conceptual categories maintained through labels that say little about the actual Japaneseness or Westernness of the objects themselves. A toilet labeled "Western," for example, is not necessarily like any found in "the West" (unless imported from Japan), not with its heated seat, variety of automatic washers and dryers, bidets, and faux flushing sound. Moreover, an object or practice can have different degrees of Japaneseness and Westernness, so that *wa-* and *yō-* are discrete categories as well as points along a continuum.

A sense of distinction between Japan and the West arises even when *wa-* and *yō-* are not specifically applied as labels. For example, Dalby points out that the kimono did not arise as native Japanese clothing until the Meiji era (1868–1912), when people in Japan felt a need to articulate what they themselves wore; *kimono* (literally, "object of wearing") then took on the sense of "what Japanese wear" in opposition to "what foreigners/Westerners wear" (1993: 59).

3. When people in Japan meet me, a Japanese-American, they sometimes ask me what I have for breakfast, rice or bread, making the food I choose a way of understanding who I am in relation to my hyphenated identity. Likewise, a middle-aged Japanese housewife in Aomori characterized her husband for me as one who will only eat rice for breakfast and adamantly refuses bread. By this she means that her husband is stubbornly Japanese.

4. These boundaries and meanings are shifting. In terms of their ubiquity, McDonald's and the 7-Eleven convenience store may be considered local Japanese

institutions. Indeed, there is an oft-told story of the Japanese child who, upon visiting the United States and seeing a McDonald's, exclaims excitedly, "Look! There's a McDonald's here, too!" The contrast between this story and the early promotion of McDonald's in Japan as a particularly American institution, in spite of founder Den Fujita's claim to the contrary (Ohnuki-Tierney 1997: 172–73), suggests that boundaries and meanings change with familiarity: McDonald's has by now been in Japan long enough (since 1971) to feed generations of Japanese, and thus the context has changed. It's not so much that the child was unaware of the American origins of McDonald's but that McDonald's is now only one of many fast-food shops that sell hamburgers and a frankly Japanese fabrication of "America." See Tobin 1992 for further discussions of Japan and its shifting relationship with things from Euro-America.

5. Japanese words meaning nostalgia include *kyōshū* (incl. homesickness), *kaiko no jō* (yearning for the old days), and the English-derived *nosutarujia* ("nostalgia").

6. The category "internal exotic" stands in contrast to the tripartite construction put forth by Ohnuki-Tierney: 1) internal others (minorities); 2) external others (foreigners); and 3) self (dominant social group) (1998: 31). Here, I look at "others" within the "self"/dominant social group in Japan, or, as Ohnuki-Tierney phrases it, the "unmarked majority" (ibid.).

7. In 1984, when the "Discover Japan" campaign was supplanted by an "Exotic Japan" campaign encouraging travel to non-Japanese, Asian-influenced areas within the country, Japan became the site of its own originary spaces and the repository of non-Japanese Asian ones (Ivy 1995). Here "Japan" stretched its borders to encompass the premodern Silk Road Asia (Samarkand, Kashmir, T'ang China, Korea), using the traces of that Asia found within its own national borders.

8. Robertson notes that the concept *furusato* invokes both time and space: the first half, *furu(i)* (old), signifies pastness, and the second half, *sato*, signifies natal, rural place (1991: 4).

9. The concept of a separate genre of music called *min'yō* was a modern invention borrowed from the German *volkslied* (folk song) (Hughes 1985: 12).

10. I am grateful to Merry White for pointing out that even the public mailboxes in Tokyo express this split: separate boxes are labeled Tokyo or *chihō* (provinces).

11. This process is not unique to Japan, as demonstrated in several examples, including that of American country and western music, that are collected in Gerald Creed and Barbara Ching's (1997) edited volume on rural identity and cultural/national hierarchies.

12. For more on *nihonjinron*, including an extensive bibliography of primary and secondary materials in Japanese and English, see Mouer and Sugimoto 1986; Yoshino 1992.

13. One often-invoked example of Japanese spirit is *yamato damashii* (the spiritual strength of the Yamato clan, the "original" Japanese). During World War II, the rationale for Japan's fortitude against all odds was said to be attributable to *yamato damashii*, which gave Japanese soldiers the edge against all others (Lebra 1976: 163).

14. Joy Hendry (1993) generalizes this public performativity as "wrapping culture," which is how she refers to not only the ubiquitous, obligatory gift-giving in Japan but, more to the point for our purposes, the critical coding given social interaction through wrapping itself.

15. A closely related concept is *katachi* (shape, form). The Nō performer and theater specialist Komparu Kunio theorizes that *kata* derives from *kami* (god) and *ta* (paddy or hand); the *-chi* (spirit) of *katachi* indicates mystical powers: "The character takes shape (*katachi*) . . . when the outer forms (*katachi*) indicating the inner soul (*chi*) are added to the standard patterns (*kata*)" (1983: 221).

Chapter 2: Inventing Enka

1. This chapter is not intended to be a detailed history of popular music in Japan but to provide an account of those aspects most relevant to the invention of enka.

2. The categories listed were, in order given: 1) enka; 2) *poppusu* ("pops"); 3) *mūdo kayō*; 4) *mūdo kōrasu gurūpu* (mood chorus group); 5) *seishun kayō* (adolescent popular song); 6) *fōku kayō* ("folk"; urban folk); 7) *gurūpu saunzu* ("group sounds"; pop group); and 8) *saike kayō* ("psychedelic" pop songs).

3. In the Japanese language, different readings of characters derive from two basic sources, the Chinese reading and the Japanese reading. Even within these two, however, different readings of the same character are possible, especially for native Japanese readings. Moreover, individuals may choose to read characters "creatively," giving a character an unusual, archaic, or fanciful reading within certain bounds, which allows for the structural character/word-play found in literature and various naming practices. The different characters used to write enka are one small example.

It is not uncommon for a historical discussion of enka to separate the term from the genre. For example, one Japanese newspaper article on enka begins its historical section with "*Enka to iu kotoba no rūtsu o tadoreba* . . . " ("If we are to trace the roots of the word enka . . . ") (Anonymous 1987: 14).

4. There are, of course, exceptions, most notably Misora Hibari, discussed below. Moreover, such typing of a singer and his or her songs may be a function of the "genre-making" (or "genre-izing") that took place primarily in the 1970s.

5. The following description of enka in various historical periods is based largely on Okada 1982 and Nakamura 1991, except where otherwise noted.

6. The *en-* (presentation; speech) is taken from *enzetsu* (oration, public speech); the *-ka* is another reading (Chinese) of the character for *uta* (song).

7. For more on the history of Western music in Meiji Japan, see Malm 1971.

8. Although Sakurai credits Kaminaga Ryōgetsu for first adding violin to enka performances, I have not been able to confirm or refute this claim. Sakurai sees little relation between the enka he sang in the 1920s and the enka of today.

In 1993 I saw Sakurai perform at Ueno Shitamachi Fūzoku Shiryōkan (Ueno Shitamachi Popular Historical Museum) in a 1920s bar setting specially constructed for his performance. When I interviewed him in February 1993, 83-year-old Sakurai was lively, energetic, and very much a showman. His eyes twinkled when he launched into a story, and he interspersed bits of song to illustrate his points. He stood straight, walking with a bounce to his step that made his neatly combed, earlobe-length gray hair shake ever so slightly. He strikes me as a survivor: he survived the Great Kantō Earthquake of 1923, he survived World War II (one of only four survivors in his military unit in the Philippines), he outlived his wife and raised four children by himself, and he has survived all other enkashi. See Yano 1998: 249–50 for more on the interview with Sakurai.

9. In general, however, these performers were regarded, according to one music teacher, as nothing more than *kawara-kojiki* or *kawara-mono* ("people of the river bank"; beggar; outcast). See Ohnuki-Tierney for a general analysis of the close historical relationship between entertainers, wanderers, and outcasts, and for an explanation of *kawara-mono* (1987: 85–86).

10. However, some enka songs adhere to a 7-5 syllabic meter, adding rests to accommodate a 4/4 musical meter (Anonymous 1990: 11).

11. According to Nakamura, "Kachūsha no uta" (Kachusha's Song) may be considered "firmly in the spirit of the modern popular song production" in its "conscious attention to audience susceptibilities by both composer and lyricist, and in their estimate of audience impact" (1991: 264–65).

12. Silverberg (1998) points out that café waitresses of the 1920s and 1930s became a focal point of gendered modernity in Japanese urban life.

13. For a discussion of "*Koga merodii*," including its appeal and its influence on subsequent Japanese popular song, see Minami 1987: 486–91.

14. For example, *beesubōro* (loan word for "baseball") thus became *yakyū* (literally, "field ball"), an invented word meaning baseball.

15. One example is that of Dick Mine, a Japanese singer, who began his career singing jazz. During this period, he switched to songs that would today be called enka.

16. In Japan, World War II is encompassed within and better known as the Pacific War (*Taiheiyō Sensō*) and overlaps with the Sino-Japanese War (*Nitchū Sensō*), both of which extended from 1937 to 1945.

17. Atkins points out that rather than simply banning jazz, military and police authorities suggested ways to control and incorporate certain elements of jazz in creating music that would serve the purposes of the state (1998: 363).

18. Yasukuni Shrine was built in 1869 and dedicated to the souls of those who have died since 1853 in defense of the country. Since its inception it has had a close and important relationship to the Japanese government and imperial institution. Because it enshrines war dead and promoted zealous nationalism during World War II, it came under intense scrutiny at the end of the war, particularly by those who sought to police nascent militarism in Japan and preserve the separation of church and state.

19. In 1994, the lavish, multilevel, technologically elaborate Misora Hibari-kan museum, which traces her life in song and film, was built in Arashiyama, Kyoto. At Iwaki city in Fukushima prefecture, a theme park, to be called Hibari Memorial Park, is planned. Another museum, Hibari Memorial Pavilion, is planned in Isogo-ward, Yokohama, her birthplace (Anonymous 1993f: 38; Anonymous 1994f: 39). As of 2000, however, only the Kyoto museum had been built and opened.

20. The Broadcasting Law mandates the following duties for NHK (Japan Public Broadcasting): "1) to broadcast high-quality programs that will both satisfy the demands of the public and elevate the country's cultural level; 2) to broadcast local as well as national programs; and 3) to contribute to the preservation of traditional culture and foster and publicize modern cultural events" (Takagi 1983: 172).

21. Unlike radio, whose early history predated the opening of commercial radio stations, television developed both public and private broadcast stations almost from its outset. In fact, NHK entered the television broadcasting scene in 1957, four years after Nippon Television Network Corporation (NTV) had begun commercial broadcasting.

22. According to Kawabata, the distinction between *hō-ban* and *yō-ban* is threefold, based on: 1) the nationality of the original record; 2) the performer's nationality; and 3) the language of the song's lyrics (1991: 335). Using these criteria, Kawabata lists the following types of music as *hō-ban*: enka, pop-oriented *kayōkyoku*, "new music," "light music" *kayōkyoku*, folk songs and traditional music, educational and children's songs, music for animation, light semiclassical music composed by Japanese composers, and karaoke; and the following as *yō-ban*: rock and disco, jazz and fusion, popular vocals, movie music, and Western classical music (1991: 331, Table 4).

23. For example, a brief survey of record labels at a Honolulu, Hawai'i, store specializing in Japanese popular music reveals that until about 1973, Nippon Columbia, the major enka-producing company, categorized what are now considered enka as *ryūkōka*; since 1973, record labels have designated certain newly released songs as enka.

Chapter 3: Producing Enka

1. In June 2000, a record producer for Kitajima Productions indicated to me in conversation that a number of these subdivisions have since closed.

2. The genre divisions in Table 3.1 are those of the music industry, as noted by Oricon. Although Oricon lists four genres, record producers and fans generally compare enka with "pops."

3. Price does not explain differences in buying habits: in the United States, CDs tend to be more expensive than cassettes, but in Japan, the price of CDs is equal to or lower than that of cassettes.

4. Different people offer different numbers. One producer at Crown Records, for example, defines an enka hit as one that has sold more than 100,000 copies; a "pops" recording, however, is not a hit unless it has sold 300,000 to 500,000 copies. A producer at Century Records considers any enka recording that has sold 50,000 copies to be a hit.

5. I use the word "record" here and "album" elsewhere to mean all forms of audio recordings, whether audiodisc, audiocassette, or audio compact disc (CD). The proliferation of new forms makes any collective reference to audio recordings awkward, so I have chosen to fall back on these dated but useful terms.

6. One record producer told me about a new male singer who debuted in May 1991. His debut song was about winter, and it did not sell well until the autumn of that year. In April 1993, nearly two years after the song's release, a news media party was held at a posh hotel in Tokyo to celebrate its sales, which had by then topped 200,000, thus making it a hit.

7. In fact, I spoke with several singers, composers, and lyricists who told me that they would not necessarily choose to perform enka were it not for the money. One veteran composer, Yoshioka Osamu, began his career writing children's songs; another, Sone Yoshiaki, wrote and performed rockabilly (early rock and roll) before settling on enka. Both men currently compose enka at least in part because of its profitability.

8. Some examples from a Euro-American context might include rereading certain novels, watching reruns of television shows, attending an opera (when one knows the music, libretto, and plot), listening to Beethoven's Fifth Symphony, watching a Shakespeare play. " Newness" is relative: one may attend a performance of a familiar Shakespeare play, for example, to appreciate an avant-garde staging.

9. Within a span of five months, from December 1992 through April 1993, Toshiba-EMI record company put no less than five collections of enka rereleases on the market. The five: *Yūsen Enka Hitto 20* (20 Cable Enka Hits; TOCT-6865; 12/16/92), *Saikin Enka Bessuto 16* (16 Best of the Latest Enka; TOCT-6899; 1/20/93), *Nihon Rettō Enka Tabi—Haiwei Enka* (Travels through Enka of the Japanese Archipelago—Highway Enka; TOCT-6916; 3/24/93), *Onna no Enka—Bessuto 16* (Women's Enka—Best 16; TOCT-8005; 4/28/93), and *Otoko no Enka—Bessuto 16* (Men's Enka—Best 16; TOCT-8006; 4/28/93). A note of interest: on the last two albums the word enka is written using different ideographs (see Chapter 2). The

ideographs on the women's album mean " love song" and have strong sexual connotations; the more neutral ideograph on the men's album means simply "performed songs."

10. The enka audience's appetite for things familiar also extends to concerts. The manager of one very popular enka star reports that the singer limits himself to two relatively new songs per concert and dedicates the rest of his performance to older hits.

11. This difference may be more of degree than of kind. I am not suggesting that no credit is given to the arranger of a song in Euro-America. In certain contexts in Euro-American music publications, arrangers are duly noted, especially when the arrangement itself is significant (for example, different arrangements of standard songs in a medley, or a band or choral arrangement of pieces). In Japan, however, the arranger is consistently given prominent separate billing on a nearly equal footing with the lyricist and the composer. If the order of names indicates any kind of hierarchy, "lyricist, composer, and arranger" is standard.

12. This practice finds a parallel in karaoke machines, which rate a singer's performance according to its closeness to the original.

13. The Oricon yearbooks are a compendium of lists that may be considered at least partial determinants of rank in the Japanese music industry. Among the lists in 1993 are the following: 1) year's top 100 single releases; 2) year's top 100 CDs; 3) year's top 100 cassettes; 4) year's top 100 albums; 5) artist sales rankings for past three years; 6) record company sales rankings for past three years; 7) top-selling lyricists; 8) top-selling composers; 9) top-selling music arrangers; 10) top-selling new singers; 11) top-requested songs on radio and cable broadcasting; 12) top-selling yōgaku; 13) production company and publishing company sales rankings; 14) top-selling videos; and 15) weekly top 100 sales lists. In addition, numerous yearly music awards also determine and express rank; the oldest of these is the Nihon Rekōdo Taishō (Japanese Record Awards; since 1959).

14. Gambaru is invoked in enka in various contexts, for example, during a concert, when a singer says she will persevere to the end of the performance; in an interview, when a singer says he will persevere to be chosen for the NHK Kōhaku Uta Gassen; in an exhortation to fans to promote a singer's new release. Singers of all ranks also invariably express the need to gambaru.

15. Tarento are a ubiquitous part of radio and television talk shows, game shows, and commercials (Miller 1995). In many cases, they have no particular talent—except that of promoting their image.

16. The reformulation of this song is somewhat unusual. In this case, its arrangement is being changed "to appeal more to a female audience," and even a few of its lyrics have been altered (Anonymous 1994b: 28).

17. One indication of the comparative activity level of record companies is the number of new single enka releases. During the period from June 1992 to June 1993, the following companies released new enka recordings: Nippon Crown Records (91), Nippon Columbia (65), Teichiku Records (48), King Records (38), Toshiba-EMI (30), Victor Entertainment Corp. (30), Tokuma Japan Communications (21), Taurus Records (16), Sony Music Entertainment (15), Pony Canyon (11), BMG Victor (11), Polydor (8), Century Records (7), Vap Records (6), Polystar (5), Warner Music Japan, Inc. (4), Apollon (3), Nihon Enka-phone (3), NEC Avenue (1), Ubaaru (1) (compiled from *Enka Jānaru*, nos. 43–49, July 25, 1992–July 25, 1993).

Comparing the number of these new releases with the capital-based size of these companies (see Appendix A) gives some indication of the place of enka in each company. For example, Nippon Columbia, by far the largest record company, puts out a large number of enka records, but this number is not necessarily so large in proportion to its size. By comparison, Nippon Crown Records, a medium-sized record company, puts out the greatest number of enka records, making enka a proportionately large part of company operations. At Teichiku Records, too, the proportion of enka to other releases within the entire company is very large, comparable to that at Nippon Crown Records.

18. In 1992–93, Teichiku and Nippon Crown Records put out enka releases at a rate of 48.0 : 1 (number of releases : capital) and 36.4 : 1, respectively. The following are the rates, in descending order, for other record companies during the same period: Taurus Records (16.0 : 1), Century Records (13.2 : 1), Tokuma Japan Communications (7.8 : 1), Pony Canyon (5.5 : 1), Polystar (5.6 : 1), King Records (4.8 : 1), Warner Music Japan, Inc. (4.0 : 1), BMG Victor (3.8 : 1), Victor Music Industries (3.0 : 1), Apollon (2.0 : 1), Toshiba-EMI (1.8 : 1), Polydor (1.7 : 1), Vap (1.2 : 1), Nippon Columbia (1.0 : 1), Sony Music Entertainment (33.1 : 1).

According to an article in *Enka Jānaru*, the following companies debuted enka shinjin in the nine-month period from October 1992 to June 1993: Nippon Crown Records (6), Teichiku (5), Victor Entertainment Corporation (4), Century Records (2), Nippon Columbia (2), King Records (2), Sony Music Entertainment (2), Tokuma Japan Communications (1), Taurus Records (1), Vap (1), Pony Canyon (1), Apollon (1), and Toshiba-EMI (1). The article also lists one shinjin for Ubaaru, but I have no further data on that company (Anonymous 1993a: 52–53).

19. Because enka is primarily a solo genre, there are very few groups. Although duets (male and female) are a significant part of the repertoire, singers who record duets together do not necessarily form any kind of group; in fact, these singers are sometimes under contract to entirely different record and production companies.

20. Additional information includes place of birth, a list of previous show business activities, and blood type. In Japan, blood type is considered an important part

of one's vital statistics, and a whole pseudo-scientific folklore is built around it. Although ostensibly cited as important information in case of an accident or emergency, blood type also becomes one of a person's, and even a group of people's (e.g., Japanese), character attributes. For more on blood ideology in Japan, see Hayashida 1976.

21. Spring is not only the season of birth, it is also the beginning of the fiscal, academic, and employment year in Japan.

22. For more on the iemoto system in English language sources, see Hsu 1975, Ortolani 1969, Read and Locke 1983, Smith 1998, and Yano 1993. The standard work in Japanese is Nishiyama 1982.

23. *Aidoru* singer is a nickname given to the teenage female and male singers who emerged in the 1970s and early 1980s as the packaged product of talent agencies. Known for their looks and upbeat personalities more than for their singing ability, they were made-for-television creations whose extreme popularity faded by the decade's end. Only a handful of these former aidoru have been able to maintain careers in show business beyond their teen years. Nagayama's transformation into an enka singer may be seen as a reflection of her lack of success as an aidoru singer and of the passing of the aidoru era. For more on Japanese pop aidoru and their popularity in other Asian countries, see Aoyagi 2000.

24. A biography of Nagayama calls her transformation *"enka tenshin"* (switching occupations to enka), noting that the promotional advertisements for her first enka single, "Higurashi" (Cicada), used the catch-phrase *"enka gannen"* (first year of enka) (Anonymous 1999: 16); see also Nagayama's home page http://www.jvc-victor.co.jp/studio/yoko/index.html.

25. This kind of information becomes a standard component of a singer's *"purofiiru"* ("profile"), a brief one-sheet reference used for publicity purposes.

26. In certain cases, any deviation from the ideal form becomes the subject of good-natured ribbing. One particularly tall, large-framed female singer overcomes her nonideal body by smiling tirelessly and giggling with her mouth covered, projecting a stage persona that is unfailingly nonaggressive and girlish. As if in compensation for her size, she tends to diminish her body through inwardly focused gestures and demure movements.

This definition of the ideal body for a female enka singer contrasts with the other female bodies glorified in the Japanese media, which emphasize a more Western-derived look: large breasts, long legs, full hips.

27. Unlike customs of dress in Western societies, kimono wearing is an art and an etiquette taught by certified teachers as one of the traditional arts of Japan. For more on kimono in English, see Dalby 1993.

28. Itsuki had one of his stage names for only a day, and even before his debut, while he was a high school student, he performed under yet another name.

29. "Kokoro-zake" (*Sake of the Heart*), with lyrics by Miura Yasuteru, music by Yamaguchi Hiroshi; recorded by the female singer Fuji Ayako (Sony Records SRDL-3533). The four teachers and their lessons: 1) anonymous, mini-lesson, *Karaoke Fan* 11 (119): 162; 2) anonymous, mini-lesson, *Enka Jānaru*, 43: 75; 3) composer Miki Takashi, full lesson, *Karaoke Fan* 11 (122): 162–63; 4a) composer Ichikawa Shōsuke, full lesson, *Karaoke Enka Kashō-hō III*, 28–31; 4b) composer Ichikawa Shōsuke, full lesson, April 19, 1993, television broadcast of NHK *Karaoke Enka Kashō-hō III*.

30. A number of songs might be written for a debuting singer and recorded on demonstration tapes. From these tapes, two songs are selected as side-A and side-B of a single release. According to a seasoned enka composer, one must strategize carefully in making these selections. For the debut release of a young female shinjin, for example, he composed a rhythmic, energetic, *akarui* (light) song for side-A, chosen because of her youth, and a slower, more typically enka one for side-B. The contrast, he felt, would show off the new singer's versatility.

31. The *Oricon Yearbook* lists the following information in given order: stage name, given name, birthdate, record and/or production companies (with contact phone number), debut song, debut date.

32. One indication of their success is that they issue a second record. This is not to say that their debut record was a big hit, but only that it sold well enough to warrant a second record.

33. Ivy interprets the giving of "naked" money to performers of *taishū engeki*, a genre with which enka is closely connected, as a kind of social transgression (1995: 234).

34. Singing a duet with someone is a highly valued form of intimacy akin to sharing a part of oneself. From the reaction of participants I witnessed here and on other occasions, I would surmise that when the duet partner is a professional singer or someone prestigious, the singing bestows some of the professional's status on the participant. Moreover, many feel a sensual thrill in comingling their voice with that of a professional singer.

35. These estimates were given to me by Japanese acquaintances, who suggest that guests would probably have treated the debut party much like a wedding and given gifts accordingly.

36. My bouquet of a dozen red roses cost ¥5,000 ($45).

37. It is in the lyrics that enka finds some of its most tangible ties with the past (see Chapter 5).

38. This is not unlike the advanced publicity given to movies in the United States and elsewhere.

39. The only ostensible connection I could see between the singer and the festival was that the festival was celebrating the blossoming of *fuji* (wisteria) and the singer's stage name had the word "*fuji*" in it.

40. In general, these songs tend to be non-enka songs, although this process has also generated some enka hits.

41. Sometimes a product may have some connection to singing: in 1993, the handsome young male singer Koganezawa Shūji could be seen in advertisements for a throat spray. But most products—antacids, futon, or cosmetics, for example—do not.

Chapter 4: Enka on Stage

1. Fox is theorizing from his analysis of American country and western music, a genre that has many parallels with enka. The "re-naturalizing" conventions of country music are also common to enka.

2. Certain practical features of live enka concerts are noteworthy. They can take place on any day of the week, not only on weekends. Evening performances are early, usually at 6:30 P.M., due both to the age of the enka audience and to the heavy use of public transportation, which tends to shut down around midnight. Ticket prices for regular concerts in 1991–93 ranged from ¥1,900 ($17) for the cheapest seat at a lower-ranked singer's concert to ¥11,000 ($100) for the most expensive seat at a higher-ranked singer's concert. The median price was ¥3,000 ($27) for the lowest-priced seats and ¥8,000 ($73) for the most expensive. In addition to these regular concerts and recitals, enka singers also perform at *shōtai* (private) concerts, at which the host companies entertain their clients. These fully paid up concerts are a boon to promoters, who have seen sales of enka concert tickets drop steadily in recent years. As a result of these shōtai performances, which take singers out of the normal concert circuit, however, regular fans do not get to see their favorite stars in concert as often as before.

3. The printed program often identifies not only the order in which the songs will be performed but also those moments set aside for interactions with fans—for example, the aforementioned *fuan purezento kōnā* (fan present corner), the *duetto kōnā* (duet corner; singing duets with individual fans on stage), or the *tōku kōnā* (talk corner), during which the singer is expected to fill in with stage patter and sometimes encores.

4. This format is similar to taishū engeki, with which enka is closely associated.

5. One of the most skilled at this sort of chatting is the veteran singer Kitajima Saburō, whose performance I describe in the Prologue. His stories, which combine hardship with humor, range from reminiscences of his early career struggles to the minor difficulties he encountered in getting to the concert hall amid heavy traffic. His patter is warm, chatty, and familiar, not unlike the conversation of a beloved uncle.

6. At one of the enka concerts I attended, the "duet corner" became an opportunity to poke fun at the non-enka crowd. Instead of asking for volunteers from the

audience to sing a duet with the star, concert staff had selected a passer-by at random beforehand, a scruffy-looking twenty-one-year-old male with long, peroxided hair in the style of a rock-and-roll singer, not at all the type of person likely to know or admire enka. The announcer brought out a gold lamé blazer for the man to wear while singing with the star, who was dressed in a dazzling gown. The announcer also revealed that the song lyrics had been written out for the amateur in simple *hiragana* syllabary (easily read by even a seven-year-old child). Following comments about how well the two looked together, they began their duet, one of the singer's enka hits. To my surprise, the amateur did seem to know at least some of the song, perhaps because of preshow coaching. The singer's reaction, however, was one of mock horror. During an orchestral interlude, she turned her head to the audience, her eyes wide, her hand covering a staged laugh, as if to say, "My god, where did they get this guy?!" When he made the occasional mistake, the singer helped him along as one would a child, with infinite patience. At the end, the amateur, who had responded throughout with good humor, was presented with an autographed photo of the star and a tape of their duet. What seemed especially ironic to me about this display of gawking and finger-pointing was its target. Members of the enka world may be mocked by detractors among the young and intellectual sectors of Japanese society for being out of step with the times, but here, in the delimited world of the enka concert, enka fans took great delight in playing insiders able to mock an outsider.

7. See Appendix B for a list of regular mass media enka programs in the Tokyo area in 1992.

8. An Osaka radio station owner told me that no station in the Kansai area (Osaka, Kyoto, Kobe, and surroundings) broadcasts a program devoted exclusively to enka; instead, enka is included on more general, popular music programs.

9. NHK is a prime producer of enka shows on television, as on radio. Among the five commercial television stations in the Kantō area, Terebi Tokyo (TV Tokyo) produces the majority of enka broadcasts, including both regular shows and specials. Some of the latter, for example, special spring or summer shows, are seasonal. Others consist of the televised concerts of top stars or their biographies. Still others are nostalgic retrospectives of popular music, in particular, that of the Shōwa era.

10. *Hanamichi* refers to a special elevated passageway used on the kabuki and the nō stage. *Hana* (flower, gift) suggests its possible origin as a platform on which gifts from fans, attached to a flowering branch, were laid for the actors (Shively 1978: 16). Since *hanamichi* designates a special runway for dramatic entrances and exits, a symbolic transition between the world in front of the curtain and the world behind it, I take *Enka no Hanamichi* (the hanamichi of enka), the title of the show, as an evocation of a theatrical pathway to the imaginary of enka.

11. The following is a list of singers who appeared on the program five or more times between January 1992 and July 1993, and how often they appeared. Male singers who appeared most frequently: Horiuchi Takao (8), Itsuki Hiroshi (6), Yoshi Ikuzō (5), Hosokawa Takashi (5), and Mori Shin'ichi (5). Female singers who appeared most frequently: Kawanaka Miyuki (8), Kobayashi Sachiko (8), Sakamoto Fuyumi (8), Fuji Ayako (7), Kōzai Kaori (7), Kei Unsuku (7), Ōtsuki Miyako (7), Godai Natsuko (6), Ishikawa Sayuri (6), Jinno Mika (5), Nakamura Mitsuko (5), and Yashiro Aki (5). During that period, female singers outnumbered males by 130 to 69, or nearly two to one. These performers represent mid- to upper-ranked enka singers who sing mostly "mood" enka (*mūdo-kayō*), with some "pops"-style (*poppusu-kei*) enka, but not much do-enka.

12. The extent to which, in the enka world of the early 1990s, scripts and songs were still written out by hand is striking, given the proliferation of word processors and computers in other areas of Japanese daily life.

13. Late-night television in Japan—shows broadcast between midnight and 5:00 A.M.—a genre unto itself in the 1990s, is dominated by the young and often the risqué. In its no-holds-barred attitude, late-night programming can be wildly irreverent, and to an American, shockingly explicit, especially those shows that veer over into soft pornography.

14. The Oricon charts are similar to those published by *Billboard* in the United States, but in Japan they are predictive rather than reflective. In general, for example, they are available two weeks in advance of the week to which they refer; because of the early taping of *Enka TV*, however, they are made available to its producers four weeks in advance.

15. Kawashima says that older people sometimes complain that the one-camera technique makes them dizzy.

Chapter 5: Clichés of Excess

1. I am grateful to Merry White, herself a fan of jazz and of country and western music, for pointing out this specific kind of appeal.

2. I took the initial one hundred titles from the following sources: 1) songs performed on the television program *Enka no Hanamichi* between July 1992 and July 1993; 2) most often requested karaoke songs, compiled by and published in the monthly magazine *Karaoke Fan* between August 1992 and August 1993; 3) songs with high Oricon-projected sales, as published in *Enka Jānaru* between August 1992 and August 1993; 4) songs selected for English translation by Mr. Harry Urata, my teacher in Hawai'i, and published serially as "Karaoke Korner" in *Hawaii Pacific Press* through August 1993; 5) the 1992 and 1993 editions of the annual pocket-sized songbooks of popular enka songs selected and distributed to his pupils by Mr. Noda Hisashi, my teacher in Japan; 6) songs taught by the composer and teacher

Mr. Ichikawa Shōsuke in the NHK televised series *Karaoke Enka Kashō-hō I, II, and III* in the years 1991–93; and 7) a list of the hundred most popular karaoke songs in 1992, compiled and published by Nihon Amachua Kayō Renmei (NAK). After compiling this list, I decided to investigate certain themes, in particular, the concepts of "furusato" and "mother" discussed in Chapter 7, and selected additional songs to explore these issues. As a result, the corpus is not as tidy as that I had initially proposed, and songs about "mother" may be overrepresented. I have used the following songbooks as references: *Furusato Enka Dai-zen-shū* (*Furusato Enka* Collection), comp. Nagata Gyōji (Tokyo: Do-re-mi Ongaku Shuppansha, 1992), containing 234 songs; and *Enka no Kokoro* (The Heart of Enka), comp. Imai Iwao (Tokyo: Do-re-mi Ongaku Shuppansha, 1992), containing the lyrics of 1,612 songs. All the songs in the corpus are included in at least one of the collections that style themselves "enka" songbooks.

The breakdown of the corpus of songs by decade is as follows: 1950s, 3; 1960s, 5; 1970s, 12; 1980s, 36; 1990s, 59. The Japanese language is a heavily gendered one, and in most instances, whether a song is sung from a man's or a woman's point of view is clear from the language or the stereotypical situation. The breakdown by gender is as follows: men's, 33; women's, 76; duets, 4; ambiguous, 2. The fact that women's songs outnumber men's songs by two to one reflects the general trend I discuss in Chapter 3.

3. This is not to say that no waka is composed today, but only that it carries with it an aura of tradition and historicity, following set forms.

4. This may be one reason why, according to one enka teacher, young people and others less knowledgeable about the genre prefer not to sing enka songs with serifu, and thus tend not to sing do-enka.

5. "Ringo Oiwake" (1952) was sung by Misora Hibari, whose early career as a child singer and movie star was built on her image as a plucky war orphan.

6. Mita, whose study covers the years 1828-1963, gathered his songs from the 497 titles listed in the "Annual Table of Japanese Songs" at the end of Shigure Otowa's *Collected Songs and Ballads of Japan* (*Nihon Kayōshū*) (Tokyo: Shakai Shisōsha, 1963), eliminating those duplicated in the annual lists or those whose lyrics could not be verified. He identified 25 emotional categories, assigned the songs to these categories, and then analyzed them chronologically. The goal of Mita's study was to develop a history of emotion in modern Japan based on its expression in popular song. My goal, by contrast, is a more synchronic one: to look at the production and consumption of popular music in the 1990s—including that of older songs—in order to probe the meanings given to enka.

7. This excerpt is taken from a serifu and is therefore not in verse form.

8. I used various methods to identify the musical kata of enka. Several Japanese manufacturers of electronic keyboards include enka as one of the available

preprogrammed musical style selections. Of those available to me, Kawai offered the greatest range. When I visited a Honolulu showroom in November 1994, I found no fewer than four keyboard models with an enka selection, each with slight variations. Moreover, each keyboard offers not only a rhythmic pattern, but also an accompaniment pattern, an introduction and ending pattern (rhythm alone or with accompaniment), and an "arrangement expander," which gives a slightly more elaborate variation on the rhythm and/or accompaniment. Further increasing the possibilities, the Kawai model includes a "one-finger ad-lib" feature: pressing any of seventeen keys generates different melodic patterns (chromatically from the G below middle C to the B above middle C). For this study, I used a Kawai Personal Keyboard MS50. Theoretically, one could derive an extensive list of rhythms, accompaniment patterns, and melodic phrases from the electronic keyboard, but in my experience these seemed meaningful only if one already knew something about each genre.

The bimonthly magazine *Enka Jānaru* features a music "*seminā*" (seminar) and contest, in which readers send in original enka songs to be ranked and critiqued by judges, who include professional composers and record producers. I drew on the judges' comments about winning entries and on the specific comments published as "*sakkyoku kurinikku*" (song composition "clinic") to further refine my conceptualizations of the musical language of enka. I also analyzed several broadcasts of the "Music Academy" section of the late-night television show *Enka TV* (broadcast dates in 1992: Aug. 8, 15; Oct. 3, 10, 24; Nov. 7, 14, 21; Dec. 5, 12, 19; in 1993: Jan. 9, 16, 23; Feb. 6; Apr. 3, 24; May 8) discussed in the chapter. In this segment, the popular music composer and program cohost Sone Yoshiaki uses various musical means to convert other forms of popular music into enka, thus helping to define enka's musical parameters.

Finally, and most significantly, I simply listened to the music. Although in the course of this study I listened to hundreds of songs whose characteristics have left their imprint in my aural memory, I selected 30 performances of 28 songs (noted by an asterisk in Appendix C) for analysis. Of these performances, 20 are by female singers and 10 by male singers; of the songs, 19 are classified as women's songs and 9 as men's songs. Using these methods, I have identified what I consider to be the musical patterns of enka. These kata and my interpretations are my own construction, not necessarily those of composers. For a more exhaustive analysis of the musical characteristics of enka, see Okada 1991. My purpose in the following description is to provide a context for more detailed comments about subjective kata later on.

9. According to Kitahara Michio (1966: 280), the introduction of Scottish and Irish pentatonic music into Japan through school songs greatly influenced the adoption of yonanuki scales in Japanese popular songs such as enka. For more on the establishment of the Japanese public school music education program during the Meiji

era, as well as its subsequent effects on certain aspects of musical life in Japan, see Malm 1971: 265–77 and Okada 1991: 285–86.

10. I do not have comparable data for Euro-American popular songs in any genre. However, my analysis of twelve popular jazz songs revealed a range that varied from an octave to a perfect twelfth, four notes wider than an octave, with a median of a minor ninth. My analysis of fifteen Euro-American Christmas songs, including popular songs and Christian hymn-type songs, showed an even narrower range of a major third to a major ninth, one note wider than an octave, with a median of an octave.

11. This musical example is written in the key of C minor for purposes of comparison with Example 2. However, Sone plays chords in whatever key is appropriate to the piece he is demonstrating.

12. The low vocal range in these songs contrasts with the very high range of some min'yō folk songs sung by female singers, especially the high *hayashi kotoba* (sung or shouted interjections) performed by one or more female singers to accompany some forms of min'yō.

13. This low-pitched female voice can also be heard in Kinomiya Ryōko's narration for the television program *Enka no Hanamichi* (see Chapter 4).

14. In conversation, these *aizuchi* (listener utterances) range from the formulaic, "Is that so?" ("*Aa, sō desu ka ?*") to empathetic grunts, moans, or breathy exhalations. Aizuchi vary according to sex role, status, age group, and social situation.

15. In these and other examples of music and text, the syllables are written nonsemantically, omitting hyphens between the syllables of one word and dashes for those syllables spanning more than one note. For the sake of text and note correspondences, long vowels are written out, rather than indicated with a macron.

16. The special attention paid to the end (and endings) of events also extends to other aspects of performance. The final day in a series (e.g., a two-week sumō wrestling tournament or an enka singer's month-long performing engagement, as described in Chapter 1), is called *senshūraku* (a close; a finish) and is marked by special activities.

17. As I discovered during my own enka singing lessons, slowing down the vibrato is very difficult for one unaccustomed to Japanese vocal production or style.

18. This vocal gesture has become standardized to the extent that, during one performance I attended, two singers singing a duet coordinated their yuri precisely, beginning and ending at the same time and with vibrato of approximately the same wave pattern.

19. The tremolo technique of guitar and mandolin playing (CK-3) common in enka shares some of these characteristics with yuri.

20. In Japan, there are formulaic ways of expressing degrees of exertion in everyday activities. A group carrying something heavy might shout "*Yoisho!*" or one of its

abbreviated variants; someone rising from a seated position might mumble it softly. Young children often mimic their elders in exclaiming "Yoisho" as they lift an object or stand up.

21. The rolled "r" is not standard Tokyo-dialect Japanese. In asking Japanese people of different ages, regions, socioeconomic backgrounds, and education levels about its significance, I have received a variety of responses. These include associations with 1) intense emotion; 2) yakuza (organized crime); 3) shitamachi (downtown); 4) Kansai (Osaka and environs); 5) working class; and 6) older forms of Japanese. Although I have not been able to verify these associations, it is worth noting that the only consensus, at least among these informants, is that it is nonstandard.

22. My analysis is based on the following materials: 1) cartoon figures of singers used as cover art for *Enka Jānaru*, March 1989 to November 1994; 2) depictions in advertisements or on record jackets of 22 male and 71 female singers, published in *Enka Jānaru*, May 1989 to November 1994; and 3) observations of live and televised enka performances, April 1992 to December 1994. These interpretations of body poses and gestures are my own. In identifying bodily kata, I have chosen to emphasize the patterning of emotional expression, with the understanding, however, that not all physical expression is culturally patterned.

23. The kimono itself contributes to an "aesthetic of the back," according to which the obi (sash) and the fabric design are best displayed. In Japan, the *ushiro sugata* (back form) of a female in a kimono has long been an important element in the aesthetics of the body (Dalby 1993: 328).

The notion of "reading" someone's back includes attentiveness to both the physical and the emotional state of the other person. I was impressed, for example, when a Japanese mother mentioned to me that she could tell her six-year-old son was happy and growing by the feel of his back as she scrubbed him in the bath.

Chapter 6: Consuming Enka's Imaginary

1. Sepp Linhart's description of *sakariba* (amusement quarters) activities reveals the life—drinking after hours, male domain, song—in which enka plays an integral part. The sakariba occupies a liminal space between work and home, a "zone of liberty" in which a (male) worker can relax and refresh himself for the next day's work (Linhart 1986: 238; cf. Allison 1994).

2. I take karaoke to be a form of consumption here, especially as it is conceived by record and production companies, even though karaoke also produces enka on the amateur level.

3. Robertson (1998) does not necessarily attribute all female fandom to homoeroticism, but she does suggest that lesbianism is a recurring theme of titillation in the discourse of Takarazuka fandom.

4. See Curtis 1983: 126–78 for more on the role of kōenkai in Japan's current political structure.

5. Here (Shinichi Mori Fan Club), not only is *kōenkai* translated as " fan club," but the order of the singer's name is given in the standard Western order (given first name, family surname).

6. This reserved stage manner stands in direct contrast to Mori's mingling with the audience discussed in Chapter 4. The point here is that each type of action is a performance, a kind of kata. Mori is, as required, the serious, unsmiling enka singer on stage and the friendly, roving handshaker off stage.

7. Takie Sugiyama Lebra discusses *omoiyari* as "among the virtues considered indispensable for one to be really human, morally mature, and deserving of respect" (1976: 38).

8. In the 1990s, Japan introduced prepaid telephone cards, which could be used to make phone calls at a slightly discounted rate, and by the end of the decade, most public telephones accepted them. Today, many in Japan collect these telephone cards, but for collectors, a card that has been used even once (as indicated by a perforation) is worthless. The telephone cards sold by the Mori Shin'ichi Kōenkai cost ¥1000 ($9) each.

9. Min'on is one of Japan's largest music promotion organizations.

10. Red is the color of youth; coupled with white, it is also the color of festivals and celebration.

11. The cherry tree, recognized for the fleeting beauty of its blossoms, is a well-known icon of Japanese culture and aesthetics.

12. According to the head of the Hawai'i fan club, Mori has a home in Honolulu and travels there about once a year.

13. In 1972, a *sunakku* ("snack"; bar) in Kobe offered patrons the then unique opportunity to sing like the professionals using professional karaoke tapes and equipment (Ogawa 1989: 1). The success of this enterprise marked the beginning of the wildly successful phenomenon of karaoke for public participation. Initially, karaoke became associated with the world of bars—male patrons (especially middle-aged businessmen), female hostesses, nightlife, alcohol, and enka.

Karaoke's global consumption suggested opportunities for many kinds of music, including enka, to be shared across national boundaries. For example, as of 1994, Sega Enterprises Ltd. had plans to link Japan, South Korea, Taiwan, Hong Kong, and the United States through karaoke network stations. Linked by telephone lines and computer stations, singers in one country could choose from songs available in any of the other countries (Anonymous 1994a: B6).

14. "Singability" does not necessarily mean that a song is written within a pitch range accessible to the general public. If a professional singer's recording is considered too high or too low, the karaoke version of the song will be pitched at the

general public's level. In addition, laser disc machinery can easily change keys within a four-step range.

15. In these contests, the judging ranges from fair to arbitrary. Many larger national contests do an initial screening of contestants through a preliminary tape, which the judges hear "blind." Some large local contests, however, have a different set of judges for each level of screening. One enka composer/judge described the procedure: the initial 200 or so contestants compete before lower-ranked judges in a large preliminary round; the 40 who are thus selected then compete before another set of higher-ranked judges in a featured public performance.

One questionable aspect of contest judging is the system of "revolving" judges. Although procedures usually limit each contestant to one verse, hearing even 200 contestants can take a long time, perhaps four hours or more. For this reason, as I saw at some of the contests I attended, the judges listen on a revolving basis: four judges are always listening and scoring at any one time, but a total of eight judges take turns on the panel over the course of the contest. Thus, because no individual judge listens to or scores all the contestants, no individual judge can conclude, based on his or her own evaluation, that a particular contestant is better than all the rest. Instead, the judgment is a consensual one based on the scoring of the group as a whole. This system explains why judges may often be seen conferring with one another during a contestant's performance. It may also in part explain why it is permissible for the teacher of one or more of the contestants to serve as a judge. Impartiality is either disregarded or assumed to be built into the system. The judges themselves are usually friendly with one another and know if a contestant is the student of a fellow judge. Thus, although the outcome of contests may not be fixed as such, according to one karaoke contest judge with whom I spoke, it is not inconceivable that among contestants whose skill is nearly equal, judges may favor a fellow judge's student over the others out of respect for that judge. In some cases, the favor passes from one judge to another in the following year. Thus, the results reward skill, but they also acknowledge social obligation.

16. Her testimonial specifies that her singing was (re)born and changed, but the headline states that she was.

17. *Kuripu* or "Creap" is a popular (if unfortunately named) nondairy creamer sold in Japan.

Chapter 7: Enka as Engendered Longing

1. This is not to suggest that the songs female songwriters write would necessarily be different from those men write, only that the possibility of expressing heterogenous female subjectivities might increase if women were the creators of these words and notes.

2. The use of English words in Japanese lyrics is more typical of "pops" songs.

3. Social drinking creates and affirms homosocial masculine ties. In the extreme, this kind of male bonding through drink even extends to animals. For example, as reported in a 1994 television program about a monkey trainer (male) and his head monkey (also male), the trainer tried different tactics to rejuvenate the monkey's lackluster performance. Finally he took the monkey off to an isolated spot, where they drank sake and, according to the television commentator, had a "heart-to-heart talk." Subsequently, the monkey rallied and was able to resume performing. Commentators on the program marveled at the effectiveness of the "heart-to-heart talk," lubricated by sake, in reaffirming the male-male bond between trainer and monkey.

4. Japan has a long history of crossing in performance. The most well known example is the *onnagata* (male actor playing the part of a woman) of the kabuki stage, whose artistry, highly developed since the seventeenth century, brings the depiction of femininity to dizzying heights. Less well known in the West, but no less popular in Japan, is the Takarazuka all-female revue established in the early twentieth century, in which designated female performers play the roles of men (see Robertson 1989, 1992a, 1992b, 1992c, 1998).

5. Two cultural elements help to illuminate crossing in Japanese performance. One is the Buddhist-derived concept of *henshin* (transformation), which informs much of traditional Japanese theater. Henshin is that process by which one being may metamorphose into another, both on and below the surface (Gunji 1991). The other is the Confucian-based concept of *yin-yang*, a set of organizing principles that emphasize, among other things, the dual nature (in this case, male and female) residing within all beings. The assumption of yin-yang gives spiritual substance to kata-derived presentations of gender. One comes up with gendered kata not out of thin air, but plumbed from within the depths of oneself.

6. It was newsworthy when, in 1991, four years after her debut and a succession of men's song hits, Sakamoto released a woman's song for the first time, "Hi no Kuni no Onna" (A Woman of Volcanic Land).

7. In this respect, middle-aged and older female fans of Mikawa Ken'ichi are not unlike the female fans of Liberace (né Wladziu Valentino Liberace, 1919–1987), a flamboyant American entertainer (pianist) whose lavish outfits and lifestyle garnered him considerable fame. Unlike Mikawa, however, Liberace's homosexuality was a constant, if furtive, topic of gossip and the subject of countless tabloid exposés, including his death from allegedly AIDS-related causes. None of this kind of lurid speculation surrounds Mikawa.

8. The implication of the label "Shitamachi no Tamasaburō" is that whereas the Tamasaburō of kabuki comes from what is today considered the "high culture" of Japan, Shitamachi no Tamasaburō comes from "low culture." This kind of homage to a well-known performer has been extended, so that there are now other cross-

gendered performers labeled "X [name of place or troupe] no Shitamachi no Tamasaburō" (the Shitamachi-no-Tamasaburo of X).

9. Compare this with that of the *otokoyaku*, or female player of men's roles, in Takarazuka. According to Robertson, the fascination of many fans with otokoyaku is that a woman is allowed to transgress the codified boundaries of femininity and masculinity (1998: 82). The otokoyaku, like the onnagata, is consumed as a signifier of the "in-between" one, whose role interacts with the biological sex of the actor. Otokoyaku and onnagata do not perform, respectively, Man or Woman, but create and administer spaces of their own making.

10. According to an informant, this is one song that can be either a man's or woman's song.

11. Daniels and Cosgrove draw parallels between Erwin Panofsky's notions of iconography as "the identification of conventional, consciously inscribed symbols" and Clifford Geertz's project of interpreting culture as a text of decipherable symbols (1988: 2–4).

12. One such nostalgically scenic railway line takes passengers from Kanaya (Shizuoka prefecture), roughly 200 kilometers southwest of Tokyo, into the mountains to Senzu and then over Sessokyo Gorge to Ikawa.

13. Tansman lists enka's "mythic places" as the *roji* (alleyway), harbor, train station, and rural town (1996: 116).

14. Although there is no way of knowing whether the place name contributed to the song's success, the lyricist reconstructed the process of song-writing to imply that it had.

Epilogue

1. The Rashōmon reference is to "Yabu no Naka," a 1922 short story by Akutagawa Ryūnosuke (1892–1927), which presents seven versions of a rape-murder, each told from the perspective of a different participant, observer, or passer-by. The point of the story is that there is no absolute truth, only different perspectives, each with its own intrinsic truth. It became the basis for Akira Kurosawa's acclaimed 1950 film *Rashōmon*.

2. This melody, by the nineteenth-century Scottish poet Robert Burns, is played electronically at various intersections in the Tokyo/Yokohama area to signal a green pedestrian crossing light.

References

Abt, Dean
　1987　Music video: Impact of the visual dimension. In *Popular Music and Communication*, ed. James Lull. Newbury Park, Calif.: Sage Publications.

Adorno, Theodor
　1990　On popular music. In *On Record: Rock, Pop, and the Written Word*, ed. Simon Frith and Andrew Goodwin. London: Routledge.

Allison, Anne
　1994　*Nightwork: Sexuality, Pleasure, and Corporate Masculinity in a Tokyo Hostess Club*. Chicago: University of Chicago Press.
　1996　*Permitted and Prohibited Desires: Mothers, Comics, and Censorship in Japan*. Boulder, Colo.: Westview Press.

Anderson, Benedict
　1983　*Imagined Communities*. London: Verso.

Anonymous
　1987　Nihonjin ni wa enka ga niau (Enka is well-suited to Japanese people). *Nihon Keizai Shimbun*, Jan. 18: 14–15.
　1990　Enka: Japan's elegiac ballad. *The East* 25 (6): 7–13.
　1991　Hiruma wa misesu ga senryō!? (During the day, is your wife being held captive!?). *Sentoraru Ribingu* (Central Living) 11/16: 16.

1992a Kokoro-zake. *Enka Jānaru* 43 (7/25): 75.
1992b Kokoro-zake. *Karaoke Fan* 11 (119): 162.
1992c Ōen shitaku naru kashu no jōken to wa? (What are the conditions for a singer who wants to gain public backing?). *Konfidensu* (Confidence) 26 (1335): 21–37.
1993a '93 enka dētā ('93 enka data). *Enka Jānaru* 48: 51–53.
1993b Anata o butai de yori utsukushiku miseru: Meekyappu-hō (Make-up methods to show oneself off more beautifully on stage). *Karaoke Taishō* 13 (4): 14–17.
1993c '93 kayō-kai saikin jōhō ('93 recent news of the popular music world). *Karaoke Fan* 12 (126): 25–29.
1993d "Enka no Hanamichi" no miryoku (The appeal of "Enka no Hanamichi"). *Karaoke Taishō* 13 (6): 13–16.
1993e Kotoshi mo Kōhaku ni tāgetto Kanmuri Jirō (Kanmuri Jirō, who will again make the Kōhaku his target this year). *Enka Jānaru* 50: 44.
1993f Misora Hibari Pavilion in Kyoto. *Kokiku* 19 (12): 38.
1994a International karaoke network planned by Sega. *Honolulu Star-Bulletin*, May 31: B6.
1994b "Josei-ka" shite hitto ni (Looking toward a "feminized" hit). *Enka Jānaru* 53: 28.
1994c Kadokawa Hiroshi kashu 20-shūnen kinen: Zenkoku karaoke konkūru (Singer Kadokawa Hiroshi's 20th year commemoration: National karaoke contest). *Kokiku* 20 (4): 39.
1994d Kore wa shiranakatta, gei-mei no yurai (Here's something you did not know—the origin of stage names). *Enka Jānaru* 52: 47–49.
1994e Mikasa Yūko no "Kiso Koi Garasu" Nagano de Dai-hitto Kigan (At Nagano, Mikasa Yuko prays for a big hit in her song "Kiso Koi Garasu"). *Kokiku* 20 (6): 38.
1994f Misora Hibari Museum—A phenomenal success. *Kokiku* 20 (5): 39.
1995   Teresa Ten. *Kokiku* 21 (1): 13.
1999   Yōko no enka. *Uta no Techō* 7 (73): 14–17.

Aoyagi Hiroshi
 2000 Pop idols and the Asian identity. In *Japan Pop! Inside the World of Japanese Popular Culture*, ed. Tim Craig. Armonk, N.Y.: M. E. Sharpe.

Appadurai, Arjun
 1981 The past as a scarce resource. *Man* 16: 201–19.

Arita Yoshio
1991   Enka wa shinda ka? (Has enka died?). *Asahi Jānaru*, Dec. 27: 21–26.

Asahi Shimbun Sei-bu Honsha
1992   *Hana ga Aru: Gendai o Utsushi-dasu Hitobito* (There are blossoms: People who cast light upon our times). Tokyo: Ishobō Yūgen-gaisha.

Atkins, E. Taylor
1998   The war on jazz, or jazz goes to war: Toward a new cultural order in wartime Japan. *positions* 6 (2): 345–94.

Bachnik, Jane M., and Charles J. Quinn, Jr., eds.
1994   *Situated Meaning: Inside and Outside in Japanese Self, Society, and Language*. Princeton: Princeton University Press.

Befu Harumi
1993   Nationalism and nihonjinron. In *Cultural Nationalism in East Asia: Representation and Identity*, ed. Harumi Befu. Berkeley: University of California, Institute of East Asian Studies.

Benedict, Ruth
1946   *The Chrysanthemum and the Sword: Patterns of Japanese Culture*. New York: Meridian.

Bennett, John W.
1967   Japanese economic growth: Background for social change. In *Aspects of Social Change in Modern Japan*, ed. Ronald P. Dore. Princeton: Princeton University Press.

Bensman, Joseph
1983   Introduction: The phenomenology and sociology of the performing arts. In *Performers and Performances: The Social Organization of Artistic Work*, ed. Jack B. Kamerman and Rosanne Martorella. South Hadley, Mass.: J. F. Bergin Publishers.

Bestor, Theodore C.
1989   *Neighborhood Tokyo*. Stanford: Stanford University Press.

Bourdieu, Pierre
1977   *Outline of a Theory of Practice*. Cambridge: Cambridge University Press.
1984   *Distinction: A Social Critique of the Judgement of Taste*. Cambridge: Harvard University Press.

Boyarin, Jonathan
1994   Space, time, and the politics of memory. In *Remapping Memory: The Politics of Timespace*, ed. Jonathan Boyarin. Minneapolis: University of Minnesota Press.

Brandon, James
1978   Form in Kabuki acting. In James Brandon, William Malm, and Donald Shively, *Studies in Kabuki*. Honolulu: University Press of Hawai'i.

Brower, Robert H.
1983   Waka. In *Kodansha Encyclopedia of Japan*, ed. Itasaka Gen. Vol. 8. Tokyo: Kodansha.

Ching, Leo
1996   Imaginings in the empires of the sun. In *Contemporary Japan and Popular Culture*, ed. John Whittier Treat. Honolulu: University of Hawai'i Press.

Clammer, John
1995   Consuming bodies: Constructing and representing the female body in contemporary Japanese print media. In *Women, Media and Consumption in Japan*, ed. Lise Skov and Brian Moeran. Honolulu: University of Hawai'i Press.

Conner, Judith, and Mayumi Yoshida
1984   *Tokyo City Guide*. Tokyo: Ryuko Tsushin Co.

Creed, Gerald W., and Barbara Ching
1997   Introduction: Recognizing rusticity: Identity and the power of place. In *Knowing Your Place: Rural Identity and Cultural Hierarchy*, ed. Barbara Ching and Gerald Creed. New York: Routledge.

Curtis, Gerald L.
1983   *Election Campaigning Japanese Style*. New York: Kodansha International.

Dalby, Liza Crihfield
- 1983 *Geisha.* New York: Vintage Books.
- 1993 *Kimono: Fashioning Culture.* New Haven: Yale University Press.

Daniels, Stephen, and Denis Cosgrove
- 1988 Introduction: Iconography and landscape. In *The Iconography of Landscape,* ed. Denis Cosgrove and Stephen Daniels. Cambridge: Cambridge University Press.

Davis, Darrell William
- 1996 *Picturing Japaneseness: Monumental Style, National Identity, Japanese Film.* New York: Columbia University Press.

Davis, Fred
- 1979 *Yearning for Yesterday: A Sociology of Nostalgia.* New York: Free Press.

De Certeau, Michel
- 1984 *The Practice of Everyday Life.* Berkeley: University of California Press.

DeVos, George
- 1973 *Socialization for Achievement.* Berkeley: University of California Press.

Doi Takeo
- 1971 *The Anatomy of Dependence.* Tokyo: Kodansha.
- 1986 *The Anatomy of Self: The Individual vs. Society.* Tokyo: Kodansha.

Donald, James
- 1993 How English is it? Popular literature and national culture. In *Space and Place: Theories of Identity and Location,* ed. Erica Carter, James Donald, and Judith Squires. London: Lawrence and Wishart.

Dore, Ronald
- 1958 *City Life in Japan: A Study of a Tokyo Ward.* Berkeley: University of California Press.

Dower, John W.
- 1993 *Japan in War and Peace: Selected Essays.* New York: New Press.

Embree, John F.
- 1939 *Suye Mura, A Japanese Village.* Chicago: University of Chicago Press.

Field, Norma
1989 Somehow: The postmodern as atmosphere. In *Postmodernism and Japan*, ed. Masao Miyoshi and H. D. Harootunian. Durham: Duke University Press.

Fox, Aaron
1992 The jukebox of history: Narratives of loss and desire in the discourse of country music. *Popular Music* 11(1): 53–72.

Frith, Simon
1987 The industrialization of popular music. In *Popular Music and Communication*, ed. James Lull. London: Sage Publications.

Frye, Northrop
1976 *Secular Scripture: A Study of the Structure of Romance*. Cambridge: Harvard University Press.

Fujie, Linda
1989 Popular music. In *Handbook of Japanese Popular Culture*, ed. Richard Gid Powers and Hidetoshi Kato. New York: Greenwood Press.

Fujitani, Takashi
1993 Inventing, forgetting, remembering: Toward a historical ethnography of the nation-state. In *Cultural Nationalism in East Asia*, ed. Harumi Befu. Berkeley: University of California, Institute of East Asian Studies.

Gans, Herbert J.
1974 *Popular Culture and High Culture*. New York: Basic Books.

Gellner, Ernest
1983 *Nations and Nationalism*. Oxford: Oxford University Press.

Gladney, Dru
1998 Making and marking majorities. In *Making Majorities: Constituting the Nation in Japan, Korea, China, Malaysia, Fiji, Turkey, and the United States*, ed. Dru Gladney. Stanford: Stanford University Press.

Gledhill, Christine
1987 The melodramatic field: An investigation. In *Home Is Where the Heart Is*, ed. Christine Gledhill. London: British Film Institute.

Gluck, Carol
1993 The past in the present. In *Postwar Japan as History*, ed. Andrew Gordon. Berkeley: University of California Press.

Gondō Atsuko
1988 Meiji-Taishō-ki no enka ni okeru yōgaku juyō (The reception of Western music in the enka of the Meiji and Taishō periods). *Tōyō Ongaku Kenkyū* (The Study of Eastern Music) 53: 1–23.

Goodman, Roger, and Kirsten Refsing, eds.
1992 *Ideology and Practice in Modern Japan*. London: Routledge.

Gunji Masakatsu
1991 *Henshin no Shō* (On transformation). Tokyo: Shiromizu-sha.

Hall, Stuart
1985 The rediscovery of ideology: The return of the repressed in media studies. In *Subjectivity and Social Relations: A Reader*, ed. Veronica Beechey and James Donald. Milton Keynes: Open University Press.

Hamm, Charles, and Andrew Lamb
1980 Popular music. In *The New Grove Dictionary of Music and Musicians*, ed. Stanley Sadie. Vol. 15. London: Macmillan Publishers.

Hatfield, Elaine, John T. Cacioppo, and Richard L. Rapson
1994 *Emotional Contagion*. Cambridge: Cambridge University Press.

Havens, Thomas R. H.
1978 *Valley of Darkness: The Japanese People and World War Two*. New York: Norton.

Hayashida, Cullen
1976 Identity, Race, and the Blood Ideology of Japan. Ph.D. diss., University of Washington.

Hendry, Joy
1993 *Wrapping Culture: Politeness, Presentation, and Power in Japan and Other Societies*. Oxford: Oxford University Press.

Herd, Judith Ann
1984   Trends and taste in Japanese popular music: A case-study of the 1982 Yamaha World Popular Music Festival. In *Popular Music*, ed. Richard Middleton and David Horn. Vol. 4: *Performers and Audiences*. Cambridge: Cambridge University Press.

Hobsbawm, Eric, and Terence Ranger, eds.
1983   *The Invention of Tradition*. New York: Cambridge University Press.

Hoshino Tetsurō
n.d.   *Enka Enka Enka*. Tokyo: Chūō Aato Shuppan.

Hosokawa Shūhei
1999   'Salsa no tiene frontera': Orquesta de la Luz and the globalization of popular music. *Cultural Studies* 13 (3): 509-34.

Hsu, Francis L. K.
1975   *Iemoto: The Heart of Japan*. New York: Schenkman.

Hughes, David
1985   *The Heart's Home Town: Traditional Folk Song in Modern Japan*. Ph.D. diss. (Music), University of Michigan.

IASPM-Japan (International Association for the Study of Popular Music, Japan Branch)
1991   *A Guide to Popular Music in Japan*. Tokyo: IASPM-Japan.

Ichikawa Shōsuke
1992a   Ichikawa Shōsuke, Miyako Harumi: Uta, jinsei, soshite ashita e (Ichikawa Shōsuke, Miyako Harumi: Songs, life, and tomorrows). *NHK Shumi Hyakka: Karaoke Enka Kashōhō II* (NHK Special Interest Hobbies: The Art of Karaoke Enka Singing II). Tokyo: Nihon Hōsō Shuppan Kyōkai.
1992b   [Various articles], *NHK Shumi Hyakka: Karaoke Enka Kashō-hō II* (NHK Special Interest Hobbies: The Art of Karaoke Enka Singing II). Tokyo: Nihon Hōsō Shuppan Kyōkai.
1993a   Kokoro-zake, *NHK Shumi Hyakka: Karaoke Enka Kashō-hō III* (NHK Special Interest Hobbies: The Art of Karaoke Enka Singing III). Tokyo: Nihon Hōsō Shuppan Kyōkai.

1993b   Kokoro-zake, *NHK Shumi Hyakka: Karaoke Enka Kashō-hō III* (NHK Special Interest Hobbies: The Art of Karaoke Enka Singing III), April 19 broadcast.

Imai Iwao, compiler
1992   *Enka no Kokoro* (The heart of enka). Tokyo: Do-re-mi Ongaku Shuppansha.

Iritani Toshio
1991   *Group Psychology of the Japanese in Wartime*. London: Kegan Paul International.

Ivy, Marilyn
1993   Formations of mass culture. In *Postwar Japan as History*, ed. Andrew Gordon. Berkeley: University of California Press.
1995   *Discourses of the Vanishing: Modernity, Phantasm, Japan*. Chicago: University of Chicago Press.

Jenkins, Henry
1992   *Textual Poachers: Television Fans and Participatory Culture*. New York: Routledge.

Kalland, Arne
1995   Culture in Japanese nature. In *Asian Perceptions of Nature: A Critical Approach*, ed. O. Bruun and Arne Kalland. London: Curzon Press.

Kasulis, Thomas P.
1993   The body—Japanese style. In *Self as Body in Asian Theory and Practice*, ed. Thomas P. Kasulis, Roger T. Ames, and Wimal Dissanayake. Albany: State University of New York Press.

Kasza, Gregory
1988   *The State and the Mass Media in Japan, 1918–1945*. Berkeley: University of California Press.

Kawabata Shigeru
1991   The Japanese record industry. *Popular Music* 10 (3): 327–45.

Keith, Michael, and Steve Pile
- 1993   Introduction, Part 1: The politics of place; Introduction, Part 2: The place of politics. In *Place and the Politics of Identity*, ed. Michael Keith and Steve Pile. London: Routledge.

Kelly, William W.
- 1986   Rationalization and nostalgia: Cultural dynamics of new middle-class Japan. *American Ethnologist* 13 (4): 603–18.
- 1993   Finding a place in metropolitan Japan: Ideologies, institutions, and everyday life. In *Postwar Japan as History*, ed. Andrew Gordon. Berkeley: University of California Press.

Kinsella, Sharon
- 1995   Cuties in Japan. In *Women, Media, and Consumption in Japan*, ed. Lise Skov and Brian Moeran. Honolulu: University of Hawai'i Press.

Kitahara Michio
- 1966   *Kayokyoku* [sic]: An example of syncretism involving scale and mode. *Ethnomusicology* 10 (3): 271–84.

Koizumi Fumio
- 1980   Japan VII. Music since 1868. 2. Popular music. In *The New Grove Dictionary of Music and Musicians*, ed. Stanley Sadie. Vol. 9. London: Macmillan.
- 1984   *Kayōkyoku no Kōzō* (The Structure of Popular Songs). Tokyo: Tōjusha.

Komota Nobuo, Shimada Yoshifumi, Yazawa Tamotsu, and Yokozawa Chiaki
- 1980   *Nihon Ryūkōka-shi (Sengo-hen)* (A History of Japanese Popular Songs: Postwar). Tokyo: Shakai Shisō-sha.
- 1981   *Nihon Ryūkōka-shi (Senzen-hen)* (A History of Japanese Popular Songs: Prewar). Tokyo: Shakai Shisō-sha.

Komparu Kunio
- 1983   *The Noh Theater: Principles and Perspectives*. New York: Weatherhill.

Kondo, Dorinne K.
- 1990   *Crafting Selves: Power, Gender, and Discourses of Identity in a Japanese Workplace*. Chicago: University of Chicago Press.

Lasch, Christopher
- 1984   The politics of nostalgia. *Harper's*, Nov.: 65–70.

Lebra, Takie Sugiyama
- 1976   *Japanese Patterns of Behavior*. Honolulu: University Press of Hawai'i.
- 1987   The cultural significance of silence in Japanese communication. *Multilingua* 6: 343–57.
- 1992   Self in Japanese culture. In *Japanese Sense of Self*, ed. Nancy Rosenberger. Cambridge: Cambridge University Press.

Lefebvre, Henri
- 1991   *The Production of Space*. Trans. Donald Nicholson-Smith. Oxford: Basil Blackwell.

Leppert, Richard
- 1993   *The Sight of Sound*. Cambridge: Cambridge University Press.

Lewis, George
- 1987   Patterns of meaning and choice: Taste cultures in popular music. In *Popular Music and Communication*, ed. James Lull. Newbury Park, Calif.: Sage Publications.

Linhart, Sepp
- 1986   Sakariba: Zone of 'evaporation' between work and home? In *Interpreting Japanese Society*, ed. Joy Hendry. 2nd ed. London: Routledge.

Lowenthal, David
- 1985   *The Past Is a Foreign Country*. Cambridge: Cambridge University Press.

Lutz, Catherine A.
- 1988   *Unnatural Emotions: Everyday Sentiments on a Micronesian Atoll and Their Challenge to Western Theory*. Chicago: University of Chicago Press.

Malm, William P.
- 1971   The modern music of Meiji Japan. In *Tradition and Modernization in Japanese Culture*, ed. Donald H. Shively. Princeton: Princeton University Press.

Marubashi Fujio
1993 Kobayashi Sachiko to tomo ni (Along with Kobayashi Sachiko). [Script for "Hatsuratsu Sutajio 505," no. 377, for broadcast 5/19].

Masuda Koh, ed.
1974 *Kenkyūsha's New Japanese-English Dictionary*. 4th ed. Tokyo: Kenkyusha.

Middleton, Dwight R.
1989 Emotional style: The cultural ordering of emotions. *Ethos* 17 (2): 187–201.

Miki Takashi
1992 Kokoro-zake. *Karaoke Fan* 11 (122): 162–63.

Miller, Laura
1995 Crossing ethnolinguistic boundaries: A preliminary look at the *gaijin tarento* in Japan. In *Asian Popular Culture*, ed. John Lent. New York: Westview Press.

Minami Hiroshi
1987 *Shōwa Bunka, 1925–1945* (Shōwa Era Culture, 1925–1945). Tokyo: Keisō Shobō.

Mita Munesuke
1992 *Social Psychology of Modern Japan*. Trans. Stephen Suloway. London: Kegan Paul International.

Moeran, Brian
1995 Reading Japanese in Katei Gahō: The art of being an upperclass woman. In *Women, Media and Consumption in Japan*, ed. Lise Skov and Brian Moeran. Honolulu: University of Hawai'i Press.

Moon Okpyo
1989 *From Paddy Field to Ski Slope: The Revitalisation of Tradition in Japanese Village Life*. Manchester and New York: Manchester University Press.

Mori Shin'ichi
1992a [Letter]. *The Shinichi Mori News* 153: 3.
1992b [Letter]. *The Shinichi Mori News* 160: 3.
1992c Talk essay: Kuyashikute (On regretting). *The Shinichi Mori News* 156: 2.

1993a   Message. *The Shinichi Mori News* 171: 1.
1993b   Talk essay: Nagai me de (With greater perspective). *The Shinichi Mori News* 164: 2.

Mori Shin'ichi Kōenkai [Mori Shin'ichi Fan Club]
1987   Unpublished poll.
1992a   Fuan no hiroba (Fans' corner). *The Shinichi Mori News* 153: 3.
1992b   Fuan no hiroba (Fans' corner). *The Shinichi Mori News* 154: 3.
1992c   Fuan no hiroba (Fans' corner). *The Shinichi Mori News* 156: 3.
1992d   Fuan no hiroba (Fans' corner). *The Shinichi Mori News* 157: 3.
1992e   Fuan no hiroba (Fans' corner). *The Shinichi Mori News* 159: 3.
1992f   Fuan no hiroba (Fans' corner). *The Shinichi Mori News* 160: 3.
1993a   Fuan no hiroba (Fans' corner). *The Shinichi Mori News* 161: 3.
1993b   Fuan no hiroba (Fans' corner). *The Shinichi Mori News* 162: 3.
1993c   Fuan no hiroba (Fans' corner). *The Shinichi Mori News* 169: 3.
1993d   Fuan no hiroba (Fans' corner). *The Shinichi Mori News* 170: 3.
1993e   "Mori-san to denwa deeto" repōto (Report on "Telephone Date with Mori-san"). *The Shinichi Mori News* 168: 2.

Morris-Suzuki, Tessa
1998   *Re-inventing Japan: Time, Space, Nation.* Armonk, N.Y.: M. E. Sharpe.

Mouer, Ross, and Yoshio Sugimoto
1986   *Images of Japanese Society: A Study in the Social Construction of Reality.* London: Kegan Paul International.

Mulvey, Laura
1989   *Visual and Other Pleasures.* Bloomington: Indiana University Press.

Nagata Gyoji, ed.
1992   *Furusato to Enka Daizenshū* (Collection of Furusato and Enka). Tokyo: Do-Re-Mi Ongaku Shuppansha.

Nakamura Toyo
1991   Early pop song writers and their backgrounds. *Popular Music* 10 (3): 263–82.

Nihon Amachua Kayō Renmei (NAK)
n.d.   NAK no nakama: Nyūkai go-annai (NAK members: Guide to admission). Pamphlet.

Nippon Hōsō Kyōkai (NHK)
    1992   Nihonjin to kayōkyoku: Iku tabi kaeru tabi sasurau tabi (Japanese and popular song: Travels going forth, travels returning home, wandering travels). Television program broadcast Feb. 11.

Nishiyama Matsunosuke
    1982   *Iemoto no Kenkyū* (Studies of Iemoto). Tokyo: Yoshikawa Kōbunkan.

Nosco, Peter
    1990   *Remembering Paradise: Nativism and Nostalgia in Eighteenth-Century Japan.* Cambridge: Harvard University, Council on East Asian Studies.

Nostrand, Richard L., and Lawrence E. Estaville, Jr.
    1993   Introduction: The homeland concept. *Journal of Cultural Geography* 13 (2): 1–4.

Nowada Masatoshi
    1992   Jinsei ga suki, uta ga suki (We Love Life, We Love Song). [Script for "Hatsuratsu Sutajio 505," no. 351, Oct. 28].

Ogawa Hiroshi
    1989   Karaoke-ron joron (Toward a theory of karaoke). Paper presented at a conference of the International Association for the Study of Popular Music, Japan branch, Tokyo, Nov.

Ohnuki-Tierney, Emiko
    1987   *The Monkey as Mirror: Symbolic Transformations in Japanese History and Ritual.* Princeton: Princeton University Press.
    1990   The ambivalent self of the contemporary Japanese. *Cultural Anthropology* 5 (2): 197–216.
    1997   McDonald's in Japan: Changing manners and etiquette. In *Golden Arches East: McDonald's in East Asia*, ed. James L. Watson. Stanford: Stanford University Press.
    1998   A conceptual model for the historical relationship between the self and the internal and external others. In *Making Majorities*, ed. Dru Gladney. Stanford: Stanford University Press.

Okada Maki
    1982   Enka. In *Ongaku Dai-jiten* (Encyclopedia of Music), ed. Shimonaka Kunihiko. Vol. 1, 252. Tokyo: Heibonsha.

1991 Musical characteristics of *enka*. *Popular Music* 10 (3): 283–303.

Oricon Co., Ltd.
 1992 *Orikon Nenkan 1992 Nenban* (1992 Oricon Yearbook). Tokyo: Oricon Co.
 1993 *Orikon Nenkan 1993 Nenban* (1993 Oricon Yearbook). Tokyo: Oricon Co.
 1998 *Orikon Nenkan 1998 Nenban* (1998 Oricon Yearbook). Tokyo: Oricon Co.

Ortolani, Benito
 1969 Iemoto. *Japan Quarterly* 16 (3): 297–306.

Painter, Andrew
 1996 Japanese daytime television, popular culture and ideology. In *Contemporary Japan and Popular Culture*, ed. John Whittier Treat. Honolulu: University of Hawai'i Press.

Plath, David W.
 1980 *Long Engagements: Maturity in Modern Japan*. Stanford: Stanford University Press.

Raz, Jacob
 1992 Self-presentation and performance in the yakuza way of life: Fieldwork with a Japanese underworld group. In *Ideology and Practice in Modern Japan*, ed. Roger Goodman and Kirsten Refsing. London: Routledge.

Read, Cathleen B., and David L. Locke
 1983 An analysis of the Yamada-ryū sōkyoku iemoto system. *Hōgaku* 1 (1): 20–52.

Reader, Ian
 1987 Back to the future: Images of nostalgia and renewal in a Japanese religious context. *Japanese Journal of Religious Studies* 14 (4): 287–303.

Reiber, Beth
 1990 *Frommer's Tokyo*. New York: Simon and Schuster.

Robertson, Jennifer
 1989 Gender-bending in paradise: Doing "female" and "male" in Japan. *Genders* 5: 50–69.
 1991 *Native and Newcomer: Making and Remaking a Japanese City*. Berkeley: University of California Press.

1992a   Doing and undoing "female" and "male" in Japan: The Takarazuka Revue. In *Japanese Social Organization*, ed. Takie S. Lebra. Honolulu: University of Hawai'i Press.

1992b   The "magic if": Conflicting performances of gender in the Takarazuka Revue of Japan. In *Gender in Performance: The Presentation of Difference in the Performing Arts*, ed. Laurence Senelick. Hanover, N.H.: University Press of New England.

1992c   The politics of androgyny in Japan: Sexuality and subversion in the theater and beyond. *American Ethnologist* 19 (3): 419–42.

1998   *Takarazuka: Sexual Politics and Popular Culture in Modern Japan*. Berkeley: University of California Press.

Sakurai Toshio
1993   Personal Communication.

Schodt, Fredrik L.
1996   *Dreamland Japan: Writings on Modern Manga*. Berkeley: Stone Bridge Press.

Seidensticker, Edward
1983   *Low City, High City*. San Francisco: Donald S. Ellis.

Senelick, Laurence
1993   Boys and girls together: Subcultural origins of glamour drag and male impersonation on the nineteenth-century stage. In *Crossing the Stage: Controversies on Cross-dressing*, ed. Lesley Ferris. London: Routledge.

Shield, Renee Rose
1980   Country corn: Performance in context. In *The Ethnography of Musical Performance*, ed. Norma McLeod and Marcia Herndon. Norwood, Pa.: Norwood Editions.

Shillony, Ben-Ami
1981   *Politics and Culture in Wartime Japan*. Oxford: Clarendon Press.

Shively, Donald H.
1978   The social environment of Tokugawa kabuki. In James P. Brandon, William P. Malm, and Donald H. Shively, *Studies in Kabuki: Its Acting, Music, and Historical Context*. Honolulu: The University Press of Hawai'i.

Silverberg, Miriam
1998 The cafe waitress serving modern Japan. In *Mirror of Modernity: Invented Traditions of Modern Japan*, ed. Stephen Vlastos. Berkeley: University of California Press.

Singleton, John
1995 Gambaru: A Japanese cultural theory of learning. In *Japanese Schooling: Patterns of Socialization, Equality, and Political Control*, ed. James J. Shields, Jr. University Park: Pennsylvania State University Press.

Singleton, John, ed.
1998 *Learning in Likely Places: Varieties of Apprenticeship in Japan*. Cambridge: Cambridge University Press.

Skov, Lise, and Brian Moeran
1995 Introduction: Hiding in the light: From Oshin to Yoshimoto Banana. In *Women, Media and Consumption in Japan*, ed. Lise Skov and Brian Moeran. Honolulu: University of Hawai'i Press.

Smith, Robert J.
1983 *Japanese Society: Tradition, Self, and the Social Order*. Cambridge: Cambridge University Press.
1998 Transmitting tradition by the rules: An anthropological interpretation of the iemoto system. In *Learning in Likely Places: Varieties of Apprenticeship in Japan*, ed. John Singleton. Cambridge: Cambridge University Press.

Sogabe Hiroshi
1992 [Script for "Enka no Hanamichi," no. 728, for broadcast 1/24/93].

Sorensen, Janet
1997 Writing historically, speaking nostalgically: The competing languages of nation in Scott's *The Bride of Lammermoor*. In *Narratives of Nostalgia, Gender, and Nationalism*, ed. Jean Pickering and Suzanne Kehde. New York: New York University Press.

Stewart, Kathleen
1992 Nostalgia—A polemic. In *Rereading Cultural Anthropology*, ed. George E. Marcus. Durham: Duke University Press.

1993 Engendering narratives of lament in country music. In *All That Glitters: Country Music in America*, ed. George Lewis. Bowling Green, Ohio: Bowling Green State University Popular Press.

Stewart, Susan
1993 *On Longing: Narratives of the Miniature, the Gigantic, the Souvenir, the Collection*. Durham: Duke University Press.

Sturken, Marita
1997 *Tangled Memories: The Vietnam War, the AIDS Epidemic, and the Politics of Remembering*. Berkeley: University of California Press.

Takagi Noritsune
1983 Broadcasting. In *Kodansha Encyclopedia of Japan*, ed. Itasaka Gen. Vol. 1. Tokyo: Kodansha.

Tansman, Alan
1996 Mournful tears and sake: The postwar myth of Misora Hibari. In *Contemporary Japan and Popular Culture*, ed. John Whittier Treat. Honolulu: University of Hawai'i Press.

Tobin, Joseph J.
1992 Introduction: Domesticating the West. In *Re-Made in Japan: Everyday Life and Consumer Taste in a Changing Society*, ed. Joseph Tobin. New Haven: Yale University Press.

Traphagan, John W.
2000 *Taming Oblivion: Aging Bodies and the Fear of Senility in Japan*. Albany: State University of New York Press.

Treat, John Whittier
1996a Introduction: Japanese Studies into Cultural Studies. In *Contemporary Japan and Popular Culture*, ed. John Whittier Treat. Honolulu: University of Hawai'i Press.
1996b Yoshimoto Banana writes home. In *Contemporary Japan and Popular Culture*, ed. John Whittier Treat. Honolulu: University of Hawai'i Press.

Ueda Jinichiro, ed.
1992 *Asahi Shimbun Japan Almanac*. Tokyo: Asahi Shimbun.

Vlastos, Stephen
    1998   Tradition: Past/present culture and modern Japanese history. In *Mirror of Modernity: Invented Traditions of Modern Japan*, ed. Stephen Vlastos. Berkeley: University of California Press.

Weiner, Michael, ed.
    1997   *Japan's Minorities: The Illusion of Homogeneity*. London: Routledge.

Williams, Raymond
    1965   *The Long Revolution*. Harmondsworth, U.K.: Penguin.
    1973   *The Country and the City*. New York: Oxford University Press.
    1977   *Marxism and Literature*. Oxford: Oxford University Press.

Williams, Rosalind
    1991   The dream world of mass consumption. In *Rethinking Popular Culture: Contemporary Perspectives in Cultural Studies*, ed. Chandra Mukerji and Michael Schudson. Berkeley: University of California Press.

Willis, Paul
    1978   *Profane Culture*. London: Routledge and Kegan Paul.

Wilson, Jean
    1993a   Enka no hanamichi. *Eye-Ai* 17 (196): 18–21.
    1993b   Enka: The music people love or hate. *Japan Quarterly* 40: 283–91.
    1995   Exclusive interview with Itsuki Hiroshi. *Eye-Ai* 19 (215): 18–22, 49–51.

Wrong, Dennis H.
    1995   *Power: Its Forms, Bases, and Uses*. New Brunswick, N.J.: Transaction Publishers.

Yano, Christine Reiko
    1993   The iemoto system: Convergence of achievement and ascription. In *Transactions of the International Conference of Orientalists in Japan*, 72–84. Tokyo: Tōhō Gakkai.
    1998   Defining the modern nation in Japanese popular song, 1914–1932. In *Japan's Competing Modernities: Issues in Culture and Democracy 1900–1930*, ed. Sharon Minichiello. Honolulu: University of Hawai'i Press.

Yoshino Kōsaku
    1992   *Cultural Nationalism in Contemporary Japan*. London: Routledge.

Index

Adorno, Theodor, 24
Aidoru (idol singer), 59, 62, 214n23
Aizuchi (listener utterances), 107, 221n14. *See also* Performer-audience interaction
Akogare (longing), 23, 90, 120, 148, 162, 174, 183; for furusato, 40, 70, 153. *See also* Desire
Amae(ru) (dependency), 22, 68, 69, 133, 177
Anderson, Benedict, 19
Antiheroes, 154, 168, 179, 185
Apprentice, 57–58
Audience response, 78–80, 83. *See also* Aizuchi; Performer-audience interaction
Auditioning, 59–60

Back, showing one's, 118–19, 159, 222n23
Baiorin enka (violin enka), 32
Befu, Harumi, 22
Bestor, Theodore, 21
Bijin, enka (enka beauties), 61, 172
Blues (burūsu), 36, 41, 43, 128
Body, 14, 17, 91, 121; kata of, 114–20, 222n22
Bourdieu, Pierre, 3, 23, 44, 91

Boyarin, Jonathon, 17
Breast, see *Mune*
Broadcasts: radio, 82–84; television, 84–89, 168–71, 220. *See also* NHK
Burakumin (outcaste), 185
Burūsu, see Blues

Center-periphery, 19–20, 179
Character goods (kyarakutā gudzu), 2, 131, 133. *See also* Souvenir
Chihō (provinces), 19–20, 207n10. *See also* Furusato; Rural/rusticity
Class, 106, 143; blue-collar/working-, 7, 20, 23–24, 88, 159; white-collar/middle-, 7, 20, 23, 88, 91
Cliché, 93–94, 122, 162
Collective memory, see Memory
Compositional Kata (CK), 103–9
Confucian values, 50, 65, 225
Consumption, 4–6, 13, 17; of enka, 9, 91, 124–25, 141, 144, 147
Country and western music, 2–3, 77, 80, 90, 113, 150, 216n1
Cover version, of song, 49–50
Creative license, 51; *See also* Kosei
Crying, 93, 102, 121, 182–83; gendered, 98–99. *See also* Namida; Tears

"Crying song" (naki-bushi), 3–4
Cultural nationalism, 23, 42, 89, 178. See also "Japan"
Culture, high vs. low, 225–26n8

Davis, Fred, 15
De Certeau, Michel, 5
Debut, 50, 60, 70–71, 81 215n30; party, 71–72, 215n35
Dentō, see Tradition
Dependency, see Amae
Desire, 14–16, 65, 122, 161, 174; vs. social order, 167, 183. See also Nostalgia
Do-enka ("real" enka), 36, 42–43, 64–65, 92, 112, 219n4. See also Enka: subgenres of
Dōsa-mawari (performing place-to-place), 74
Doryoku, see Effort
Dream (yume), 94–95
Drinking, 100, 150, 225. See also Sake
Duty, see Giri

Effort, 16, 48, 74–76, 113, 128. See also Gambaru
Emotion, 22–23, 128; construction of, 3–5, 26, 67–68, 102, 109, 112–13, 153; aestheticized, 25, 62, 99, 152, 166; kata of, 26, 90, 122–23; in various genres, 92–93, 219; embodied, 120–21
Empathy (omoiyari), 69, 102, 112, 131, 167, 177, 179, 182, 223; between fans and performers, 132, 139–41
Endings of performances, 81, 89, 221n16
Enka: defining, 29–31, 41–42, 208n6, 211–12n9; history of, 30–42 passim; as a narrative genre, 31–32, 108, 172; as conservative, 41–42, 45, 73; subgenres of, 42–43, 218; decline of, 43–44; popularity of, 125–26; themes in, 148, 170, 182
Enka no Furusato (Hometown of Enka; TV show), 168–69
Enka no Hanamichi (lit., "Flower Way"/Stage Passage of Enka; TV show), 85, 170–71
Enkashi (enka singer/caller), 31, 33, 35
Enka TV (TV show), 86–88, 220
Entertainment world, see Geinō-kai
Erotic, 30, 41, 87, 159–60. See also Sexuality
Ethnocentrism, 13, 22, 65
Evanescence, 162–63, 183
"Exocentrism," 13

Familiarity, 48, 50, 122. See also Repetition
Fan club, see Kōenkai
Fan party (fuan no tsudoi), 136
Fans: characterizations of, 1–2, 6–7, 44, 74, 86; as elderly, 83, 225; male vs. female, 83, 127; as promoters, 74–75, 130–31
Fate, 163, 165, 168
Female: roles, 5, 80, 150; vs. male, 55–56; subjectivity, 57, 122, 224. See also Mother
Femaleness, construction of, 68, 122, 149–51, 166, 174, 214
Femininity, 56, 59, 61–62, 68–69, 112, 157
Feudalism, 23, 36
Floating world, see Ukiyo
Fluids of intimacy 178–79. See also Namida; Tears
Freedom and people's rights movement (jiyū minken undō), 31
Frith, Simon, 25
Fuan kurabu (fan club), see Kōenkai
Fuan no tsudoi, see Fan party

Fuji Ayako (singer), 69
Furu-kusai (outdated), 8, 86. *See also* Old-fashioned
Furusato (hometown), 17–21, 33, 40, 42, 168–75, 178, 207n8; and men, 97, 148
Furusato-zukuri (*furusato*-making), 21, 85

Gambaru (perseverance), 48, 75, 126, 167; of singers, 45–46, 52–53, 60–61, 66, 70, 212n14. *See also* Effort
Gaze, 114–16
Gei-mei (stage name), 65–66
Geinō-kai (entertainment world), 10, 63
Geisha, 36
Gender: construction of, 62, 98, 148, 161; crossing, 64, 123, 126, 156–61, 222, 225–26; vocal production of, 67, 106, 112; embodiment of, 113–21 *passim*
"Genre-izing," 41–42
Gesture, 118, 120. *See also* Body
Gift-giving, 208; at debut party, 71–72; to performers, 79–80, 215n35. *See also O-miyage*
Giri (duty), 168; vs. *Ninjō* (human feelings), 15, 42, 153, 183
Godai Natsuko (singer), 172
"Good wife, wise mother," *see Ryōsai-kenbo*
Guitar, 105–6
Gunka (military songs), 32, 38

Hanagoe (nasal voice), 110
Hardship (*kurō*), 70, 80. *See also* Effort; *Gambaru*
Hatsuratsu Sutajio 505 (Lively Studio 505, radio show), 83–84
Hayashi kotoba (sung or shouted interjections), 221n12
Headmaster, *see Iemoto*
Heart, *see Kokoro*

Heartbreak, 69, 96, 99, 165–66
Hierarchy, 22–23, 50, 89, 133
Hiru-oke (daytime karaoke), 142, 144
Hit song, 47, 184, 211n4; making of a, 26, 49, 53, 62, 73, 143
Homeland/hometown, *see Furusato*
Homogeneous, 4, 18
Homosociality, 154–55, 225n3
Honne (private feelings), 24, 26, 100
Hō-ban (Japanese-originated recordings), 40–41, 210n22
Horiuchi Takao (singer), 43, 75
Hosokawa Shūhei, 13

Ichikawa Shōsuke (composer), 67–69, 142, 218–19n2
Identity construction, 4, 7, 14, 23, 26
Idol singer, *see Aidoru*
Iemoto (headmaster), system of teaching, 57, 65. *See also Uchi-deshi*
Image construction, 61–65
Imaginary: of enka, 3–4, 9, 22, 58, 76, 85, 114, 147, 217; of nation, 19, 179; of romance, 162, 167; of *furusato*, 170, 172, 178
Imēji-zukuri (image-making), *see* Image construction
Imitation, 49, 137
In-group, *see Miuchi*
Inaka (countryside), 19–20. *See also Furusato*; Rural/rusticity
Instruments: Japanese, 8, 32, 86, 102–3, 107; Western, 32, 34, 37–38, 41–42, 92, 103, 105–6
Intellectuals, 8, 32–33
"Internal exotic," 8–9, 15–16, 24, 173, 207n6
Intimacy, 68, 80, 82, 90, 105, 178, 182, 215; construction of, 78–79, 84, 112,

120, 151; staged by *kōenkai*, 135, 137, 138
Introspection boom, 13–14, 42
Itsuki Hiroshi (singer), 43, 66, 118, 145
Ivy, Marilyn, 15, 159

"Japan," 6, 8, 13, 15, 19, 22–24, 126, 179; as traditional, 8, 45, 76, 168, 172; vs. "the West," 13–15, 87–88, 126, 161, 206n2
Japan Public Broadcasting, see NHK
Japanese-American, see *Nikkeijin*
Japaneseness, 4, 7, 14, 22, 125, 175; as natural/biological 6, 18, 54, 65, 178, 184
Jazz, 38–39, 221n10
Jenkins, Henry, 5
Jidai-geki, see Period drama
Jigoe (chest voice; natural voice), 109–10
Jiyū minken undō, see Freedom and people's rights movement
Josei rashii (feminine), 68–69

Kabuki, 8, 74, 78, 107, 114
Kadai-kyoku (theme song), 144–45
Kae-uta (substitution song), 31–32
Kakegoe (shouts), 78–80. See also *Aizuchi*; Performer-audience interaction
Karaoke, 8, 71, 141–47 passim, 223n13; consumption and, 7, 44, 126–27, 144–45, 222n2; *taikai* (karaoke contest) 58, 137–38, 144–46, 224n15; *bokkusu* ("karaoke box"; private karaoke rooms for rent), 141–42; *sākuru* (karaoke circles), 142; *hiru-oke* (daytime karaoke), 142, 144
Kasulis, Thomas, 26
Kata (patterned form), 24–27, 92, 102, 219–20n8; of emotion, 26, 90, 122–23; and promotion, 46, 64, 76; of performance, 49, 69, 78, 80–81, 156; in *kōenkai*, 139–40; gendered, 157–59; of romance, 163, 165. See also Compositional kata; Performative kata
Kayōkyoku (mainstream Japanese popular music), 29
Kelly, William, 5, 21
Kimono, 63, 151, 157, 172, 206, 214, 222; *bijin* (kimono beauties), 61; and gender, 116, 161
Kitajima Saburō (singer), 1–2, 43, 65, 145, 172, 182, 183, 185, 216n5
Ko-bushi (ornamentation), see Vocal Techniques
Kōenkai (fan clubs, support groups), 71, 80, 127–29, 183; as community, 134, 139; promotional activities of, 79, 138. See also Fans; Mori Shin'ichi Kōenkai
Koga Masao (composer), 36, 37, 39
Koga merodii (Koga melody), 37, 42
Kōhaku Uta Gassen (Red and White Song Contest), 7, 50, 88–89, 172
Kokoro (heart/soul), 7, 84, 96–97, 100, 102, 104, 134, 150, 171; of Japan, 57, 178. See also *Onna-gokoro*; *Nihonjin no kokoro*
"Kokoro-zake" ("Sake of the Heart"; song title), 67–69, 73
Korea, 30; singers from, 9, 43, 123, 185
Kosei (individuality; originality), 26, 90–91, 123. See also Singers: creative license of
Koto (zither), 8, 103. See also Instruments: Japanese
Kouta (ballad form), 32, 36
Kurai (dark, somber), 68, 86, 128
Kurō (hardship), see *Gambaru*

Index

Kyanpein (promotional campaign), 73–74, 145
Kyarakutā gudzu, see Character goods

Lefebvre, Henri, 18
Life-stages and consumption patterns, 5–7, 88, 145. See also Youth culture
Loneliness, see *Sabishii*
Longing, see *Akogare*

Male: as controller of consumption, 5, 57, 69; vs. female singer, 55–56
Maleness, 5, 54–55, 122, 152–55
Manipulation, 16, 64–65
Marketing, 5, 40. See also Promotion
Masculinity, 61, 153, 157, 178. See also Maleness
Matsuri (festival), 74, 169, 171, 172
Melodrama, 90
Memory, 5, 17, 97
Mikawa Ken'ichi, 158–59, 161, 225n7
Miki Takashi (composer), 67–69
Military songs, see *Gunka*
Mimicry, 141. See also Imitation
Mimi ni hairu (entering the ears), 46, 73–74, 91, 130, 133, 144
Mi-narai (learning by looking), 58. See also *Uchi-deshi*
Min'yō (folk song), 18, 32, 207n9, 221n12; *shin-* (new folk song), 33
Misora Hibari (singer), 39, 121, 210n19, 219n5
Mita Munesuke, 33, 93
Miuchi (in-group, insiders), 84, 106, 183
Miyako Harumi (singer), 43, 68
Modernity, 13–14, 28, 168
Monomane (mimicry), 141. See also Imitation
Mood song, 29, 41. See also *Mūdo enka*

Mori Shin'ichi (singer), 43, 65–66, 81, 128–41, 145, 157, 175
Mori Shin'ichi Kōenkai, 127–40
Mother, 38, 128–29, 135–36; of singer, 71–72; and *furusato*, 169, 175–76; and child, 174–75, 177–78
Mūdo enka, 43, 106. See also Enka: subgenres of
Mūdo-kayō (mood music), 29, 41
Multi-sited ethnography, 10
Mune (breast; chest), 96, 174. See also *Kokoro*
Music, Western, see *Yō-ban*; *Yōgaku*
Musical arranger, 50, 212n11
Musical genres, 29; switching, 209n15, 211n7, 214n23
"Musical habitus," 91
"Music overheard," 7, 24, 44, 124, 179

Nagayama Yōko (singer), 58–59
NAK (Nihon Amachua Kayō Renmei, Japan Amateur Popular Song Federation), 145–47, 218–19n2
Nakayama Shimpei (composer), 34, 36
Naki-bushi (crying song), 3–4
Naku (to cry), see Crying. See also *Namida*; Tears
Namida (tears), 4, 38, 94, 98–99. See also Crying; Tears
Naniwa-bushi (Osaka song), 36, 172; influence on enka, 31–33, 42
Narrative genre, enka as, 67, 73, 93, 107, 112, 172
Nation, 4, 15, 19, 168; and mother, 175, 177–78
National culture, 4–5, 8, 19, 22, 149, 156, 167
Nationalism, 23, 36, 38, 184
Natsu-mero (nostalgic melody), 27. See also Nostalgia

Newcomer, see *Shinjin*
NHK (Nippon Hōsō Kyōkai; Japan Public Broadcasting), 6–7, 19, 83, 88–89, 141, 210n20, 217n9; history of 35, 40. See also *Kōhaku Uta Gassen*
Nihon, see "Japan"
Nihon Amachua Kayō Renmei (Japan amateur popular song federation). See NAK
Nihonjin no kokoro (heart/soul of Japanese), 4, 7, 9, 29, 184
Nihonjinron (treatises on being Japanese), 22, 42, 65
Nihon no uta (song of Japan), 4, 122, 125, 149, 184
Nikkeijin (Japanese-American), 10–11, 58, 64–65
Ninjō (human feelings) vs. *giri* (duty), 15, 42, 153, 183
Nippon Hōsō Kyōkai. See NHK
Noguchi Ujō (lyricist), 34, 36
Non-Japanese, 6; enka singers, 9, 56, 58, 185
North country, 19, 170, 173
Nostalgia, 4, 14–18, 24, 57, 65, 181–83, 207n5; and *furusato*, 18, 170, 178; commercial production of, 84–85, 89, 184
Nyū myūjikku (new music), 42–43

Obligation, see *Giri*
Old-fashioned, 42, 45, 73, 86. See also *Furu-kusai*
O-miyage (souvenir gift), 79. See also Souvenir
Omoiyari, see Empathy
Omote (surface, front side), 24, 26
One-night stand, see *Wan naito rabu*
Onna-gokoro (heart of a woman), 97, 99, 114, 117, 148–49. See also Femaleness

Onnagata (male performer of female roles), 159–60, 225n4
Onnarashii (feminine), see Femininity
Onsen (hot springs), 169
Oricon Yearbook, 50, 212n13, 218n14
Otherness, 7, 16, 24, 173. See also "Internal exotic"
Otoko-michi (path of a man), 97, 148, 152–54. See also Maleness
Otokorashii (masculine), see Masculinity

Painter, Andrew, 82, 84
Pan-Asia, 9, 207n7
Passivity, 112, 151, 166
Past, construction of, 3–4, 15–17, 26–27, 75, 85, 169, 181–82,
Patterning. See *Kata*
Penlights, see Performer-audience interaction
Pentatonic scale, see *Yonanuki onkai*
Performance, 25, 77–78, 122, 155, 224n15; format of, 2–3, 89, 216n2
Performative Kata (PK), 103–4, 109–14, 151, 155, 172
Performer-audience interaction, 2, 62, 77–81, 216, 223; *kata* of 14–41
Performer-audience relationship, 78–80, 82, 83, 168, 183–84; imaginary, 128–39 *passim*, 216
Period drama (*jidai-geki*), 2, 172
Periphery, 7–8, 19, 179
Perseverance, see *Gambaru*
Poppusu ("pops" music), 29, 211n2; *-kei* enka (pops-style enka), 43. See also Enka: subgenres of
Poses, 115–17
Promotion, 71, 73–75, 129–30, 143
Provincial, 19, 182. See also Rural/rusticity

Purofiiru (profile) of singers, 59, 213n20, 214n25

Radio, *see* Broadcasts
Rank, 50–53, 85, 212n13. *See also* Hierarchy
Recitative, *see Serifu*
Recording companies: history of, 35–36, 41, 46; image of, 53–54
Recordings, 35, 211n9. *See also Hō-ban*; Sales of recordings
Recruitment, 57–58
Red and White Song Contest, *see Kōhaku Uta Gassen*
Redundancy, *see* Repetition
"Re-naturalize," 77–78, 81–82, 216n1
Repetition, 46, 48–49, 144, 154, 184; and promotion, 73–74; musical, 105, 107, 108. *See also Kata*
Resonance, 78–80
Rokku (rock music), 29, 46–47
Rōkyoku (narrative song), 31–32, 36
Romance, 99, 161–62, 181; gendered 148, 163–68, 177
Rural/rusticity, 7, 18–21, 24, 169
Ryōsai-kenbo ("good wife, wise mother"), 150, 168
Ryūkōka (popular music), 33–34, 36, 210n23

Sabishii (loneliness), 33, 40, 70
Sakamoto Fuyumi (singer), 43, 58, 64, 157
Sake, 91, 101. *See also* Drinking
Sales of recordings, 5–6, 40–41, 46–47, 87
Saxophone, 105–6. *See also* Instruments, Western
Senpai-kōhai (senior-junior) relations, 51. *See also* Hierarchy

Serifu (recitative), 43, 92–93, 219n4
Sexuality, 121–22, 126, 160. *See also* Erotic
Shakuhachi (end-blown flute), 103. *See also* Instruments, Japanese
Shamisen (lute), 32, 86, 103, 107. *See also* Instruments, Japanese
Shinichi Mori News, 132. *See also* Mori Shin'ichi Kōenkai
Shinjin (newcomer), 54, 56–57, 61, 64, 70–71, 85
Shinjuku Koma Gekijō, 80, 181
Shitamachi (downtown), 20, 172
Shitamachi no Tamasaburō (downtown's Tamasaburō), 159. *See also* Umezawa Tomio
Shittori shita (wet/moist), 67, 69. *See also* Fluids of intimacy
Shōjo (premarital female), 59–60
Singers: creative license of 26, 51, 64, 90–91, 123; male vs. female, 55–56; profiles of, 59, 213–14; criteria for selecting, 61–62; constructing image of, 63–66; training of, 63, 66–70
Soeda Azembō (composer/singer), 32
Sone Yoshiaki (composer), 86–87, 104–105, 111, 211n7, 219–20n8
Song: cultural definitions of, 49–50
Souvenir, 16, 65, 79–80. *See also* Character Goods
Spirituality, 8, 22, 26, 48, 153
Stage names, 65–66
Stewart, Kathleen, 14, 90
Stewart, Susan, 16
Stratification, *see* Hierarchy
Sturken, Marita, 17
Surface, *see Omote*

Tai-appu ("tie-up"; media promotional collaboration), 71, 75

Taiko (drum), 103. *See also* Instruments, Japanese
Taishū engeki (theater of the masses), 74, 78, 159–60, 216n4
Taiwan, 9
Takarazuka, 126, 2254, 226n9
Tarento ("talent" show personality), 53, 212n15
"Taste culture," 3, 23. *See also* Bourdieu, Pierre; Class; Life stages; Youth culture
Tatemae (public face), 24, 26, 96, 100
Tears, 99–102, 120–21, 135–36, 179; shared, 4, 80, 167; and national culture, 8, 103, 168. *See also* Crying; Namida
Television, *see* Broadcasts
Terebi Asahi (TV Asahi), 86
"Textual poaching," 5
Textured sound, 105, 110, 113, 128
Things made, *see* Tsukutta mono
Toba Ichirō (singer), 43, 58, 126
Tokyo, 19–20, 172
Tōshindai (life-sized), 62, 79, 81
Tourism, 169, 207n7
Tradition, 6, 42, 73, 168; invention of, 21, 28–29, 41–42
Truck drivers, *see* Performer-audience relationship
Tsukutta mono, 16, 26, 54, 63, 183. *See also* Kata

Uchi-deshi (live-in apprentice), 57–58
Ukiyo (floating world), 85, 95–96
Umezawa Tomio, 159–160
Underdog, 45; enka as, 47–48; Japan as, 48, 75
Ura (under or back side), 24. *See also* Back
Uragoe (head voice; falsetto), 110

Urban vs. rural, 19–21, 24, 40, 88

Vibrato, *see* Vocal Techniques: *yuri*
Violin enka, *see* Baiorin enka
Vocal techniques, 69, 93, 112, 222; *yuri* (vibrato), 39, 43, 105, 111–12, 221n12m 221n17; *ko-bushi* (ornamentation),43, 67–68, 87–88, 104–5, 111, 143; whisper, 84, 93, 112; *jigoe* (chest voice; natural voice), 109–10; *hanagoe* (nasal voice), 110; *uragoe* (head voice; falsetto), 110
Voice: training, 66–70; marking exertion, 113, 221–22n20

Wa- (Japanese) vs. *Yō-* (Western), 13, 206n2. *See also* "Japan"; Japaneseness
Waka (Japanese vernacular poetry), 92, 102, 205n4, 219n3
Wandering as a theme, of popular song, 37; of dreams, 95–96, 209n9
Wan naito rabu (one-night stand), 161–62
Wareware nihonjin ("we Japanese"), 22
"West, the," *see* "Japan"
Western music, *see* Yō-ban; Yōgaku
Wet vs. dry, 102, 125
World War II, and popular music, 37–38

Yakuza (gangsters), 15, 26
Yamanote (uptown), 20, 172
Yaruki (inner drive), 61. *See also* Gambaru
Yashiro Aki (singer), 43, 156–57
Yō- (Western), 13, 206n2
Yō-ban (foreign-originated recordings), 40–41, 210n22

Yōgaku (imported Western music), 29, 47

Yonanuki onkai (pentatonic scale), 34–40 *passim*, 43, 103, 105, 128, 220–21n9

Yoshino Kōsaku, 13

Yoshioka Osamu (composer), 73, 173, 211n7

Youth culture, 8, 42, 217

Yum, see Dream

Yuri (vibrato), see Vocal Techniques

Harvard East Asian Monographs
(*out-of-print)

*1. Liang Fang-chung, *The Single-Whip Method of Taxation in China*
*2. Harold C. Hinton, *The Grain Tribute System of China, 1845–1911*
3. Ellsworth C. Carlson, *The Kaiping Mines, 1877–1912*
*4. Chao Kuo-chün, *Agrarian Policies of Mainland China: A Documentary Study, 1949–1956*
*5. Edgar Snow, *Random Notes on Red China, 1936–1945*
*6. Edwin George Beal, Jr., *The Origin of Likin, 1835–1864*
7. Chao Kuo-chün, *Economic Planning and Organization in Mainland China: A Documentary Study, 1949–1957*
*8. John K. Fairbank, *Ching Documents: An Introductory Syllabus*
*9. Helen Yin and Yi-chang Yin, *Economic Statistics of Mainland China, 1949–1957*
*10. Wolfgang Franke, *The Reform and Abolition of the Traditional Chinese Examination System*
11. Albert Feuerwerker and S. Cheng, *Chinese Communist Studies of Modern Chinese History*
12. C. John Stanley, *Late Ching Finance: Hu Kuang-yung as an Innovator*
13. S. M. Meng, *The Tsungli Yamen: Its Organization and Functions*
*14. Ssu-yü Teng, *Historiography of the Taiping Rebellion*
15. Chun-Jo Liu, *Controversies in Modern Chinese Intellectual History: An Analytic Bibliography of Periodical Articles, Mainly of the May Fourth and Post–May Fourth Era*
*16. Edward J. M. Rhoads, *The Chinese Red Army, 1927–1963: An Annotated Bibliography*
17. Andrew J. Nathan, *A History of the China International Famine Relief Commission*

Harvard East Asian Monographs

*18. Frank H. H. King (ed.) and Prescott Clarke, *A Research Guide to China-Coast Newspapers, 1822–1911*

19. Ellis Joffe, *Party and Army: Professionalism and Political Control in the Chinese Officer Corps, 1949–1964*

*20. Toshio G. Tsukahira, *Feudal Control in Tokugawa Japan: The Sankin Kōtai System*

21. Kwang-Ching Liu, ed., *American Missionaries in China: Papers from Harvard Seminars*

22. George Moseley, *A Sino-Soviet Cultural Frontier: The Ili Kazakh Autonomous Chou*

23. Carl F. Nathan, *Plague Prevention and Politics in Manchuria, 1910–1931*

*24. Adrian Arthur Bennett, *John Fryer: The Introduction of Western Science and Technology into Nineteenth-Century China*

25. Donald J. Friedman, *The Road from Isolation: The Campaign of the American Committee for Non-Participation in Japanese Aggression, 1938–1941*

*26. Edward LeFevour, *Western Enterprise in Late Ching China: A Selective Survey of Jardine, Matheson and Company's Operations, 1842–1895*

27. Charles Neuhauser, *Third World Politics: China and the Afro-Asian People's Solidarity Organization, 1957–1967*

28. Kungtu C. Sun, assisted by Ralph W. Huenemann, *The Economic Development of Manchuria in the First Half of the Twentieth Century*

*29. Shahid Javed Burki, *A Study of Chinese Communes, 1965*

30. John Carter Vincent, *The Extraterritorial System in China: Final Phase*

31. Madeleine Chi, *China Diplomacy, 1914–1918*

*32. Clifton Jackson Phillips, *Protestant America and the Pagan World: The First Half Century of the American Board of Commissioners for Foreign Missions, 1810–1860*

33. James Pusey, *Wu Han: Attacking the Present through the Past*

34. Ying-wan Cheng, *Postal Communication in China and Its Modernization, 1860–1896*

35. Tuvia Blumenthal, *Saving in Postwar Japan*

36. Peter Frost, *The Bakumatsu Currency Crisis*

37. Stephen C. Lockwood, *Augustine Heard and Company, 1858–1862*

38. Robert R. Campbell, *James Duncan Campbell: A Memoir by His Son*

39. Jerome Alan Cohen, ed., *The Dynamics of China's Foreign Relations*

40. V. V. Vishnyakova-Akimova, *Two Years in Revolutionary China, 1925–1927*, tr. Steven L. Levine

Harvard East Asian Monographs

*41. Meron Medzini, *French Policy in Japan during the Closing Years of the Tokugawa Regime*

42. Ezra Vogel, Margie Sargent, Vivienne B. Shue, Thomas Jay Mathews, and Deborah S. Davis, *The Cultural Revolution in the Provinces*

*43. Sidney A. Forsythe, *An American Missionary Community in China, 1895–1905*

*44. Benjamin I. Schwartz, ed., *Reflections on the May Fourth Movement.: A Symposium*

*45. Ching Young Choe, *The Rule of the Taewŏngun, 1864–1873: Restoration in Yi Korea*

46. W. P. J. Hall, *A Bibliographical Guide to Japanese Research on the Chinese Economy, 1958–1970*

47. Jack J. Gerson, *Horatio Nelson Lay and Sino-British Relations, 1854–1864*

48. Paul Richard Bohr, *Famine and the Missionary: Timothy Richard as Relief Administrator and Advocate of National Reform*

49. Endymion Wilkinson, *The History of Imperial China: A Research Guide*

50. Britten Dean, *China and Great Britain: The Diplomacy of Commercial Relations, 1860–1864*

51. Ellsworth C. Carlson, *The Foochow Missionaries, 1847–1880*

52. Yeh-chien Wang, *An Estimate of the Land-Tax Collection in China, 1753 and 1908*

53. Richard M. Pfeffer, *Understanding Business Contracts in China, 1949–1963*

54. Han-sheng Chuan and Richard Kraus, *Mid-Ching Rice Markets and Trade: An Essay in Price History*

55. Ranbir Vohra, *Lao She and the Chinese Revolution*

56. Liang-lin Hsiao, *China's Foreign Trade Statistics, 1864–1949*

*57. Lee-hsia Hsu Ting, *Government Control of the Press in Modern China, 1900–1949*

58. Edward W. Wagner, *The Literati Purges: Political Conflict in Early Yi Korea*

*59. Joungwon A. Kim, *Divided Korea: The Politics of Development, 1945–1972*

*60. Noriko Kamachi, John K. Fairbank, and Chūzō Ichiko, *Japanese Studies of Modern China Since 1953: A Bibliographical Guide to Historical and Social-Science Research on the Nineteenth and Twentieth Centuries, Supplementary Volume for 1953–1969*

61. Donald A. Gibbs and Yun-chen Li, *A Bibliography of Studies and Translations of Modern Chinese Literature, 1918–1942*

62. Robert H. Silin, *Leadership and Values: The Organization of Large-Scale Taiwanese Enterprises*

63. David Pong, *A Critical Guide to the Kwangtung Provincial Archives Deposited at the Public Record Office of London*

Harvard East Asian Monographs

*64. Fred W. Drake, *China Charts the World: Hsu Chi-yü and His Geography of 1848*
*65. William A. Brown and Urgrunge Onon, translators and annotators, *History of the Mongolian People's Republic*
 66. Edward L. Farmer, *Early Ming Government: The Evolution of Dual Capitals*
*67. Ralph C. Croizier, *Koxinga and Chinese Nationalism: History, Myth, and the Hero*
*68. William J. Tyler, tr., *The Psychological World of Natsume Sōseki*, by Doi Takeo
 69. Eric Widmer, *The Russian Ecclesiastical Mission in Peking during the Eighteenth Century*
*70. Charlton M. Lewis, *Prologue to the Chinese Revolution: The Transformation of Ideas and Institutions in Hunan Province, 1891–1907*
 71. Preston Torbert, *The Ching Imperial Household Department: A Study of Its Organization and Principal Functions, 1662–1796*
 72. Paul A. Cohen and John E. Schrecker, eds., *Reform in Nineteenth-Century China*
 73. Jon Sigurdson, *Rural Industrialism in China*
 74. Kang Chao, *The Development of Cotton Textile Production in China*
 75. Valentin Rabe, *The Home Base of American China Missions, 1880–1920*
*76. Sarasin Viraphol, *Tribute and Profit: Sino-Siamese Trade, 1652–1853*
 77. Ch'i-ch'ing Hsiao, *The Military Establishment of the Yuan Dynasty*
 78. Meishi Tsai, *Contemporary Chinese Novels and Short Stories, 1949–1974: An Annotated Bibliography*
*79. Wellington K. K. Chan, *Merchants, Mandarins and Modern Enterprise in Late Ching China*
 80. Endymion Wilkinson, *Landlord and Labor in Late Imperial China: Case Studies from Shandong by Jing Su and Luo Lun*
*81. Barry Keenan, *The Dewey Experiment in China: Educational Reform and Political Power in the Early Republic*
*82. George A. Hayden, *Crime and Punishment in Medieval Chinese Drama: Three Judge Pao Plays*
*83. Sang-Chul Suh, *Growth and Structural Changes in the Korean Economy, 1910–1940*
 84. J. W. Dower, *Empire and Aftermath: Yoshida Shigeru and the Japanese Experience, 1878–1954*
 85. Martin Collcutt, *Five Mountains: The Rinzai Zen Monastic Institution in Medieval Japan*
 86. Kwang Suk Kim and Michael Roemer, *Growth and Structural Transformation*
 87. Anne O. Krueger, *The Developmental Role of the Foreign Sector and Aid*

Harvard East Asian Monographs

*88. Edwin S. Mills and Byung-Nak Song, *Urbanization and Urban Problems*
89. Sung Hwan Ban, Pal Yong Moon, and Dwight H. Perkins, *Rural Development*
*90. Noel F. McGinn, Donald R. Snodgrass, Yung Bong Kim, Shin-Bok Kim, and Quee-Young Kim, *Education and Development in Korea*
91. Leroy P. Jones and Il SaKong, *Government, Business, and Entrepreneurship in Economic Development: The Korean Case*
92. Edward S. Mason, Dwight H. Perkins, Kwang Suk Kim, David C. Cole, Mahn Je Kim et al., *The Economic and Social Modernization of the Republic of Korea*
93. Robert Repetto, Tai Hwan Kwon, Son-Ung Kim, Dae Young Kim, John E. Sloboda, and Peter J. Donaldson, *Economic Development, Population Policy, and Demographic Transition in the Republic of Korea*
94. Parks M. Coble, Jr., *The Shanghai Capitalists and the Nationalist Government, 1927–1937*
95. Noriko Kamachi, *Reform in China: Huang Tsun-hsien and the Japanese Model*
96. Richard Wich, *Sino-Soviet Crisis Politics: A Study of Political Change and Communication*
97. Lillian M. Li, *China's Silk Trade: Traditional Industry in the Modern World, 1842–1937*
98. R. David Arkush, *Fei Xiaotong and Sociology in Revolutionary China*
*99. Kenneth Alan Grossberg, *Japan's Renaissance: The Politics of the Muromachi Bakufu*
100. James Reeve Pusey, *China and Charles Darwin*
101. Hoyt Cleveland Tillman, *Utilitarian Confucianism: Chen Liang's Challenge to Chu Hsi*
102. Thomas A. Stanley, *Ōsugi Sakae, Anarchist in Taishō Japan: The Creativity of the Ego*
103. Jonathan K. Ocko, *Bureaucratic Reform in Provincial China: Ting Jih-ch'ang in Restoration Kiangsu, 1867–1870*
104. James Reed, *The Missionary Mind and American East Asia Policy, 1911–1915*
105. Neil L. Waters, *Japan's Local Pragmatists: The Transition from Bakumatsu to Meiji in the Kawasaki Region*
106. David C. Cole and Yung Chul Park, *Financial Development in Korea, 1945–1978*
107. Roy Bahl, Chuk Kyo Kim, and Chong Kee Park, *Public Finances during the Korean Modernization Process*
108. William D. Wray, *Mitsubishi and the N.Y.K, 1870–1914: Business Strategy in the Japanese Shipping Industry*

Harvard East Asian Monographs

109. Ralph William Huenemann, *The Dragon and the Iron Horse: The Economics of Railroads in China, 1876–1937*
110. Benjamin A. Elman, *From Philosophy to Philology: Intellectual and Social Aspects of Change in Late Imperial China*
111. Jane Kate Leonard, *Wei Yüan and China's Rediscovery of the Maritime World*
112. Luke S. K. Kwong, *A Mosaic of the Hundred Days:. Personalities, Politics, and Ideas of 1898*
113. John E. Wills, Jr., *Embassies and Illusions: Dutch and Portuguese Envoys to K'ang-hsi, 1666–1687*
114. Joshua A. Fogel, *Politics and Sinology: The Case of Naitō Konan (1866–1934)*
*115. Jeffrey C. Kinkley, ed., *After Mao: Chinese Literature and Society, 1978–1981*
116. C. Andrew Gerstle, *Circles of Fantasy: Convention in the Plays of Chikamatsu*
117. Andrew Gordon, *The Evolution of Labor Relations in Japan: Heavy Industry, 1853–1955*
*118. Daniel K. Gardner, *Chu Hsi and the "Ta Hsueh": Neo-Confucian Reflection on the Confucian Canon*
119. Christine Guth Kanda, *Shinzō: Hachiman Imagery and Its Development*
*120. Robert Borgen, *Sugawara no Michizane and the Early Heian Court*
121. Chang-tai Hung, *Going to the People: Chinese Intellectual and Folk Literature, 1918–1937*
*122. Michael A. Cusumano, *The Japanese Automobile Industry: Technology and Management at Nissan and Toyota*
123. Richard von Glahn, *The Country of Streams and Grottoes: Expansion, Settlement, and the Civilizing of the Sichuan Frontier in Song Times*
124. Steven D. Carter, *The Road to Komatsubara: A Classical Reading of the Renga Hyakuin*
125. Katherine F. Bruner, John K. Fairbank, and Richard T. Smith, *Entering China's Service: Robert Hart's Journals, 1854–1863*
126. Bob Tadashi Wakabayashi, *Anti-Foreignism and Western Learning in Early-Modern Japan: The "New Theses" of 1825*
127. Atsuko Hirai, *Individualism and Socialism: The Life and Thought of Kawai Eijirō (1891–1944)*
128. Ellen Widmer, *The Margins of Utopia: "Shui-hu hou-chuan" and the Literature of Ming Loyalism*
129. R. Kent Guy, *The Emperor's Four Treasuries: Scholars and the State in the Late Chien-lung Era*
130. Peter C. Perdue, *Exhausting the Earth: State and Peasant in Hunan, 1500–1850*

Harvard East Asian Monographs

131. Susan Chan Egan, *A Latterday Confucian: Reminiscences of William Hung (1893–1980)*
132. James T. C. Liu, *China Turning Inward: Intellectual-Political Changes in the Early Twelfth Century*
133. Paul A. Cohen, *Between Tradition and Modernity: Wang T'ao and Reform in Late Ching China*
134. Kate Wildman Nakai, *Shogunal Politics: Arai Hakuseki and the Premises of Tokugawa Rule*
135. Parks M. Coble, *Facing Japan: Chinese Politics and Japanese Imperialism, 1931–1937*
136. Jon L. Saari, *Legacies of Childhood: Growing Up Chinese in a Time of Crisis, 1890–1920*
137. Susan Downing Videen, *Tales of Heichū*
138. Heinz Morioka and Miyoko Sasaki, *Rakugo: The Popular Narrative Art of Japan*
139. Joshua A. Fogel, *Nakae Ushikichi in China: The Mourning of Spirit*
140. Alexander Barton Woodside, *Vietnam and the Chinese Model.: A Comparative Study of Vietnamese and Chinese Government in the First Half of the Nineteenth Century*
141. George Elision, *Deus Destroyed: The Image of Christianity in Early Modern Japan*
142. William D. Wray, ed., *Managing Industrial Enterprise: Cases from Japan's Prewar Experience*
143. T'ung-tsu Ch'ü, *Local Government in China under the Ching*
144. Marie Anchordoguy, *Computers, Inc.: Japan's Challenge to IBM*
145. Barbara Molony, *Technology and Investment: The Prewar Japanese Chemical Industry*
146. Mary Elizabeth Berry, *Hideyoshi*
147. Laura E. Hein, *Fueling Growth: The Energy Revolution and Economic Policy in Postwar Japan*
148. Wen-hsin Yeh, *The Alienated Academy: Culture and Politics in Republican China, 1919–1937*
149. Dru C. Gladney, *Muslim Chinese: Ethnic Nationalism in the People's Republic*
150. Merle Goldman and Paul A. Cohen, eds., *Ideas Across Cultures: Essays on Chinese Thought in Honor of Benjamin L Schwartz*
151. James Polachek, *The Inner Opium War*
152. Gail Lee Bernstein, *Japanese Marxist: A Portrait of Kawakami Hajime, 1879–1946*

Harvard East Asian Monographs

153. Lloyd E. Eastman, *The Abortive Revolution: China under Nationalist Rule, 1927–1937*
154. Mark Mason, *American Multinationals and Japan: The Political Economy of Japanese Capital Controls, 1899–1980*
155. Richard J. Smith, John K. Fairbank, and Katherine F. Bruner, *Robert Hart and China's Early Modernization: His Journals, 1863–1866*
156. George J. Tanabe, Jr., *Myōe the Dreamkeeper: Fantasy and Knowledge in Kamakura Buddhism*
157. William Wayne Farris, *Heavenly Warriors: The Evolution of Japan's Military, 500–1300*
158. Yu-ming Shaw, *An American Missionary in China: John Leighton Stuart and Chinese-American Relations*
159. James B. Palais, *Politics and Policy in Traditional Korea*
160. Douglas Reynolds, *China, 1898–1912: The Xinzheng Revolution and Japan*
161. Roger Thompson, *China's Local Councils in the Age of Constitutional Reform*
162. William Johnston, *The Modern Epidemic: History of Tuberculosis in Japan*
163. Constantine Nomikos Vaporis, *Breaking Barriers: Travel and the State in Early Modern Japan*
164. Irmela Hijiya-Kirschnereit, *Rituals of Self-Revelation: Shishōsetsu as Literary Genre and Socio-Cultural Phenomenon*
165. James C. Baxter, *The Meiji Unification through the Lens of Ishikawa Prefecture*
166. Thomas R. H. Havens, *Architects of Affluence: The Tsutsumi Family and the Seibu-Saison Enterprises in Twentieth-Century Japan*
167. Anthony Hood Chambers, *The Secret Window: Ideal Worlds in Tanizaki's Fiction*
168. Steven J. Ericson, *The Sound of the Whistle: Railroads and the State in Meiji Japan*
169. Andrew Edmund Goble, *Kenmu: Go-Daigo's Revolution*
170. Denise Potrzeba Lett, *In Pursuit of Status: The Making of South Korea's "New" Urban Middle Class*
171. Mimi Hall Yiengpruksawan, *Hiraizumi: Buddhist Art and Regional Politics in Twelfth-Century Japan*
172. Charles Shirō Inouye, *The Similitude of Blossoms: A Critical Biography of Izumi Kyōka (1873–1939), Japanese Novelist and Playwright*
173. Aviad E. Raz, *Riding the Black Ship: Japan and Tokyo Disneyland*
174. Deborah J. Milly, *Poverty, Equality, and Growth: The Politics of Economic Need in Postwar Japan*

Harvard East Asian Monographs

175. See Heng Teow, *Japan's Cultural Policy Toward China, 1918–1931: A Comparative Perspective*
176. Michael A. Fuller, *An Introduction to Literary Chinese*
177. Frederick R. Dickinson, *War and National Reinvention: Japan in the Great War, 1914–1919*
178. John Solt, *Shredding the Tapestry of Meaning: The Poetry and Poetics of Kitasono Katue (1902–1978)*
179. Edward Pratt, *Japan's Protoindustrial Elite: The Economic Foundations of the Gōnō*
180. Atsuko Sakaki, *Recontextualizing Texts: Narrative Performance in Modern Japanese Fiction*
181. Soon-Won Park, *Colonial Industrialization and Labor in Korea: The Onoda Cement Factory*
182. JaHyun Kim Haboush and Martina Deuchler, *Culture and the State in Late Chosŏn Korea*
183. John W. Chaffee, *Branches of Heaven: A History of the Imperial Clan of Sung China*
184. Gi-Wook Shin and Michael Robinson, eds., *Colonial Modernity in Korea*
185. Nam-lin Hur, *Prayer and Play in Late Tokugawa Japan: Asakusa Sensōji and Edo Society*
186. Kristin Stapleton, *Civilizing Chengdu: Chinese Urban Reform, 1895–1937*
187. Hyung Il Pai, *Constructing "Korean" Origins: A Critical Review of Archaeology, Historiography, and Racial Myth in Korean State-Formation Theories*
188. Brian D. Ruppert, *Jewel in the Ashes: Buddha Relics and Power in Early Medieval Japan*
189. Susan Daruvala, *Zhou Zuoren and an Alternative Chinese Response to Modernity*
190. James Z. Lee, *The Political Economy of a Frontier: Southwest China, 1250–1850*
191. Kerry Smith, *A Time of Crisis: Japan, the Great Depression, and Rural Revitalization*
192. Michael Lewis, *Becoming Apart: National Power and Local Politics in Toyama, 1868–1945*
193. William C. Kirby, Man-houng Lin, James Chin Shih, and David A. Pietz, eds., *State and Economy in Republican China: A Handbook for Scholars*
194. Timothy S. George, *Minamata: Pollution and the Struggle for Democracy in Postwar Japan*
195. Billy K. L. So, *Prosperity, Region, and Institutions in Maritime China: The South Fukien Pattern, 946–1368*
196. Yoshihisa Tak Matsusaka, *The Making of Japanese Manchuria, 1904–1932*

Harvard East Asian Monographs

197. Maram Epstein, *Competing Discourses: Orthodoxy, Authenticity, and Engendered Meanings in Late Imperial Chinese Fiction*
198. Curtis J. Milhaupt, J. Mark Ramseyer, and Michael K. Young, eds. and comps., *Japanese Law in Context: Readings in Society, the Economy, and Politics*
199. Haruo Iguchi, *Unfinished Business: Ayukawa Yoshisuke and U.S.-Japan Relations, 1937–1952*
200. Scott Pearce, Audrey Spiro, and Patricia Ebrey, *Culture and Power in the Reconstitution of the Chinese Realm, 200–600*
201. Terry Kawashima, *Writing Margins: The Textual Construction of Gender in Heian and Kamakura Japan*
202. Martin W. Huang, *Desire and Fictional Narrative in Late Imperial China*
203. Robert S. Ross and Jiang Changbin, eds., *Re-examining the Cold War: U.S.-China Diplomacy, 1954–1973*
204. Guanhua Wang, *In Search of Justice: The 1905–1906 Chinese Anti-American Boycott*
205. David Schaberg, *A Patterned Past: Form and Thought in Early Chinese Historiography*
206. Christine Yano, *Tears of Longing: Nostalgia and the Nation in Japanese Popular Song*